THE FAMILY DOCTOR SPEAKS:

THE TRUTH ABOUT SEED PLANTING

EQUIPPING BELIEVERS FOR EVANGELISM

ROBERT E. JACKSON JR., M.D.

The Family Doctor Speaks: The Truth About Seed Planting
Equipping Believers for Evangelism

Photography and Cover Design: Hannah R. Miller, HRMillerphotography.com

All Scripture references are from the New American Standard Bible, unless otherwise noted.

ISBN 978-1-940645-57-5

Courier Publishing, Greenville, South Carolina
CourierPublishing.com

TABLE OF CONTENTS

INTRODUCTION

When people ask me what I do, I tell them I am an ROCD — a regular old country doctor. I do hatching, patching, matching and dispatching; in other words, I take care of families from the cradle to the grave. I don't really do the hatching part anymore since I quit delivering babies in the year 2000, but you get the picture.

Truly, family medicine is the best gig in town. The patients who don't like me don't come back. The ones who do like me come back repeatedly. They become my best friends; they ask for my advice, which I love to dispense — and they pay to see me. What could be better than that?

Now here is the tricky part. My patients pay me to tell them the truth. They want to know the truth about their health status (i.e., blood pressure, blood sugar, cholesterol, weight, etc.). They may not like what they hear, but it is my job to tell them the truth.

Sometimes they disbelieve me when I tell them they have become a diabetic or a hypertensive. Sometimes they are offended when I write the diagnosis of obesity on their chart, and they say indignantly, "Dr. Jackson, really, can't you write down something other than obesity?"

"What do you want me to write? Really fat? Obese is the correct medical terminology."

"But, Doctor, I've been heavy all of my life."

"Yes, ma'am. I understand that. I've been ugly all of my life, and I can't do anything about that, but we can do something about your weight."

The hardest part of all is when I have to tell the truth about a cancer diagnosis. As I write this, I am waiting on repeat lab tests to verify my suspicion of a cancer diagnosis for one of my long-term patients. If the lab tests confirm my suspicions, I will have to tell the truth to her and her husband next week. I am already dreading that conversation, but this is part of my job.

This book contains some hard truths — hard because most Christians I know do not regularly or routinely participate in evangelism, even though all of us know we should. We will explain the reasons why we don't and how to overcome these deficits. We will discuss in each chapter a different facet of seed planting that, if applied, will move us closer to becoming effective seed planters.

◆   ◆   ◆   ◆   ◆

I stood in the rain outside a motel in downtown Atlanta with a friend named David. We had participated in evangelism training and had just finished a door-to-door evangelistic outreach in the inner city of Atlanta with miserable results. Nobody would talk to us. We were soaking wet, and I was discouraged. I stood with David, surveyed a long line of yellow cabs parked in front of the hotel, and finally said, "Follow me."

I picked a cab at random, opened the door, stuck my head in, and spoke to the driver, "Hi, my name is Robert, and this is David. We're talking to people about their relationship with the Lord Jesus. You want to talk?"

The cab driver, a pudgy fifty-year-old guy, sat behind the steering wheel eating a sandwich and staring at me like I was an alien. He swallowed twice, then replied, "Sure, why not? I'm not going anywhere."

We piled in, me in the front seat and David in the back. I commenced to sharing my testimony while David prayed. Then I read a gospel presentation from a gospel tract. Before we finished, the windows were all fogged up, and this fifty-year-old cab driver was weeping. Turns out, his father was a Methodist minister, and he had been running from the Lord (and his dad) all of his adult life. Before we left, he prayed a sinner's prayer and said, "I can't wait to call my dad. He won't believe this."

As indicated earlier, the theme of this book is seed planting. How many times had this cab driver's father planted a gospel seed in his son's heart? How many times had his mother and father prayed over him in fifty years? Do you think it an accident that a college student would pick a cab at random, or was that divinely orchestrated in answer to his father's prayers? Was his heart prepared for the "word (seed) implanted, which is able to save your souls" (James 1:21)?

As you read through this book on principles of seed planting, you will recognize several themes repeated over and over. These are abiding in the Word and prayer (daily quiet time), submission to Holy Spirit (being filled), preparation (training), and church membership/ministry. Becoming an effective seed planter is a characteristic of a Christian's life that flows out of abiding in Christ through His Word and prayer. It also flows automatically out of allowing Holy Spirit to control our lives. I place a premium on evangelistic training, but without being filled with Holy Spirit and abiding in the Word and prayer, we will never become consistent, effective seed planters.

More than that, the effective seed planter ministers in concert with a body of believers, with the family of God. I don't know any really effective seed planter who is a maverick (i.e., a loner). We all need each other, and our unique gifts supplement one another.

I know you are saying to yourself, "Why does he keep saying 'seed planter' instead of the time-honored expression 'soul winner'"? I use the term "seed planter" because that is all you and I can do — plant the seed of the gospel. The soul winning is up to Holy Spirit, who is responsible for conversion and who imparts new life. You and I cannot change a person's heart or mind; only Holy Spirit can. He "convicts of sin and righteousness and judgment" (John 16:8). We are responsible to plant the seed, pray over it, and leave the results to God. That takes a heavy weight off of you and me. This doesn't mean we aren't emotionally involved, because we do carry a burden for our spiritually lost family and friends, driving us to pray, share the gospel, and invite them to evangelistic events. Nevertheless, we understand the final results are up to God.

My best teaching is by sharing events in my life and then extracting the lessons Holy Spirit has taught me. Please enjoy these evangelistic adventures in which God has allowed me to participate over the last forty years. Each story is true. All of the characters are real. The names and circumstances have been changed a bit in some of the stories to protect the innocent or the guilty, as the case may be. If a full name has been provided, then those individuals have given me permission to provide their names and stories intact. I trust you will benefit from the lessons I have learned, but remember, the vitamin most lacking in most Christians' lives is Vitamin A — application! Reading about these lessons does you no good unless you apply them to your life!

DEDICATION

I dedicate this book to the college students of the Clemson University Campus Crusade for Christ from 1973-1977, who adopted me into their Christian subculture at a formative time in my spiritual journey. They helped me transition into a true evangelical with a love for God's Word and a sincere desire to share the love of Jesus Christ with others. These students accepted me with all of my warts and began to slowly mentor/disciple me until I caught a vision for doing the same.

Mike Garber and Ken Kelly taught me about the Spirit-controlled life. Ralph Vick taught me the Bible in a small group discipleship group for two years. He also taught me how to share the gospel one-on-one over that same two-year period of time. I am thankful for the entire group teaching me how to worship God seriously and enthusiastically. I'm forever grateful for their constant challenge to fulfill the Great Commission by making disciples. More than that, they taught me the finer points of a multiplying discipleship strategy.

I recently attended a reunion of that group of students at Clemson in April 2018. It was the first time I had seen some of them in thirty-five years or more. Most of them were still active in Christian ministry of one sort or another, doing the things they taught me to do forty years ago.

You guys and gals were and are an amazing group of God-fearing, Spirit-filled, ministry-minded Christian people. I'm honored to have been a part of you, and I'm thankful that God brought me across your path at that strategic time in my life. God used you to shape the ensuing years of my life. For that I am eternally grateful.

You all know who you are. This book is dedicated to each of you.

ACKNOWLEDGEMENTS

I freely acknowledge that this book would not be possible without the loving and patient input of my beautiful bride, Mrs. Carlotta. She types with lightning speed what I write out in longhand. She corrects my grammar, checks all the facts, and creates the footnotes. In short, she does all the stuff I hate to do. She will have stars in her crown.

Special thanks to my wonderfully talented daughter, Hannah, who designed the front and back covers, took all the photos, and made the promotional videos. She is the bomb!

I am grateful to Rev. Michael Cloer, Rev. Jim Goodroe and Rev. Bobby Jackson (my beloved first cousin) for reading my book to approve my doctrine/theology. (After all, I am a physician, not a theologian.) Their oversight is a blessing and a comfort. Their collective endorsement of the book is also appreciated.

Finally, I must acknowledge and thank my family, friends, neighbors and patients, whose stories make up the backbone of this book. Without their willingness for me to share their stories, there would be no book and no lessons to share. Without their stories, there would be no lessons in seed planting for me to share with you.

FOREWORD

As I watched an infomercial of Chuck Norris working out on his Total Gym machine, I wondered how many people would buy one of those if Brother Chuck was an obese chain-smoker? I suppose it would not be many, if any, because everyone is turned off by those who do not practice what they preach.

I have known Robert Jackson for nearly thirty-five years and would testify in any courtroom that he is a man who lives out everything he has written about in this book. In one of my first conversations with him as his new pastor in 1984, he looked me straight in the eye and asked, "Tell me, preacher man, are you a soul-winner?" When I said that I was, he immediately said, "Good! I'm on nights next week at the hospital, so let's go out one afternoon."

Thus began a lifelong friendship where I have watched him witness, mentor, disciple and leave a legacy that only heaven will unfold.

Robert is not interested in simply recording decisions but also in making disciples. He is the essence of what is referred to as a Great Commission Christian. This means he is intentional about evangelism and disciple-making.

The International Mission Board of the Southern Baptist Convention defines disciple-making as *the Christ-commanded, Spirit-empowered duty of every disciple of Jesus to evangelize unbelievers, baptize believers, teach them the word of Christ, and train them to obey Christ as members of His church who make disciples on mission to all nations.*

In this book, Dr. Jackson not only allows us to follow him as he goes about every individual aspect of this definition, but he also challenges us and instructs us in how we can be Great Commission Christians also. Through these pages we can observe the person, the process, and the principles involved in being disciple makers.

After reading it completely, then reading it again a second time carefully, I would recommend this book to every pastor, every missionary, every small group leader — in fact, every Christ follower who is serious about fulfilling the Great Commission. You will be both inspired and instructed, enlightened and encouraged. Before you finish, you will already be saying to yourself, "If he can do that, so can I."

Dr. Michael Cloer, Pastor
Englewood Baptist Church
Rocky Mount, North Carolina

1

KEEP ON PLOWING

"Dr. Jackson, my foot is killing me. I can't walk on it. I can't stand on it. You have got to help me!"

Lenny hobbled into the exam room — one shoe on, one shoe off, leaning on his wife with visible distress on his face. Limping on his heel, he carefully prevented anything from touching his left big toe, which was obviously hot, red and swollen. While tears welled up in his eyes from the pain, I noticed his flushed face and his markedly elevated blood pressure, a sure sign he had been drinking excessive alcohol again, even though he had sworn off the booze repeatedly after each gout attack. This was his third gout attack of the year. Missing too much work, he had already informed me his boss had warned him about his absences.

"Is this the same foot as last time?"

"Ow, ow, no sir, right foot last time. This is killing me."

His wife helped him onto the exam table. I could tell she was none too happy. His wife of twenty years, Angela, was a petite, pretty little lady who had borne him two adorable kids. She grew up Baptist, attending church every Sunday with her parents. During their tenth year of marriage, Lenny began drinking alcohol intermittently, then much too frequently until his alcohol consumption produced a serious rift between them. On this particular visit, when I explained to him the alcohol contributed to his recurrent gout attacks and his elevated blood pressure, she nearly exploded.

"Why have you never told me this?" she almost shouted at him. He just shrank into his protective shell like a turtle, never saying a word. Yep, she surely was not a happy camper. "You told me your drinking didn't hurt anybody, but that isn't true, is it? That is what has been causing all of these gout attacks, the doctor visits, and absences from work; plus, it runs your blood pressure up, requiring all of the blood pressure medicine we have to pay for! If I had known you were going to turn into a drunken bum, I would never have married you!"

Well, that got stuck in Lenny's craw, because he poked his passive little turtlehead out of his shell and simply said, "I'm not a drunk. I'm not a bum. I never get drunk, and I go to work every day — well, every day I don't have gout."

I figured I better intervene before this scene degenerated into fisti-cuffs right there in my office. So I asked Lenny, "Do you ever get so intoxicated that you can't function or go to work?"

"No," he replied sullenly.

I looked at Angela slowly shaking her head negatively with disgust, and then she said, "He might as well be drunk. He never interacts with the family. All he does is come home from work, get out a six-pack, plop in front of the television, and drink beer until bedtime. We don't talk. We don't go places. He won't go to church with us. All he is to our family is a paycheck every other Friday."

At that, "Turtlehead" piped up and said, "Hey, I'm a good provider. I heard your preacher say one time that a good husband is a good provider. I pay all of the bills and you don't go hungry. What more do you want?"

In an instant, Angela commenced to crying uncontrollably with hurt-filled sobs, the painful culmination of years of spousal neglect and misunderstanding. Quizzically, Lenny looked at me like a lost puppy with an expression between "What's the matter with her?" or "Does she need psychiatric help?" Lenny was clueless in Spartanburg!

I began to speak encouraging words to Angela for a few minutes when Mr. Understanding said, "Hey, what about my big toe?" We both glared at him in such a way that he stuck his little turtlehead back into his shell immediately and just whimpered.

I gave Lenny a shot of cortisone and some indomethacin, along with a stern lecture regarding his alcohol abuse and his refusal to take his previously prescribed gout medicine. Then, in true alcoholic fashion, he insisted he didn't drink that much and couldn't see why it was a "big deal." I asked him to return in two weeks for a follow-up appointment for gout and blood pressure. Before they left, I spoke to his wife in the hallway.

"Angela, only God can change his heart. Your nagging will not do it. Your anger will not do it either. You are a Christian woman, and you should understand that. I understand your frustration, but you have to live above the fray as it will destroy you and your marriage. Pray every day that Holy Spirit will cause your husband to be born again. Otherwise, he will be addicted to alcohol for the rest of his life."

She just stared at me, trying to absorb what I had just said. Then she replied, "What about alcohol rehab programs?"

"Angela, I am not against rehab programs if a patient is willing to go. Right now, Lenny sees no reason to go. The only problem with most rehab programs is they can only change how people behave on the outside and the way they think about drugs or alcohol. Only Jesus can change a person's heart from the inside out so they never desire alcohol or drugs ever again. He needs an extreme makeover from the inside out. That's what Lenny needs. Does that make sense?"

She slowly nodded her head, but I was not certain she truly understood. Psychologists, counselors and rehab can help, but ultimately what Lenny needed was a new heart, a radical transformation from the inside out. He needed to be born again. Jesus Christ could change him into a new man. I have many patients who go to rehab, come out on the other side, and go straight back to their drinking buddies. Why? It is because their hearts have not changed, their desires have not changed.

I restated my words with, "Angela, you and I cannot change a man's heart. Rehab programs cannot change a man's heart. Only Jesus can do that. That is what regeneration and being born again is all about. Jesus can make us completely new. 'Therefore, if any man is in Christ, he is a new creature; the old things passed away; behold, new things have come' (2 Corinthians 5:17)."

She continued to stare at me like I had two heads.

"Think about it, Angela. Pray for Lenny every day, but remember, you cannot nag him into the kingdom of God." At that, she smiled, turned on her heels, and walked away.

Obediently, Lenny returned in two weeks. He was quite proud of himself as he had joined AA at Angela's insistence, reduced his drinking to two cans of beer a day, and started attending church with his wife. His blood pressure was once again normal, and his gout symptoms alleviated. So I congratulated him on his success.

Before he left, I asked him about his spiritual life. "Oh, I'm fine, Doc. Don't worry about me."

"But I am concerned about you, Lenny, and about your spiritual well-being. What does it profit my patients if I help them maintain perfect physical health, but if in the end, they lose their souls?"

He cocked his head to one side and said, "Huh?"

"Lenny, have you ever been born again?"

"You mean like Billy Graham talks about on TV?"

"Yes, exactly. Have you ever been born again?"

He paused, searching for words. His shoulders sagged. "I don't quite know what that means."

"Lenny, in John 3 a religious leader named Nicodemus came to Jesus to ask Him spiritual questions. Jesus told him, 'Unless one is born again, he cannot see the kingdom of God' (John 3:3). Nicodemus kept all of the religious rules of the day; thus, he assumed he would be acceptable to God because of his pious obedience. When Jesus said he had to be born again, Nicodemus thought He meant a physical birth, but Jesus was talking about a spiritual birth whereby the Spirit of God imparts the life of God into our spiritually dead souls. Do you know why you are spiritually dead?"

He shook his head. "No."

"Because of your sin. The Bible says the penalty of sin is death, not just physical death but spiritual death. Right now, you are spiritually dead because of sin. What is the consequence of your sin and your spiritual death?"

He shook his head again, indicating he didn't know.

"Paul told the Romans, 'The wages of sin is death' (Romans 6:23). The consequence for all sinners is to be forever separated from God in a place called hell. Obviously, that means you miss out on heaven; plus, during this life you cannot have any kind of meaningful relationship with the Heavenly Father. That is the bad news. What is the good news, Lenny?"

He shook his head again.

"The good news is that God the Father loved you enough to send His only Son, Jesus Christ, to die on the cross in our place and to pay our sin debt so we could be set free from the penalty of sin and so we could enjoy a personal relationship with God the Father through Jesus the Son. But wait! There's more! Jesus not only takes away our sin, He also gives us His righteousness as a free gift. That's important, Lenny, because how can we walk in righteousness unless He gives us something special to enable us? How can you throw off a sinful habit like excessive beer drinking if He doesn't give you His righteousness?"

Lenny was perplexed by all of this information. I asked him if it made sense. He responded that it did, but I could tell he was still confused. I gave him the book of John, asked him to read it through, and I told him I would pray for him. I would like to tell you he returned in a few weeks born again and transformed, but such was not the case.

A decade went by.

My office became a revolving door for him, with repeated attacks of gout, elevated blood pressure, medication noncompliance, and excessive beer intake. Nevertheless, we maintained a cordial, respectful relationship over years of time. Angela came to understand what I meant about praying rather than nagging. She came to appreciate that Lenny was never angry or abusive as so many alcoholics are. She became a prayer warrior on his behalf. In fact, he was what I call a "happy drunk." Angela herself said she couldn't stay mad at him because he was so happy. I reviewed the gospel with Lenny repeatedly and encouraged him to give his life to Jesus Christ. He thanked me for my concern but continued to be perplexed. He really was spiritually blind.

On one occasion, he presented early in the morning, complaining of gout pain and requesting a cortisone injection so he could attend a sporting event that weekend. Angela brought him in but left in exasperation. I looked at him in frustration and commented, "One day she may leave you for good. Are you willing to let that beautiful, God-fearing woman walk out of your life all because of a little booze?"

He looked at the floor for a moment; then he said to me, "That would be a hard decision, Doc."

Sin makes us stupid and blind.

I was shocked and heartbroken. Sin makes us stupid and blind. Years passed, years of plowing the stubborn hard ground of Lenny's heart with the truth of the gospel.

Then, one day all the plowing and praying paid off! Lenny came into my office for a blood pressure medication refill. When I walked into the exam room and before I said a word, he triumphantly announced with laughter in his voice, "Doc, before you say anything, I need to tell you something. About three months ago I got saved!" He sat there with a giant smile like a mule eating briars, looked at me, and waited expectantly for my response.

Well, you can believe my heart leaped for joy, when I all but shouted, "Lenny, are you for real? Tell me what happened."

Then he said, "Before I tell you, Doc, I want to say thank you. Thank you for all the times you shared the gospel with me and prayed for me. I know my wife prayed for me for many years, but I want to thank you for all the times you spoke the truth into my life. You will never know how thankful I am. I've told my pastor all about you. In fact, I told my whole church about you."

"Well, Lenny, you are so welcome, but tell me … tell me what happened?"

"Dr. Jackson, I don't know why, but I just started going to church with my wife a few months ago. She begged me to go for fifteen years, and I finally decided to go. The church has a new pastor, who is about my age, and for some reason I connected with him. Somehow his messages began to get through to my heart. For some reason I started going on Sunday night. I've never been to church on Sunday night in my whole life. You could not have dragged me to church on Sunday night with a team of wild horses! On this one Sunday evening, the Spirit of God just got all over me and convicted me of all my sins. I knew then I had to ask Jesus to forgive me. I knew then I had to be born again. That night I prayed to receive Christ as my Savior. He took away all my sins, Doc, and just like you told me ten times before, He took away all of my desire for alcohol. I haven't had a drink of beer since that night. I haven't even wanted one. Oh, and I meet with my pastor once a week for Bible study and discipleship, which has been a blessing and encouragement. I'm a new man, and my wife has a new husband."

I don't see Lenny much anymore. He doesn't have gout attacks or elevated blood pressure because he no longer drinks beer, but when I do see him he's getting along well in his new Christian life. As I told Angela, Lenny needed to be born again. He needed a new heart. "Therefore, if any man is in Christ, he is a new creature; the old things passed away; behold new things have come" (2 Corinthians 5:17). In Lenny's case, repeated exposure to the gospel and persistent prayer won the day.

In our lives, each of us has multiple Lennys who will not come to Christ with just one exposure to the truth. The hard, stony ground of their hearts must be broken up with persistent love and prayers, and multiple exposures to the gospel. You know who those people are in your life, and I trust Lenny's story will encourage you to persevere over time and to keep on plowing.

STUDY QUESTIONS | Chapter 1

1. What does Paul mean in Romans 1:16 by "For I am not ashamed of the gospel, for it is the power of God for salvation to everyone who believes"?

2. What is the value of AA or NA meetings? What is the danger of AA or NA meetings?

3. What ultimately changed Lenny's drinking habit?

4. What does it mean to be a new creation in Christ Jesus?

5. What finally won the day in Lenny's life, leading him to make a commitment to Jesus Christ?

2

A TWELVE-YEAR WALKABOUT

I received a call late one night during my family medicine residency program. It was my mom. She was distraught.

"Robert, can you come to Columbia and help to search for your brother, John Reed? He has been missing for three days. I've searched everywhere, and I can't find him." Even though my mother is a strong woman and weeping is not a part of her *modus operandi*, she broke down and began quietly crying on the phone. She continued, "I'm certain he is abusing drugs again. I know all of his usual haunts, but this time I can't find him. I am afraid he has overdosed. Can you possibly get off to come help me?"

It broke my heart to tell my mother I could not leave my on-call responsibilities. I was, in fact, at the hospital at that moment. It made me angry with my drug-addicted brother, who would treat my mother this way time after time, as it was not unusual for him to disappear for days. Thus, he could not maintain any kind of employment. On one occasion, he even fell asleep while intoxicated on the rocks beside the Broad River flowing through Columbia, South Carolina, becoming so severely sunburned that Mom had to have him treated in the emergency room.

My dad was a military man and loved everything about the military.

He voluntarily joined the Air Force at the beginning of the Vietnam War, leaving my mom and four children plus a growing family medicine practice in our hometown of Manning, South Carolina. He served in the Air Force for two years and in the Air National Guard for eleven years, until his untimely death at the age of forty-one. He was a loving and dedicated father, but our home was run with strict discipline, keeping all of us kids in line. After his death, my two younger brothers quickly stepped out of line by smoking pot and experimenting with other illicit drugs. The older of the two, John Reed, became attached to harder drugs, which ruled his life for the next twelve years. In the well-known Hollywood production, *Crocodile Dundee,* the main character described his long absence from polite society as a "walkabout." John Reed took a twelve-year "walkabout" from polite society, from his family, and from God.

John Reed, called JR by his friends, was a talented musician. He played the drums in a series of bands until he landed in a group in Columbia called Pyramid, which became quite popular with a large following. He was both vocalist and drummer, an unusual combination, but he easily accomplished both. Sadly, alcohol and drugs freely followed that lifestyle. The flow of drugs and booze led to several hospitalizations for drug rehab, all at my mom's expense and all to no avail. Each time he was discharged, he would return immediately to his old drinking buddies, much to my mother's chagrin.

He reminded me of a patient I discharged from a hospital on a hot summer day in the early '80s. He was still recovering from DTs (delirium tremens) — which manifested as hallucinations, tremors, confusion and profound weakness — but he had recuperated enough to be discharged home. It was ninety-nine degrees outside the hospital, so I asked the patient, "Jerry, how do you plan to get home?"

"I don't know, Doc. I guess I'll just walk."

"Jerry, you can hardly walk across the room. Do you have some family you can call?"

"No, none of them would come."

Such are the effects of chronic alcoholism.

"Where do you live, Jerry?"

"In Inman."

Inman was approximately twelve miles from the hospital. I could not imagine him walking twelve miles in ninety-nine-degree heat in his current state of health.

"Well, Jerry, I live in Inman. I'll drive you home over my lunch break," which I did. I delivered him to a little two-room shanty off the beaten path in Inman.

When we arrived, a large man with a big abdomen, wearing no shirt and carrying a beer can in one hand, looked at Jerry and unwisely advised, "Jerry, you look awful. You need a beer."

That was the last thing Jerry needed, but what could I do?

Fast forward ten years — I am now sitting in a courtroom in a murder trial. Jerry is the defendant, accused of killing a friend in a drunken brawl not long after I dropped him off. I had been subpoenaed to testify about his mental status when I treated him in the hospital. The lawyers didn't know I had dropped him off at his home shortly before the murder occurred. I remembered Jerry immediately, even though he had gained approximately eighty pounds eating prison food. Likewise, he remembered me and smiled broadly when he saw me.

My testimony did not prove beneficial to his defense in anyway, because he was ultimately convicted and sent off to prison for a very long time. He reminded me of my brother, and my brother reminded me of Jerry. Consequently, I was frightened that John Reed would end up like Jerry because he ran with a very rough crowd.

JR became so depressed he was diagnosed as bipolar by a psychiatrist and placed on strong psychiatric medications for a number of years to counteract his mood swings. I always felt the mood swings were attributable to drug abuse rather than an underlying psychiatric disorder, but I was not his doctor, so I kept it to myself. This can be an extremely confusing scenario with drug-addicted patients. On several occasions, my mom and I discussed our concerns about his diagnosis and his strong prescription medications. However, when desperate for a family member to get well, most of us will try about anything.

Many years later, JR confided that he would get so depressed and hopeless, he would lock himself in his apartment with a case of beer, listening to heavy metal music and holding a shotgun. He contemplated suicide for literally days at a time, just drinking beer, smoking pot, and listening to his heavy metal music. He really did not know why he never could bring himself to pull the trigger, although this scenario played out on multiple occasions. (As you will see later, spiritual forces were at work, of which he was unaware.)

If the drugs, booze and punk rock music were not enough, he then acquired an occult mentor who began to instruct him in the black arts. He began to read and study the satanic bible. His mentor, who seemed to have occult powers, began to teach him occult rituals and gave him a Chinese foo dog, saying, "As long as you keep this around, I will always be able to come and check up on you." I tried to warn him about the foolishness and the spiritual danger of dabbling in the occult on one occasion, but he merely laughed me to scorn and refused to listen.

Of course, I knew little to nothing about most of these things as they happened. I only found out about them after the fact years later. As I grew in my spiritual life, my brothers had less and less to do with me, affirming 2 Corinthians 6:14: "What fellowship has light with darkness?" Indeed, if I came in the front door, they went out the back door. If I questioned them about their lifestyle, they resorted to ridicule and scorn. I was fearful for both of my brothers' spiritual wellbeing because I loved my brothers and longed for fellowship with them, but the darkness in them feared the light in me. They wounded me and repeatedly stabbed me in the back as I sought to be their friend. They rejected friendly counsel and advice, and they shunned any attempt to share the gospel with them or to warn them about the consequences of their lifestyle.

JR's punk rock band prospered and became very popular. They had gigs almost every weekend and produced a couple of CDs. My other brother traveled with them as a stagehand, helping with the equipment. Booze and marijuana were always available. I remember coming home from singing in a wedding in Rock Hill, South Carolina, on one occasion. I just happened to come up behind their vehicle as they traveled from a gig in the same vicinity. There were four of them in JR's Monte Carlo.

Immediately, I recognized his car in the darkness and pulled up close behind, flashing my lights. Of course, they couldn't recognize me. All they could see were headlights, so they assumed it was a cop car following them. Their windows went down, and all manner of drug paraphernalia went out. I began to laugh uncontrollably. I hit my blinker to get them to turn off the road. That confused them because a cop would hit his blue light. I knew they were thinking I was a cop. JR slowed way down but didn't stop. I kept hitting my blinker, so finally he pulled over.

I got out and walked up slowly like a cop would, tapped on the side of the car, and put on my best cop voice, asking, "What are you boys doing in my county?" When they realized it was me, they didn't think it was funny at all, especially since they had just thrown out several hundred dollars' worth of drugs (well, the way of the wicked is hard). "Your car smells a little funny. Some of you want to ride with me to get some fresh air?"

They declined.

"Hey, I've got a new Christian tape I just bought; you'll probably enjoy it." They still declined. I just couldn't figure them out. I got back in my car and laughed all the way home.

Well, some things started happening that these brothers of mine weren't counting on. First, they weren't counting on the power of a mother's prayers. Nobody prays for a prodigal child like his mother. (Can I get an "amen"?) Our mom prayed for my brothers from the first day of their straying until the first day God brought them home. I visited my mom on multiple occasions, and we sat around her kitchen table holding hands and praying for my brothers with tears in our eyes, praying that God would intervene in their lives. I know no one cared for them more or prayed for them more than our mother.

It reminds me of the Canaanite mom who came to Jesus on behalf of her child who was ill. Well, my mom was the "Manningite" woman who came to Jesus persistently over many years of time, wrestling with Jesus like Jacob and declaring she wouldn't let go until God gave her her request.

Well, that wasn't the only thing going on behind the scenes. I heard my pastor, Ray Long, at Rock Hill Baptist Church in Inman, South Carolina, say to the congregation one Sunday, "There is something special about prayers prayed at the altar. God honors prayers prayed at the altar." Then he began to review all the prayers in the Old Testament prayed at an altar. As soon as I heard this, I knew it was true, and I made a commitment before God to go to the altar every time I was in church to pray for my brothers because God had put a heavy burden on my heart for my brothers' salvation.

'There is something special about prayers prayed at the altar. God honors prayers prayed at the altar.'

Thus began a six-year journey of going to the altar every Sunday morning, Sunday night and Wednesday night to kneel and pray for my brothers, even if no one was there but God and me. I'm sure people wondered, "What is wrong with that doctor? He goes to the altar all the time. He must have serious problems."

I didn't care what people thought about me; I only cared about my brothers' salvation, and I was convinced God honored prayers prayed at the altar, and He honored persistence in prayer. He told us so in the Bible.

More than that, I had about fifty people in our Wednesday night prayer meeting praying for my brothers. At Rock Hill Baptist, we had a group of prayer warriors who met on Wednesday nights to pray for lost people, the sick, and for families to be restored. Those years at RHBC, praying with those brothers and sisters, were some of the most exciting years of my life because we saw families restored and lost people saved. This included my brothers!

About five and a half years into this prayer journey (eleven and a half years into JR's debauchery) on a Sunday night, the Spirit of God impressed on my heart while I was praying at the altar: "It is done. JR is saved." Just like that. I knew in my heart he was saved. I just didn't know when. I never asked God to save him again. I just started to thank God for his salvation every time I went to the altar. I didn't stop going to the altar, but now I was thanking God by faith in advance for my brother's salvation.

Six months later, I spoke at a church in Walterboro, South Carolina, on "What Disgruntled Wives Tell Their Family Doctor." My brothers came to hear me because the pastor was our high school Bible teacher, Rev. David Dinkins. True to form, they left right after the service and would not stay for Sunday lunch. One hour of church was all they could stand of being around Christian people. One week later, JR called my house and asked if he and his wife could come and speak to me.

Now you have to understand, my brother had never called me but once in twelve years and that was to ask for money. I looked at my wife, Carlotta, and said, "JR is coming to get saved."

Several days later, he arrived at my house with his wife. The three of us went into my very small dining room to talk privately. He admitted they were having some marital issues, while she commenced to blaming him for all the troubles they were having in their relationship. I looked him in the eye and asked, "Have you ever been born again?"

He replied, "Sure, when I was eleven years old." I didn't want to debate that with him, but I knew he wasn't any more saved than my big dog named John the Baptist! So, as I always do when counseling with couples, I started at first base — which is assurance of salvation — because if people aren't born again and filled with Holy Spirit, they don't possess the spiritual resources to do any of the things I ask them to do, like confess their sins to one another and forgive one another.

Boiled down to the bare essence, when couples stand before the judge in divorce court, two issues ultimately divide them — unwillingness to change, and unwillingness to forgive. Holy Spirit within us provides the supernatural power to do both. Counseling always starts with first base, making certain the counselee is, in fact, a member of the family of God and indwelt by Holy Spirit.

Miraculously, all of those years of praying paid off. My brother stared at my face for twenty minutes without looking away, while I shared the gospel with him as if he had never heard it before. The whole time I was talking to him, his wife was talking rapid-fire, blaming him continually for every problem in their marriage. At the conclusion of my gospel presentation, I asked him if he understood, and he simply nodded, "Yes."I invited him to return in one week for session two. He thanked me, gathered up his wife, and left. As they walked down the driveway, she was chewing on his ear, but he was oblivious.

Three days later, JR called me on the phone in a dither. "Rob, something has happened to me."

"What?"

"I don't know. Something has happened!"

"What do you mean?"

"I can't stop reading my Bible!"

"You can't stop reading your Bible?"

"No, I can't stop. I've read it through completely one time, and I'm halfway through a second time. I haven't slept in three days. I haven't been to work. All I want to do is read my Bible."

"Sounds to me like you just got saved."

"No, I got saved when I was eleven."

"Dude, I hate to tell you this, but you haven't been any more saved than my dog."

"What do you mean by that?"

"You've had no fruit."

"No fruit?"

"Yes, the Bible says, 'You will know them by their fruits' (Matthew 7:20). All of your fruit has been rotten fruit."

"Oh, yeah, I read that. You don't think I've been saved?"

"Not by your fruit. Sounds to me like you just got saved, and now it is time to produce good fruit in keeping with repentance."

"Yeah, well, whatever, but something has happened to me, and it is something good."

JR stopped abusing drugs and booze in a single day — no more alcohol abuse, marijuana or cocaine. It took six weeks to give up smoking cigarettes (that should tell you something about the hold nicotine has on people). He called the boys in the punk rock band and told them he couldn't come back. He also gave the boot to his occult mentor. Six weeks later, he was enrolled in Columbia Bible College (now Columbia International University) and began to play drums in their praise and worship band.

He has never looked back. That has been over twenty years ago. He still leads in worship in every church of which he has been a part. He is a walking, talking evangelist everywhere he goes. He calls me his brother times two, and when we get on the phone together, we end up shouting praises to God into the phone because we get so excited about what God has done and is doing in our lives. Oh, and by the way, he quit all the psychiatric drugs about six months after his conversion and has never needed them again. Just saying!

Approximately one year later, JR invited my other brother to a Christian rock concert in Columbia, South Carolina. Now, that brother was always what I called a "GOB" — good, old boy. He was an ex-military, chain-smoking, beer-drinking good old boy. He was hard-working, tax-paying, and patriotic, but lost as a long-necked goose in a bucket of juice. He did not understand me, nor did he understand John Reed's newfound "religion." Nevertheless, just to make John Reed happy, he agreed to go to the concert. Sometime later he told me, "Halfway through the concert, I knew I needed to get saved. I knew I was a sinner, and I knew I had been fooling myself all those years about my salvation. I was ready to go down front and make a commitment to Christ, but the concert was only half over. I could hardly wait for it to end. Finally, before the concert finished, I walked down front and stood there just looking at them for ten minutes — all by myself. I was just waiting for them to wrap things up so I could talk to a counselor and get things right between God and me. My life has been completely changed ever since that day."

Now, interestingly, John Reed still maintains he became a Christian at age eleven after going to church summer camp. He returned from the camp excited about his newfound faith. He gave out gospel tracts to everyone for several months. He believes God transformed his life at this point. He cannot explain how or why he descended into debauchery for twelve years; however, he believes Holy Spirit in him prevented him from committing suicide on multiple occasions. Moreover, he had friends who became deeply involved in the occult under the leadership of their occult mentors, but he could never quite catch on. He believes it was the protection of Holy Spirit in him delivering him from further involvement in the occult.

Was it the prayer of my mom and the prayer warriors at Rock Hill Baptist Church protecting John Reed? Was it the presence of Holy Spirit in his heart? I'll be honest, it's confusing to me. My brother walked, talked and smelled like one of the devil's own for twelve years. I could not assume his church camp experience at age eleven was valid or sufficient. It may have been, and the Spirit of God may have been preserving and protecting him all those years. (He may have been what I call "a Lady Clairol Christian" — only God knows for sure.)

What are you and I supposed to do when we have a family member or friend like this? I believe you have an obligation to pray for them as if they are lost, which is what I did in John Reed's case. If they look and act like lost people, then I suggest you pray for them as if they are lost people. If it turns out they were saved all along, well, God can sort it out. He knows the intention of our hearts is to see them restored to fellowship with Him. He knows the desire of our heart and the condition of their soul.

You and I can never judge whether another person is truly lost or saved. That is God's responsibility. He is the final Judge of the living and the dead. I cannot look at any person and say with certainty that he or she is a Christian. However, I can be a fruit inspector. In fact, we are admonished in Matthew 21 to watch out for those who have rotten fruit who claim to know God. Jesus said, "You will know them by their fruits" (Matthew 7:20). If folks have good fruit, it's a good indication that they belong to Jesus. What kind of fruit? Why, the fruit of the Spirit and fruitfulness in witnessing. If folks who claim they belong to God have rotten fruit, then their claim is suspect. What kind of fruit? Why, the fruit of the flesh and no fruitfulness in witnessing.

Nevertheless, I still cannot see into people's hearts. I cannot judge their motives or whether or not they've been born again. Only God, the righteous Judge, can do that.

So, what's a Christian to do? If people you love have rotten fruit, you pray for them as if they are lost. That's what you do. And if you happen to be wrong? Well, again, God can sort it out. Better to be safe than to assume that someone with rotten fruit is a Christian just because he/she says so, to his/her eternal loss.

◆　◆　◆　◆　◆

Let's go back in time to the hot, dusty foothills of Judea. Jesus and his disciples are walking toward the region of Tyre and Sidon on the coast of the Mediterranean. This was an area mostly populated by Gentiles, but Jesus went out of His way on several occasions to travel through Gentile territory to minister to Gentile people. That's how He met the woman at the well when He traveled through Samaria, something most Jews would not do.

There was whispering in the crowd, "Mama, what are you going to do?" The whispered words came from a stout Gentile teenage boy with a determined look.

A Canaanite woman said, "I've made up my mind. I'm going to talk to the Jewish rabbi." She then looked back at her daughter who had a wild-eyed look on her face and was grinding her teeth. The closer Jesus came, the more agitated her daughter became until now she was pulling clumps of her hair out with both hands and glaring ferociously with fiery eyes.

"Mama, you can't do that. Look at those twelve big men. They are like security guards. They keep the crowds from getting too close."

"I know, but I heard from your cousin Ishmael that Jesus let little children come up to Him, and He held them and blessed them. He even rebuked those guards from keeping them away."

"But, Mama, He's a Jew, and a famous one at that. Look at all the people following Him. You won't even get close. He's not going to talk to a woman, especially a Gentile woman. I hear Hiram, our next-door neighbor, praying on his roof every morning, thanking God he's not a woman or a dog of a Gentile." At that, he turned his head and spat on the ground. "May the gods ruin his business and rot his soul."

Wiping the sweat from her brow and wide-eyed with fear, the woman looked at her son and said, "We've spent all of your deceased father's money on the medicine men in three towns, and no one has been able to help your poor possessed sister. I am a desperate woman, Ahmed. Tell me what more can I do. This Jesus is a miracle man. He heals the sick just by speaking a word. He may never come this way again. He is your poor sister's only hope."

With a deep breath and a cry of desperation, she pushed away from her son and bulled her way through the shocked crowd. She began to shout as loudly as she could, "Lord, Son of David, have mercy on me! My daughter is demon-possessed and suffering terribly!"

Her cries were so loud that they silenced the entire crowd and the procession came to a halt. She repeated her plea again, this time even louder against the backdrop of silence and buttressed by deep sobs from the bottom of her soul. Hundreds of people stopped and stared at this wretched woman, this Gentile woman, who had dared to violate the social norms and approach a Jewish male in public without an intermediary. How could she?

Oddly, Jesus just looked at the dusty ground and said nothing. The spectacle became awkward when a third time she barely choked out through her sobs, "Lord, Son of David, have mercy on me! My daughter is demon-possessed and suffering terribly!"

The crowd began to shuffle their feet nervously, waiting on Jesus' response. His disciples came to Him with some embarrassment and whispered rather urgently, "Send her away, for she keeps crying out after us."

Jesus answered quietly without looking up, "I was sent only to the lost sheep of Israel."

The Jews in the crowd nodded affirmatively. The Gentiles were perplexed and asked themselves why He was preaching and healing in their country.

Trembling and weak in her desperation, the mother came and knelt before Jesus. All she could think to say was, "Lord, help me." A torrent of tears began to flow as she realized that before her was her daughter's only hope.

Pondering for a moment, Jesus replied, "It is not right to take the children's bread and toss it to the dogs."

Tossing every cultural restriction aside, she responded quickly and with a gentle smile, "Yes, it is, Lord, but even the dogs eat the crumbs that fall from the master's table."

Instantly, Jesus threw back His head and laughed a deep, hearty laugh that echoed off the surrounding hills. The whole crowd laughed nervously, following His lead but not understanding the humor.

Then bending over, He cupped her face in both of His hands and wiped away her tears. Looking deep into her hopeful eyes, He said approvingly, "Woman, you have great faith! Your request is granted."

Immediately, she began to thank Jesus over and over, so much so that her effusive gratitude began to embarrass His disciples. Suddenly, a war whoop emanated from the crowd. Everyone turned to see Ahmed leading his sister by the hand. She was smiling, composed and peaceful. Gone were the screams and the wild-eyed, fierce expression that dominated her features for years. Gone were the glare and the clenched fists. Gone were the spitting and the grinding teeth. Those in the crowd who knew her could tell immediately that a remarkable transformation had taken place in her life. Slowly but gathering momentum, the entire Gentile crowd began to praise this Jewish miracle worker amidst whispers, "Could this be the promised Messiah?"

◆　◆　◆　◆　◆

Suppose you are the one who has a child with a serious life-threatening illness, perhaps a cancer of some sort. Can you imagine the anguish you would experience? Could you identify with this Canaanite mother? Suppose you are the one who has spent all of your insurance money and personal finances searching for a cure — to no avail. Suppose you are the one who has turned to herbal treatments or other alternative therapies — to no avail — and your child's health continues to decline. But then you hear that an international researcher has come to your town to introduce a new revolutionary treatment, especially designed for your child's particular cancer. Only a select few will be allowed in the final trials, according to the newspapers.

Would you be willing to risk the refusal, the rejection, being turned away — to represent your child? He's going to be in your town only one day. Would you interrupt his presentation on stage? Could you stop his motorcade? Would you kneel in front of God and everybody, and shout, "Sir, have mercy on me! My child has the very cancer your drug treats!"

What would it take for you to do that? What characteristics did the Canaanite woman possess that compelled her to interrupt Jesus' entourage that day? Let's examine her story a little closer.

First, **she was audacious** in that she approached a Jewish miracle worker with a large following in the midst of a busy workday. It contravened the cultural mores of the day for a woman to approach a strange man — especially for a Gentile woman to approach a Jewish man, and, even more so, a prominent teacher/rabbi. Nevertheless, her audacity was born of desperation. Scripture says, "Let us therefore draw near with confidence to the throne of grace, that we may receive mercy and may find grace to help in time of need" (Hebrews 4:16). Yet, we all listen to the enemy when he tells us that God is too busy for us. Jesus wasn't too busy for this foreign woman with no claims on His time or person — no family connections, no introduction, no friends in common.

We are family; we are connected, needing no introduction. We can come boldly and with confidence into the very throne room of God to receive mercy and obtain grace to help in our time of need. Our audacity is really confidence based on a royal invitation from the King himself.

After I joined the choir at our church, I often noticed this pretty butterfly of a girl, just a young child, run out on the stage unannounced, hug the choir director, and kiss him goodnight. He immediately stopped whatever he was doing, gave her a hug and a kiss, and sent her flitting away with her mother. He was always in the midst of conducting a seventy-plus-person choir and small orchestra; nevertheless, when this delicate little flower appeared, he stopped what he was doing to give her his full attention. She required no introduction, and she came boldly and with confidence into the presence of the maestro to receive a goodnight kiss. Such was her audacity. Why? She was his daughter. She was family. She belonged. Let us be so audacious. Don't listen to the enemy. He is the father of lies and was a liar from the beginning. God does have time for us, and like this precious little girl, we have the privilege of family.

Second, **the Canaanite woman demonstrated persistence**. The disciples complained, "Send her away, she keeps crying out after us"

(Matthew 15:23, NIV). This reminds me of the parable Jesus told of the woman who pestered the judge so much that even though he feared neither God nor man, he gave her what she wanted (Luke 18:1-8). Don't be afraid of being a bother to God. He's the one who teaches us to be persistent. He said to "pray and not to lose heart" (Luke 18:1).

Remember: Spiritual battles occur in the spiritual realms that we do not comprehend and we do not see — battles for the souls of our loved ones. The enemy of our souls wages war to ensnare and capture our children and our loved ones. If we don't persist in overcoming prayer, he will snatch them away.

Daniel persisted in prayer for twenty-one days before Michael the Archangel was able to overcome the Prince of Persia and deliver the answer to Daniel's prayer (Daniel 10:2, 12-14). What if he had relented on day twenty? What if you and I relent a day or a month too soon as we labor in persistent prayer for that precious loved one? We prayed for my brother for twelve years. What if we had given up at eleven and a half years? Matthew 7:7-8 says, "Ask, and it shall be given to you; seek, and you shall find; knock, and it shall be opened to you. For everyone who asks receives, and he who seeks finds, and to him who knocks it shall be opened."

Third, **"she knelt before Him" (Matthew 15:25, NIV) in humility,** begging, "Have mercy on me" (Matthew 15:22). This combined confession of faith and cry for mercy indicated a total dependence on Jesus Christ. She knew He alone could deliver her child. He alone can deliver your child — not the psychiatrist or counselor or medication or even the pastor. These people and things have their place, but ultimately our hope and confidence have to be in Jesus Christ. He is Jehovah Rafah, the Lord who heals.

When I first moved to Spartanburg, I attended a church that had a Monday night evangelistic outreach attended by dozens and dozens of its church people. Before they set out on their evangelistic visits, the church folks prayed at the altar for the people they planned to visit. I noticed a doctor in town, for whom I had great respect and who was a member of the church, was down at the altar with his face to the floor and his derriere up in the air. I thought to myself, "How embarrassing for him." The Spirit of God immediately stuck a spiritual dagger in my heart, saying, "He has humility and you do not," and convicted me that I should be humble, unconcerned about personal appearance and willing to pray for lost people. I made a commitment in my heart that very night to be like my doctor friend, always willing to be at the altar in humility and in prayer for myself, my family, and for lost people. The Bible teaches us in James 4:6 that "God is opposed to the proud, but gives grace to the humble."

Fourth, **the Canaanite woman had great faith**. Jesus Himself told her, "Your faith is great" (Matthew 15:28), when she implied that even a crumb from His table was sufficient to save her daughter. Jesus honors faith. "Without faith it is impossible to please [God]" (Hebrews 11:6). Why would the Canaanite woman persist if she did not have an expectation that He would have responded to her anguished plea? Why would you persist if you didn't have faith that He would answer your prayer? Faith gives confidence that my praying and God's intervening are stronger than their sinning, stronger than Satan's **binding**, stronger than Satan's **blinding**, and stronger than the world's allure. There is power in the persistent prayer of a pure-hearted prayer warrior. Do you believe this? Then go to Jesus with audacity, persistence, humility and faith on behalf of your lost family member or friend or coworker. He will no more turn you away than He turned away this Canaanite woman.

♦   ♦   ♦   ♦   ♦

I learned some important lessons from the twelve-year saga in our family life on behalf of my brothers:

1) If you have family members like my brothers, do not be discouraged. Your praying is stronger than their sinning. The persistent prayers of a pure-hearted prayer warrior will prevail.

2) Nobody will prevail in prayer like a concerned, brokenhearted mom or dad, just like Job did in Job 1:4-5.

> *The persistent prayers of a pure-hearted prayer warrior will prevail.*

3) There is something supernatural about praying at the altar. God honors prayers prayed at the altar. Why? When you and I kneel at the altar, it demonstrates humility and seriousness.

4) Corporate prayer encourages the body of Christ, knits people together forever, and wins the day in spiritual battles. When we pray with a group of like-minded prayer warriors who worship God energetically and take hold of the horns of the altar and won't let go until God releases their loved ones, we are encouraged to pray even more. More than that, our hearts become knit together forever. Those Wednesday night prayer warriors at Rock Hill Baptist Church are still my best friends — twenty-five years later — and they still ask me about John Reed's spiritual well-being when they see me. They invested in his life. I'm convinced that our united prayer was the necessary ingredient to tip the balance of power in the heavenly realm in my brother's favor. Remember when he said he sat all weekend with a shotgun under his chin but couldn't pull the trigger. He didn't know why. Loud heavy metal music played in the background urging him on, but he couldn't go through with it. He was covered by the angels of God because fifty people prayed for him every Wednesday night, I prayed at

the altar every Sunday (and really more often), and my mom prayed at her kitchen table every morning. Corporate prayer wins the day. Recruit your friends and family to pray with you.

5) God teaches us to approach the throne of grace with confidence. He will not turn you away. The devil will lie to you and tell you God is too busy or you made that request already. God teaches us that persistence in prayer and purity in heart will prevail.

STUDY QUESTIONS | Chapter 2

1. Who has God laid on your heart to pray for?

2. Why is the altar a sacred place of prayer?

3. If we know God honors prayers prayed at the altar, why don't we go to the altar to pray?

4. Why do we give up praying for our friends or family member?

5. Is there someone too hard for God to rescue?

6. Who would be the best ones for you to join with in concerted prayer?

3

PROCRASTINATION

Back when I was a "baby" doctor (a young doctor about twenty-nine years old), I was running through the hospital one day — running with my hair on fire, as usual. At the time, I got up every morning at approximately 5:00 a.m. to have my devotional, and then I left the house by 5:45 a.m. to visit three hospitals to see anywhere from five to ten medical patients and usually two obstetric patients. It wasn't unusual to have one or two patients in intensive care with either a heart attack, stroke, or congestive heart failure. We family doctors used to take care of everything in those days before hospitalists existed. I almost always had someone in the hospital with uncontrolled diabetes, asthma or pneumonia. Now, most of the time I can manage all of these as an outpatient with the availability of home glucose monitors, home nebulizer machines, and newer, long-acting, injectable antibiotics. It's a new world!

Well, back to my story. I was in a hurry, as usual, this particular day. I planned to discharge from the hospital a forty-five-year-old black man who had just had an inferior myocardial infarction (heart attack). He had been cleared by the cardiologist for discharge since he was now symptom free, and he had been given a follow-up in one month in his office. I requested him to see me in my office in one week. As I was writing his discharge orders at his bedside, the Spirit of God very plainly prompted me, "Share the gospel with him."

I stopped, looked at him, looked at my watch, and made a portentous decision. I decided to share the gospel with him when he came to my office the next week when I would not be in such a rush. I signed off on his discharge orders, patted him on the shoulder, and told him, "See you in one week."

Sure enough, one week later I saw his chart in my chart box at the office. I remembered the subtle prompting of Holy Spirit the week before and determined in my heart I would share the gospel with him that very day. As I entered the exam room across the hall from his room, I heard a loud and heavy thud. I quickly crossed the hall, opened the door to his room, and found him lying face down on the floor in full cardiac arrest! I shouted for the nurses, and we began a thirty-minute CPR attempt that ultimately failed. We never got the least pulse or BP. He was dead when he hit the floor. He is the only patient who has actually died in our medical office during my thirty-five-plus years of medical practice. Our entire staff was visibly shaken.

His two sisters were in the waiting room, so I called them into my private office to inform them of his demise. Still trembling myself, I tried to comfort them. During this difficult conversation, they informed me he was not a believer, which stabbed me in the heart as I remembered Holy Spirit had prompted me to speak to him one week previously. I didn't know what to say at that point. I really lost my composure then. I said something dumb like, "Well, he lived a good life," to which they both shook their heads negatively in unison. Then I really felt even dumber. Not only was that theologically incorrect, they knew it to be actually inaccurate. Man, I was sinking fast. Even his sisters were shaking their heads at me sadly. What must Holy Spirit be thinking?

That has been over twenty-five years ago, and as you can tell, I haven't gotten over it yet. Why? Because I procrastinated. I didn't immediately listen to the subtle prompting of Holy Spirit in my life to share the gospel. I have a conviction that when Holy Spirit tells us to share the gospel with someone, He has also prepared that person's heart on the other end. This certainly makes sense. Why would He send me to speak to someone whose heart is hardened and unprepared? Sometimes the window of opportunity is narrow — case in point with my patient's abbreviated life. That is why immediate obedience to Holy Spirit is crucial. I don't know everything that goes on behind the curtains in other people's lives. However, Holy Spirit does.

> *I have a conviction that when Holy Spirit tells us to share the gospel with someone, He has also prepared that person's heart on the other end.*

I teach my children to obey me sweetly, completely and immediately. They don't always understand the reasons why I ask them to do the things I ask them to do, but I ask them to trust me and obey me.

I don't always understand the rationale behind the prompting of Holy Spirit. Sometimes it seems foolish or illogical, but our responsibility is to trust and obey. Jesus said in John 14:15, "If you love Me, you will keep My commandments." The old hymn says, "Trust and obey, for there's no other way to be happy in Jesus, but to trust and obey."[1]

I once had a great uncle who was dying in the hospital. When I heard about it, Holy Spirit plainly prompted me to go there and share the gospel with him. Because I am an evangelist at heart, I was initially thrilled at the prospect, but my uncle's wife, who could be a bit harsh, always intimidated me. I was at my pastor's home when I heard about his condition, so we prayed for him before I set off for the hospital.

I arrived to find him and my aunt all alone in the hospital room. She was not overly pleasant or inviting as usual. I stayed about fifteen minutes to pay my respects and then left. I went back to my pastor's home to finish my visit with him but could not shake the impression that I was supposed to share the gospel with my uncle.

When I finished my visit with my pastor, Paul Sullivan, I determined to go back to the hospital once again. This time my uncle was all alone in his room. We talked for a few minutes. He was so weak he could only whisper.

Finally, I asked him about his spiritual life. He pondered for a moment; then he asked me, "What does it mean to be born again? Can you explain that to me?" I almost laughed out loud. He might as well have asked Billy Graham if he could explain that one. Well, I was on that one like a duck on a June bug. I carefully explained the entire conversation between Jesus and Nicodemus, and that being born again is a spiritual birth whereby the Spirit of God imparts the life of God to us when we, by faith, receive the Lord Jesus Christ as our Savior. I explained the role of confession of sin and repentance from sin, and I explained that salvation is a free gift of God that He extends to us by His grace.

After that brief explanation, I asked if he understood. He nodded affirmatively. I asked if he would like to pray and receive the Lord Jesus Christ as His Savior. He again nodded affirmatively. I asked him if he had ever done that before, and he shook his head negatively while tears came from both eyes and rolled down both cheeks. I then led my aging uncle in a sinner's prayer right there in his hospital bed. I talked a little more with him holding both of my hands tightly. A little later he fell asleep, and sometime the next morning my uncle died and went to Jesus.

All of my life I will regret not speaking to my patient when Holy Spirit prompted me. All of my life I will rejoice that I spoke to my uncle when Holy Spirit prompted me. Two different stories — two different endings. I believe Holy Spirit had prepared both of those men's hearts. My heart was obedient on one occasion but not on another.

♦ ♦ ♦ ♦ ♦

A retired pastor was in my office one day and shared with me this account of how his brother-in-law had become estranged from his children and grandchildren. It seems he was sharing with them information about his favorite political candidates and issues about nine years ago via email and texts when his sharing of information became obnoxious to the children. They tried to politely infer that his emails were over the top, but he didn't get the message. They had to demand that their father and grandfather cease and desist.

He became highly offended and refused to communicate with any of them for nine years. He wouldn't attend family gatherings or birthday parties. He became hard, sullen and bitter, with no amount of cajoling or pleading appeasing him.

Ultimately, his eighty-plus-year-old mother lay dying in the hospital. She was the most grieved of all the family members by his conduct. My pastor friend shared with me that he was praying for his mother-in-law one morning when he received the strongest impression from the Lord that he should go speak to his brother-in-law about being reconciled to the family. He said, "This intimidated me because I had no idea how he would respond, but I have a conviction that when God speaks to me on this end, He is also speaking to the other person on the other end."

He went to the hospital and found his brother-in-law at his mother's bedside. He called him out into the hallway and said, "I've got a message for you. I believe God prompted me this morning to tell you that you need to make things right with your kids and grandchildren. There's nothing in this world worth ruining these relationships, and you need to do it as a gift to your mama before she goes."

Immediately, he began to weep and agreed that my pastor friend was right. He went straight to his mother's bedside and informed her of his plan to make things right with his family. His mother died shortly thereafter. At the reception for friends the day before the funeral, he collected all the family and reconciled himself to every one of them.

My pastor friend was obedient to the subtle prompting of Holy Spirit leading to the reconciliation of an entire family. When God speaks to you and me on one end, He also has spoken to someone else on the other end. Though it sometimes doesn't make sense to us, our responsibility is to be obedient.

What if the apostle Philip had not been obedient to the prompting of Holy Spirit when he was led down to the desert road leading to Gaza where he met the Ethiopian eunuch? That leading official may never have heard the gospel, and the gospel may never have arrived in his country except for Philip's obedience. How many times have you and I missed opportunities to share the gospel with someone whose heart Holy Spirit has prepared, but we procrastinated for various reasons? Pray every day that God will make us sensitive to the prompting of Holy Spirit, not just sensitive but obedient — sweetly, completely and immediately.

Pray every day that God will make us sensitive to the prompting of Holy Spirit, not just sensitive but obedient — sweetly, completely and immediately.

STUDY QUESTIONS | Chapter 3

1. Why do we expect our children to obey us sweetly, completely and immediately?

2. Why should we be so careful to obey God the same way?

3. Are there really spiritual activities that go on behind the scenes of which we are not aware?

4. Why is immediate obedience to Holy Spirit important?

5. How do we discern the prompting of Holy Spirit?

6. How do we know the will of God?

4

I'VE GOT TO TELL SOMEBODY

I remember when I first met my wife, Carlotta. I sang in a trio for a Campus Crusade for Christ banquet, and we needed a pianist. One of the fellows in the trio knew Carlotta played the piano, and she graciously agreed to practice with us. Thus, our first meeting, brief and casual at the end of our junior year, occurred at the piano in the foyer of Byrnes Hall at Clemson University. As providence would have it, in the fall of our senior year I again needed a pianist to practice with me for my weekly voice lessons, and the rest is romantic history.

Even before our relationship became serious, I would suddenly break the silence in my dorm room, where my roommate Barry and I were studying, with nonstop, one-sided comments about Carlotta. Barry would frown and say, "Nobody here was talking about anybody named Carlotta." Attempting to embarrass me, Barry soon realized I was too far gone before even I realized that she was "the one" for me. I couldn't control myself. I just had to tell somebody. I couldn't keep it to myself.

Well, we married and a few years later our first daughter entered God's world. We named her Rachel; in my professional, expert medical opinion, she was the prettiest little baby ever born to mankind. I immediately had pictures developed, putting them in a little baby book small enough to fit into my white medical coat pocket, and then I proceeded to show them to every human being I saw — at every nurses' station, in every patients' room, at church, in stores, and on the streets of Spartanburg! I was one proud papa! Some things we just have to tell somebody about. I had a bad case of the "can't help its."

Now, suppose you won the Publishers Clearing House grand prize for $10 million, and they just showed up at your house with the camera crew and a three-foot-long imitation check by surprise? Would you be happy? Could you pay off your debts? Buy a new house? A new car? Give to missions? Would you call somebody? A lot of somebodies?

I call it the "law of good things." When something good happens to you, you have to tell somebody. What's the "goodest" thing that ever happened to you? Well, of course, being born again into the kingdom of God, the day you met Jesus and had your sins washed away.

> *Oh happy day (oh happy day)*
> *Oh happy day (oh happy day)*
> *When Jesus washed (when Jesus washed)*
> *Oh, when He washed (when Jesus washed)*
> *When Jesus washed (when Jesus washed)*
> *He washed my sins away (oh happy day)*
> *Oh happy day (oh happy day)[1]*

So often in Scripture when people met Jesus, they hurried away to tell everybody what He had done for them. Do you remember the woman at the well in John 4? The Bible says she returned to her town and said, "Come meet a man who told me everything I ever did" (my version of verse 29). This was a woman who had been married five times and now lived with a man. You can bet this news stirred up a little excitement among the men folk. The whole town came out to meet Him. She had to tell somebody!

When Jesus healed the Gadarene demoniac in Luke 8:26-39, the man was so overcome with joy he desired to follow Jesus. However, "[Jesus] sent him away, saying, 'Return to your house and describe what great things God has done for you.' And he went away, proclaiming throughout the whole city what great things Jesus had done for him" (Luke 8:38b-39). This man who previously lived among the tombs, naked and exposed to the elements and tormented by demons, was now completely delivered from demonic influence, completely clothed and in his right mind. He had a story to tell and he had a grateful heart. That is a powerful combination. What has Jesus delivered you from? How grateful are you? Who will you tell first?

When I was in my residency training, I met a friend from high school that I had not seen in ten years. As we talked, I quickly got to telling him about what Jesus had done in my life over the last ten years. Excited and quite animated about the changes Christ had produced in my heart and my character, I blabbed on for about ten minutes before he finally stopped me and said, "You weren't like this in high school; what happened to you?"

I stopped and thought for a moment. I wasn't really prepared for that question. So, I just said offhand, "The Holy Spirit just got a hold of me, I guess." Then I went back to describing the changes God had made in my life.

Later that night, I thought more seriously about that question. What had actually transpired in my life? I remember the day one of my college friends kicked my dorm room door open, unannounced, and shouted at me, "Jackson, I heard you were turning into a Jesus freak. Is that true?"

He said it with obvious disgust. I thought about it briefly. I had started going to weekly Bible study. I was having a daily quiet time. I was memorizing Scripture. I was going with an older, more mature

Christian and learning how to share the gospel each week in the dorms. I looked up and said, "Yeah, I guess I am."

He cussed a blue streak, slammed the door, and left, going down the hall. I never saw him again. Previously, he was a close friend. Jesus said, "I did not come to bring peace, but a sword" (Matthew 10:34). The gospel often divides.

What were the factors that turned me from a mere believer into an evangelical? I make a distinction between believers and evangelicals because there are many who sit in the pews every Sunday who *believe* the right things but never *practice* the right things. In other words, they are not obedient. James said for us to "prove [ourselves] doers of the word, and not merely hearers who delude themselves" (James 1:22). If believers never practice what they believe (i.e., share the gospel), can they truly be called evangelical? See what I mean? Somewhere in my freshman year of college, I transitioned from saying and believing the right things to doing the right things. Nobody told me to. An inner compulsion motivated by Holy Spirit compelled me to tell everyone who would listen to what God was doing in my life and what God could do for them if they would allow it.

> *He was suspicious that maybe I should consider seminary, since all I ever did was talk about Jesus and the Bible. That's what preachers do, right? No, that's what evangelical Christians do!*

I had become an evangelical so much so that my father called me at college one night to reaffirm with me that medical school was really my calling. He was suspicious that maybe I should consider seminary, since all I ever did was talk about Jesus and the Bible. That's what preachers do, right? No, that's what evangelical Christians do! Let's trace the steps of what happened in my life. First, two senior college students came by my dorm room one day and explained to me what it meant to be a Spirit-controlled Christian. I had been in church all of my life, and I had never heard an explanation of this basic, fundamental biblical truth. I began immediately to pray every day that Holy Spirit who lives in me would rule over every area of my life. I conscientiously attempted to submit every area of my life to His leadership. My spiritual growth began to skyrocket. My understanding of Scriptures increased rapidly under the instruction of Holy Spirit; my prayer life took on new vibrancy. Suddenly, my desire to share the gospel was intensified.

Jesus told his disciples in Acts 1:8 that "when Holy Spirit has come upon you, you shall be my witnesses." I certainly found this to be true. The Holy Spirit had always been in me as a believer, but I had not allowed Him to be in control of my life. Every day I was careful to confess sin in my life and to subordinate my life under God's authority as revealed in His Word. The transformation was obvious to all my friends.

Second, I made a strong commitment to a daily devotional. I had been reading a chapter a day in my Bible since I was thirteen years old, but now I had an appetite for God's Word that required much more than that. I began to spend thirty to forty minutes a day reading the Word, memorizing Scripture and praying. My Bible knowledge increased, and, hence, my relationship with the Father became much more personal and intimate. I began to worship God rather than just run through a list of prayer requests. I learned how to pray the Scriptures that I was memorizing, which enhanced my prayer life tremendously. The benefit to me? I began to experience "the peace of God which surpasses all comprehension" (Philippians 4:7). Gone were the impatience, anger, and frustration — sinful flaws in my previous character. Praise the Lord, that old worrywart vanished forever. I've learned to trust God in all things.

When I was in medical school, I read a series of missionary

biographies about well-known missionaries. As I read, I noticed a common thread in all of their lives. Prior to embarking on their missionary journeys, each of them shared two life-altering experiences that shaped the remaining years of their Christian ministries. The first was when they committed to a daily devotional, and the second was when they understood the ministry of Holy Spirit in their personal lives. They all considered those two things to have revolutionized their spiritual lives. I reflected on my own spiritual journey and had to say the same was true for me.

I was blessed shortly after all this took place to receive some quality training in evangelism. It was basic training at the time, but it started me on the right foot at a time when Holy Spirit was motivating me to speak out. God was orchestrating all the events of my life. Isn't God good?

I went from being a "do nothing, know nothing" pew sitter to a moderately well-trained, well-informed, fired-up, full-of-the-Holy-Spirit evangelical in the course of two years. I still had a lot to learn, and I was eager to do so. In fact, I'm still eager to learn — forty-plus years later. I'm eager to learn and I'm eager to share what God is teaching me. That's what prompted my friend to ask, "What happened to you? You weren't like this in high school." So now you know the long answer, and why I'm compelled to tell somebody. Who are you going to tell?

STUDY QUESTIONS | Chapter 4

1. What two life-altering experiences, shaping their ministry years, did each of the missionaries have?

2. Have you had a similar experience? Can you share your experience with the group?

3. Who helped you the most to develop a consistent daily quiet time?

4. Where did you learn the fundamentals of the Spirit-controlled life?

5. Do you feel a compulsion to share your faith?

6. With whom do you most want to share your faith?

5

Is There a Plan B?

I was in love — really, really in love. It was springtime with azaleas blooming and birds singing. My little heart was singing as well. I had just asked my girlfriend, Carlotta, to marry me and she had graciously accepted. I was scheduled to graduate from medical school in a couple of days, and Carlotta had just returned from a two-year missionary journey to the Middle East working as a nursing instructor in a Baptist hospital in Gaza. She returned a week early in order to attend my graduation. My life was full of excitement, and I was in love!

That particular day, I had arranged with one of my uncles to drive Miss Carlotta around town in his old Model A Ford, which he had kept in pristine condition. It was yellow with a black roof and running boards. It drove exceptionally smooth for its age, changing gears without difficulty. I remember clearly that my new fiancée had on a yellow dress matching that yellow Model A Ford. It's funny what we remember. We drove around town for about an hour just enjoying the springtime day, the old car, and each other's company. We ended up back at my uncle's house.

We went inside to drink iced tea and chat a bit about our future plans. Of course, we talked about Carlotta's two-year stint in the Middle East, which was filled with fascinating events. We had no definite wedding plans since we had been engaged for only two days. Then we got around to mentioning we would like to go back overseas as career missionaries when I finished my residence program.

Now before I proceed any further, you have to understand that my uncle used to take me to Sunday school when I was of elementary age and my dad was busy at the hospital. He taught young boys in Sunday school, and he was a deacon at our Baptist church.

He pondered the plans we had mentioned and then said, "Robbie, don't you think that God will make a way for all those folks over there to get to heaven even if they never hear the gospel?"

In stunned disbelief, I nearly shouted at my uncle, "No, no, a thousand times — no!"

Now I didn't really say that to my uncle. I respected him too much, but inside that's what I thought. I very carefully responded, "No, sir, I don't think so. That's why we send missionaries overseas because we don't believe God will save them by any other way. There is no Plan B. The Bible says, 'For there is no other name under heaven that has been given among men, by which we must be saved' (Acts 4:12). That name is Jesus. Jesus Himself said, 'I am the way, and the truth, and the life; no one comes to the Father but through me' (John 14:6)."

My uncle pondered my mini-sermon for a few moments, then said, "If you say so."

I could tell he was not persuaded.

My uncle's thinking is not unique among American Christians. I talk to many who are convinced that because God is good He will not allow millions of lost people who have not heard the gospel to perish apart from Christ. Like my uncle, they believe in Plan B, which is never spelled out in the Scripture. It is a figment of the imagination of weak-willed or poorly informed Christians unwilling to accept the hard truths of Scripture — first, the lost are really lost, and, second, we are responsible to take the gospel to them. Now, don't be hard on my uncle, because according to the 2016 State of American Theology Research Report by LifeWay Research and sponsored by Ligonier Ministries, 64 percent of Americans with evangelical beliefs agree with the statement "Heaven is a place where all people will ultimately be reunited with their loved ones."[1] Theologians call this universalism, the belief that God will save everyone in the end.

Let's answer this hard question: Are the lost really lost? Are unbelievers condemned to spend eternity separated away from God in a place called hell? The justification for all missionary endeavors hangs on the answer to that question. Understand clearly: If lost people (nonbelievers in Jesus Christ) are not condemned to eternal separation from the Heavenly Father, then why send our best young people to dangerous places around the world? I mean, Carlotta, my wife, had a bomb explode in front of her car in downtown Gaza one day; plus, she had guns pointed at her routinely as she crossed borders and transported supplies to the hospital. Why would we invest thousands of dollars sending missionaries overseas to preach the gospel if there is a Plan B, and God will allow them into heaven anyway? Why would we expose pagans to the gospel, give them an opportunity to reject Christ, put their soul in eternal jeopardy by that very rejection when, in fact, God intends to save them anyway? Does that make any sense? Of course not.

Our missionary endeavors are not simply humanitarian gestures to provide food for the poor and medical care for the afflicted, although compassion compels us to do those very things. Our ultimate motivation is to fulfill the Great Commission as commanded by our Lord to "go therefore and make disciples of all the nations" (Matthew 28:19).

Making disciples, followers of Christ, through the preaching of the gospel is our ultimate and primary objective. Baptism and Bible teaching follow closely.

This is not my opinion. It bears repeating — Jesus is the one who claimed to be the exclusive, one-way path to God when He said, "I am the way" (John 14:6). Then He proved the veracity of His audacious claim by His resurrection from the dead!

While in Gaza for three months as a fourth-year medical student, I met a number of Greek Orthodox and Muslim students. It had been years since any of the Muslims had converted to Christianity. Many of the Greek Orthodox students were Christian in name only. It was a generally held belief among the Greek Orthodox that Muslims could not be saved. Why was that? They had never seen or heard of a Muslim who had become a believer. These Greek Orthodox students were the opposite of my uncle. He believed God would save lost people in the far parts of the world even if they had never heard the gospel. These students, on the other hand, didn't believe Muslims could ever be saved even when they had heard the gospel! Isn't that a strange turn of events?

While Carlotta was in Gaza, a mini-revival broke out at the Gaza Baptist Hospital Nursing School. Twenty-two nursing students, all Muslim, became believers! This was truly remarkable, given that they risked rejection or death at the hands of their families. Everyone — missionaries, the Greek Orthodox students and the Muslims who witnessed this revival — was amazed. To God be the glory!

> *If you and I are not convinced in our hearts that the lost are really lost ... then we will never be assertive evangelists.*

If you and I are not convinced in our hearts that the lost are really lost, without God and without any hope of salvation, then we will never be assertive evangelists among our family and friends. More than that, we will certainly not take great pains to fulfill the Great Commission in order to reach people we don't even know in the far-flung parts of the world. What would be my motivation if I'm not even convinced that unregenerate people groups really are in peril of eternal condemnation? If I have a sneaking suspicion that God has a different plan for them, why bother? But is this what Scripture teaches? Let's examine the Scriptures more closely.

I. The invisible God has been clearly seen. In Romans 1:19, Paul teaches us God is revealing Himself to all people "because that which is known about God is evident within them; for God made it evident to them." He does this through the beauty and the complexity of the created world that He spoke into existence and sustains by the word of His power. No human being on any continent (throughout all of time) can say that God did not reveal Himself to him or her because "the heavens are telling of the glory of God; and their expanse is declaring the work of His hands" (Psalm 19:1). Furthermore, Paul said in Romans 1:20, "For since the creation of the world, His invisible attributes, His eternal power and divine nature, have been clearly seen, being understood through what has been made, so that they are without excuse." All people have a knowledge of God. He has revealed Himself to them plainly. They are without excuse.

II. All people everywhere are ungrateful rejecters of God. The apostle Paul discusses this very thing in Romans 1:21 when he states, "For even though they knew God, they did not honor Him as God, or gave thanks." When I was in India, we couldn't drive a half-mile without seeing a shrine built on the side of the road to house some family's personal deity. There are literally thousands of different man-made deities conjured in the minds of the Indian people that they worship. They reject the true knowledge of God. But not just the people of India — this happens in every country of the world, including America, where the gospel is preached continuously on radio, TV, and in churches all across the country. We underestimate how our lower nature rejects the true knowledge of God.

"But, Dr. Jackson, those people are sincere in their belief. They may not hear about Jesus. Doesn't God give them credit for their sincerity?" I read about a medical doctor, an anesthesiologist who accidentally gave his patient nitrous oxide instead of oxygen. It was a mistake, a sincere mistake, but the patient sincerely died, and this doctor paid a huge amount of money in malpractice fees to the patient's family. He was sincere all right; he was sincerely wrong, and the patient died. Being sincere does not earn merit in a court of law or with God.

God alone deserves to be worshiped, and He shares His glory with no other (Isaiah 42:8). Sincerity notwithstanding, pagan peoples are deluded, but the fact of the matter is they choose to worship false idols, the same as we do if we and they reject the true knowledge of God. All of us are idolaters at heart.

III. All people of all countries are guilty before Holy God. In Romans 3:10-12, Paul describes our condition by saying, "There is none righteous, not even one." There is not even one innocent guy living out there somewhere. All are guilty before Holy God. If any of you have children, you know what I mean. Did you ever have to teach them to rebel against your authority? No, it just comes naturally, doesn't it? I have visited some of those idyllic tribes that are portrayed in magazines. Trust me, they are not so idyllic. They lie and steal with the worst of them. They covet other men's wives and pursue revenge killings with the worst of them. Their cultures are rife with sin and depravity just like downtown Spartanburg where I live. Sin is universal. It just wears different clothes and speaks a different language. I don't know where we get off thinking that just because they don't know about Jesus, the default eternal state for them is heaven. Listen! God is a holy God. He does not allow anything corrupt in His holy dwelling. Those sinners are not going to heaven any more than you unless you and they repent, confess sin, and come to Jesus. Paul was not kidding when he said, "For there is no other name under heaven that has been given among men, by which we must be saved" (Acts 4:12). Again, he was talking about the name of Jesus.

IV. Hallelujah! God has made a way for the lost. I remember watching Al Mohler, president of Southern Baptist Theological Seminary, talk to Larry King on his television program one time.[2] Jewish Rabbi Boteach derisively asked Mohler, "Where do Jews go who don't believe in Jesus?"

I held my breath. What would he say? How would he answer? You know the rabbi was baiting him, trying to get him to back off his fundamental belief in front of a national television audience.

Reverend Mohler didn't blink or pause. He stared Rabbi Boteach down like a coon in a tree, and said, "I believe it says that those who are ... who reject Christ ... those who do not accept Christ, those who do not believe in Christ, will die, and when they are raised in the resurrection, they will face the judgment of God, and they will be consigned to hell."[3]

The audience gasped and sighed, but Mohler held his ground and spoke the truth. You see, you and I must be willing to wear the shame of the cross and bear the ridicule that comes with the preaching of the gospel message. "For the word of the cross is to those who are perishing foolishness, but to us who are being saved it is the power of God" (1 Corinthians 1:18).

Hallelujah! Yes, God has made a way for the lost. That way is through the cross of Jesus Christ. Jesus died on the cross for sinners, paid their sin debt, rose again on the third day, and by faith in Him offers us the very righteousness of God apart from the law to all who believe. That is the good news, the greatest news. *But* there is a catch!

How can folks who have never heard this good news be saved? Paul went on to ask and answer that question in Romans 10:13-15: "For whoever will call upon the name of the Lord will be saved. How then shall they call upon Him in whom they have not believed? And how shall they believe in Him whom they have not heard? And how shall they hear without a preacher? And how shall they preach unless they are sent? Just as it is written, 'How beautiful are the feet of those who bring glad tidings of good things!'"Don't you understand? Unless we send preachers of the good news, many will never hear. We as the church are the plan of God for reaching the lost world. There is no Plan B. So as John Wayne famously said, "Slap some bacon on a biscuit and let's go! We're burnin' daylight!"[4]

Time's a-wasting, brothers and sisters. As of November 2017, the Joshua Project estimates there are more than 6,672 people groups totaling 3,065,065,000 people currently classified as unreached.[5] "Unreached" means a people group does not contain an indigenous community of evangelical Christians. "Unengaged" means no church or organization is actively working to spread the gospel within that people group.

The church I attend has adopted a people group in northeast India called the Andro people. The Andro are 300,000 strong and mostly rice farmers. They are an oriental people, short in stature, and very industrious. By our standards, their living conditions would be classified as primitive. They are also classified as unreached and unengaged because the few churches present are not evangelistic. That means people are born, live and die there without ever hearing the gospel and have done so for generations. Our church aims to change that by God's grace, prayer and diligent evangelism.

What people group has your church adopted? There are plenty to choose from.

The next time a family member or friend asks you, "Don't you think

God has a special plan for all of those lost people in Africa?" don't go postal on him or her like I was tempted to with my uncle. Just be calm and rational and rehearse with them all the truths you have just learned in this chapter. Better yet, share with them your personal plan for reaching lost people locally and around the world. Whaaat? You don't have a personal plan? Then you better read the next chapter.

STUDY QUESTIONS | Chapter 5

1. What is meant by Plan B?

2. Why is there no Plan B?

3. Why are those who never hear the gospel spiritually lost? Is that fair?

4. Why can Jesus claim to be the only way?

5. What is the church's responsibility in regard to the lost?

6. What is your responsibility in regard to the lost?

7. What exactly is an unreached/unengaged people group? How many are there?

6

WHAT'S YOUR PLAN?

S tanding on a stone fountain in a market in Oradea, Romania, I
raised my voice and began to preach using an interpreter. As soon
as I spoke, my voice boomed over the noise of a thousand people in
the city square because the ground was covered with stone pavers;
plus, we were surrounded by four-story stone buildings, adding to the
megaphone effect. All the people turned, looked at me simultaneously,
and stopped what they were doing. A strange hush fell over the market
that seemed a mile long (it may have been). I have to admit my heart fell
to my feet for a brief second. I wasn't prepared for that kind of response.
My mind went blank for a split second, but then the message that I had
been preaching all week using the wordless book as an evangelistic tool
came back to me. (The wordless book has colored pages with no words.
The user explains the plan of salvation using the colors, much like the
bracelet with colored beads.) I launched into my gospel presentation by
discussing the white page, representing God's holiness; then the black
page, a symbol of our sin; the red page, Christ's blood sacrifice paying
the penalty for our sin; and so forth. My interpreter was only seventeen,
but he had learned English well; in the last four days, he had also learned
my presentation by heart. We had preached on the street all day long
each day to thousands of people. Unlike Americans, these people in

Romania were hungry to hear the gospel. Within a few seconds, several hundred were gathered around me to hear what I had to say.

I was in Romania with Carpenters for Christ on an evangelistic trip, no construction this time. We were there about one and a half years after Nicolae Ceausescu was deposed after forty years of communist rule. It was amazing to see busy people at bus stations turn aside for fifteen to twenty minutes to listen to an American preach the gospel through an interpreter. That would never happen in America. Afterwards, we opened a suitcase full of Bibles to hand out, and there was a literal stampede. We were going to give the Bibles to the ones who indicated a decision for Christ, but everyone in the crowd wanted a Bible, possession of which was forbidden for forty years under communist rule.

In a day and a half, we gave out 20,000 gospel tracts printed in their language. We never saw a single tract discarded on the ground or rejected like we would see in America. Such was the hunger for spiritual truth. However, we were in a crisis after the second day because we were out of tracts. We gathered our entire group together for supper and prayed. We asked God to provide more tracts, an impossible task in our minds. Where could we find gospel tracts in former communist Romania?

That night a Swedish mission group dropped by to say they were leaving the next day and had 40,000 Romanian gospel tracts left over. Could we use them? We all looked at each other like the children of Israel after the Red Sea parted! We were back in business. Our God is Jehovah Jireh, the Lord who provides!

Our group of evangelists traveled around the city looking for opportunities to share the gospel. My medical partner, Steve Bailes, went to a school, introduced himself, and asked permission to speak to one of the classrooms. The principal called an assembly of the entire school so he could share the gospel message with every student! In another instance, he asked permission to speak to some factory workers, and the plant manager invited all the workers together. He completely stopped production for an hour for them to hear a foreigner talk about Jesus! Imagine that in America. God certainly showed us favor during that time.

I was invited to speak to a group of about 100 medical doctors. I pondered how to address them. I decided that God honored the foolishness of preaching the cross, so I gave them the same message with the wordless book that I gave everyone else on the street all week long. That was the only group that sneered at me all week. They were too intellectual and too proud. Afterwards, I gave them an opportunity to ask questions. I supposed they would ask about my presentation. Oh, no, they wanted to know how much money American doctors make!

Communism may have been dead, but atheistic materialism was still alive. No thoughts of God for these men. In the new order, they stood to make a profitable living. They didn't need God. In most every other venue, it was not unusual for 50 percent of the audience to indicate a decision for Christ. None of these proud doctors were interested at all. None of them came up to speak to me afterwards. I was really brokenhearted for my medical colleagues. I can still see their hard faces twenty-five years later.

My wife, Carlotta, traveled to Romania with us. She was seven months pregnant at the time with our fifth child. It was not a fun or easy trip for her. She was swollen and fatigued the entire trip. Our friends thought she was crazy for going, but remember I was her obstetrician. I've delivered all but one of our children. Why would she go, you ask? That's a good question.

My wife had been pregnant or nursing a baby for all of my Carpenters for Christ trips. This time she believed God called her to go. It's that simple. I know my wife's heart. She is driven to fulfill the Great

Commission. She is driven to obey her Lord's command, "Go therefore and make disciples of all the nations, baptizing them in the name of the Father and the Son and Holy Spirit, teaching them to observe all that I commanded you; and lo, I am with you always, even to the end of the age" (Matthew 28:19-20). That's why she went to Gaza, Israel, for two years while I was in medical school (tore my heart out and stomped that sucker flat!) to serve as a nursing instructor in the Baptist hospital there. Was it adventurous? Yes. Was it dangerous? Yes. Was it hard? Yes. But she did it out of obedience to God's command, and now here she was seven months pregnant in Romania one year after the fall of communist rule, sharing the gospel in downtown Oradea. I watched her share the wordless book in the park surrounded by a crowd of people. Crazy? In the eyes of the world — yes. Obedient? In the eyes of God — yes. It's what obedient Christians do every day all over the world. We will never fulfill the Great Commission from our recliners watching television with a remote control in one hand and an iced tea in the other. If we are ever to fulfill the Great Commission, then the entire church of Jesus Christ, not just a select few professional missionaries, will have to commit to doing "whatever it takes" until the mission is accomplished.

So, let me ask you, what is your plan? What is your personal plan for fulfilling the Great Commission? Every obedient Christian should possess a carefully thought-out personal strategy for reaching the world for Jesus Christ. So what is your personal strategy? When I ask Christian friends that question, they look at me like a baby calf looking at a new gate. Most have no readily available answer. Most have never even thought about it. Most Christians give a little extra cash and pray a short prayer at the annual mission fundraising event, and that's their contribution to world missions.

Let's talk about this a little bit more. Here are a few helpful suggestions:

1) Make a list of ten names of lost people in your circle of influence. Begin to pray for them and make plans to share the gospel with them. We're fooling ourselves if we think we have a heart for reaching the world if we don't share the gospel with the people closest to us. What makes us think we would share the gospel in Iraq if we don't in our neighborhoods where we know the language and the culture?

2) Go to mission conferences and learn about missions and missionaries in other parts of the world. The more you know, the more God gets a hold of your heart. I recently attended a missions conference where missionaries told of the amazing things God was doing around the world in bringing people to Christ. My vision of God's greatness and for missions was greatly expanded. At the conference, over 100 people of various ages were commissioned as career missionaries to go to over ninety different countries around the world. My heart was moved to tears as I considered the homes and families they were leaving to obey God's call to fulfill the Great Commission. Many of them were going to the toughest, hardest, and most-resistant-to-the-gospel places on this earth. They were doing so gladly and freely and in obedience to God's command. That scene continues to impact my life today. In like manner, every Christian with a heart for missions needs to attend a similar missions conference and commissioning ceremony. The impact will last for a lifetime.

> *My heart was moved to tears as I considered the homes and families they were leaving to obey God's call to fulfill the Great Commission.*

3) Support a missionary personally with your prayers and your finances. Correspond with them frequently by email or by letter. Send them care packages. Did you know you cannot purchase grits in most foreign countries? How do our missionaries survive without grits? Go

see them if you can. Make a report back to your Sunday school class and friends. When you get personally attached, your prayers become more fervent.

4) Set aside money in your budget monthly for support of missions in general, a missionary family in particular, and your own mission trips. If you don't intentionally budget mission money, it will be spent on other items.

5) Adopt an international student, businessman or worker. There are plenty of countries where we as Americans cannot go as missionaries, but they can come to America for school or work. I suspect that most international students spend four or more years in America and never visit in the home of an American or visit in a church. They spend their entire time in America on the campus and in the mall or restaurants. Lord, forgive us!

Bakht Singh, one of the greatest evangelists in the history of India, was won to faith in Christ as a college student while in Canada by Edith and John Hayward in 1930. John Hayward met Bakht at the local YMCA and invited him to a meal at their home where he heard them pray and conduct family devotions. A devoted Hindu, he debated with them the merits of the Christian faith over many subsequent mealtimes. In time, Holy Spirit broke down his resistance, and he committed his life to Christ. His family abandoned him when he returned to India, but he immediately began to preach Christ and soon had large followings. An evangelist had been born! He was eventually responsible for planting hundreds of churches and winning thousands of Indians to Christ.[1] Where did this start? It began with a simple invitation for an international student to eat Sunday dinner at the home of caring Christian people who determined to make friends with a lonesome international student.

The same principle holds true for international businessmen and workers and their families. That's a lot easier than traveling to another country where you don't know the language or the culture in order to share the gospel. God is bringing internationals to our back doorstep by the thousands. What an amazing opportunity! "When a stranger resides with you in your land, you shall not do him wrong. The stranger who resides with you shall be to you as the native among you, and you shall love him as yourself, for you were aliens in the land of Egypt; I am the Lord your God" (Leviticus 19: 33-34).

6) Get a passport. If you don't have a passport, you're not serious about doing missions. Mission trip opportunities come up all the time for those who are prepared and willing to go. "But, Dr. Jackson, you know I can't afford to take off work and go on a mission trip. Besides, my work will never let me off." Look, Jesus is always enough. My first mission trip to Brazil in 1985 cost $1,500. That was 10 percent of my annual income at that time. I was convinced the Lord wanted me to quit talking about the Great Commission and start going on mission trips. I began to pray for God to supply my need. Two doctor friends gave a total of $700, and the rest came in $25 and $50 increments from supportive friends at church. All I could afford was $200, but God provided the rest. Jesus is always enough. Just commit to go and He will provide the rest, even the time off.

"Surely you don't want me to give up my vacation time to go on a mission trip. I only get two weeks of vacation a year."

I don't see why not. Many of my close friends and I have been doing it for thirty years — one week for family vacation and one week for a mission trip. Jesus gave up a plush and comfortable home in heaven to come to earth and gave His life to purchase your salvation. Why would you not give up your vacation to go tell someone who has never heard that Jesus saves? What is the cost of you not going? For the lost person overseas who never hears the gospel, it could mean eternal condemnation. Is your vacation or savings worth that much?

More than that, going on a mission trip changes your perspective forever. Once you see firsthand how the poverty-stricken third world lives, you learn to make do with a lot less. You learn to appreciate America and the standard of living we enjoy. I look at parking lots full of gleaming, nearly new automobiles, and I wonder where are the ox carts laden with colorful fruit? Where are the donkey carts hauling entire families to market? With every purchase I make, I stop and think, saying to myself, "I could support a child in Sudan for one month with that meal. I could support a pastor and his family in India for one month with that purchase." Every purchase now is compared to what it might accomplish on the mission field. "For where your treasure is, there will your heart be also" (Matthew 6:21). The converse is also true. If God has burdened our hearts for the lost people groups of this world, then our treasure will find its way there.

So, what's your plan? May I suggest you sit down with paper and pen and ask God prayerfully to reveal to you a personal strategy for reaching your circle of influence first and then the rest of the world. Make a plan for close to home, then expand your impact for the kingdom of God internationally. Do this, of course, in cooperation with your church or some existing mission organization. No need to recreate the wheel. As you pray about it, you will be surprised at how God will begin to give you ideas. He will then bring people and opportunities into your life as well as transforming your heart. The next thing you know, you will be a world changer, organizing mission trips, hosting missionaries in your home, and raising money for missions. Don't laugh. It happened to me. It started with one mission trip to the Middle East.

STUDY QUESTIONS | Chapter 6

1. Have you ever been to a missionary commissioning ceremony? Can you describe it? Look one up right now and make plans to go. (Call your denomination's headquarters and ask about future commissioning services.)

2. Do you have a passport? Why not? You can apply online at https://travel.state.gov.

3. What does your mission giving look like? Haphazard or budgeted?

4. Do you correspond with an individual missionary?

5. How do you reach your close circle of influence? Why is that important?

6. Do you have any overseas mission trip adventures to share? If not, then plan a trip and collect your own adventures, not for the sake of adventure but out of obedience to the Great Commission.

7. What does this saying have to do with your going on a mission trip or leading a mission trip? "If you think you look funny sitting on a horse, you'll never lead a cavalry charge."

7

A LINE UNSEEN

There is a line by human eyes unseen that crosses every path.
It is the invisible boundary between God's mercy and God's wrath.[1]

M r. B., a patient of mine a long time ago, experienced multiple heart attacks over several years of time. Because of this, he was prone to experience episodes of congestive heart failure. During a hospitalization for heart failure, I became aware he was experiencing a sense of impending doom, a very real and legitimate concern for him. I sat down with him in the coronary care unit and reviewed a gospel presentation with him. Obviously, he was very familiar with the gospel; however, he expressed a great fear of dying and admitted freely that he was not a Christian.

In fact, Mr. B. told me he had listened to J. Harold Smith, a well-known evangelist, on the radio every morning for over forty years. Because he had never made a personal commitment to Christ, he knew he had never been born again. He also was well acquainted with the eternal consequences of dying without resolving the sin issue in his life. Subsequently, he had a great fear of dying. I urged him to pray with me, to confess his sins, to repent of his former lifestyle, and to believe on the Lord Jesus Christ as his only substitute/savior. To my surprise, he stated he would really like to do that, but he simply could not. I asked for an explanation, but he could give none. I urged him to think about it seriously and to not postpone his decision too long, since we both knew his life on this earth would not last much longer.

As I was entering the coronary care unit in order to discharge him from the hospital two days later, I was met by none other than J. Harold Smith and several of his associates. Someone had told the famous evangelist about my patient, and Reverend Smith had come to the hospital to visit him and share the gospel with him. As Reverend Smith was leaving the coronary care unit, he shook my hand, stared into my eyes, and inquired about my spiritual well-being. I was impressed with his forthright manner and assured him I had been born again as an eleven-year-old boy. He quickly blessed me and then disappeared down the hallway with five young preacher boys in tow. I turned and spoke to Mr. B., who appeared to be in a blue funk. I thought he would be exceptionally pleased that the famous evangelist had taken time to come by and visit him. As it turned out, Reverend Smith had shared the gospel with him in the same way I had two days prior.

"Well," I asked, "did you ask Christ to pardon your sins and be Lord of your life?"

Mr. B. sorrowfully nodded in acquiescence.

Perceiving what had happened, I then asked him, "Did you really mean it?"

With tears streaming down his face, Mr. B. admitted that he really prayed the prayer only to please the famous evangelist. "I couldn't say 'no' to the man" was all he could say.

I reproached him. "Mr. B., you just lied to J. Harold Smith, your favorite radio preacher. I can't believe you! Do you understand the seriousness of the issue before you?" He began to sob uncontrollably and assured me he fully understood. I beseeched him, "Mr. B., would you please pray with me a genuine sinner's prayer asking Christ to be the Lord of your life?"

Looking at the floor with tears streaming down his face, he simply said, "I know I need to, but I just can't." I stared at him in amazement. I was completely bumfuzzled by this entire situation.

Two months later, Mr. B. presented to the Spartanburg Regional Medical Center emergency room in fulminant congestive heart failure. Despite heroic efforts by the emergency room staff, his life waned away slowly in the ER. He would pass into unconsciousness and then suddenly awaken. The entire scene was described to me in great detail by one of the ER nurses since I was not there. Whenever Mr. B. awakened, a hospital chaplain would talk to him about his spiritual life. The chaplain discerned that Mr. B. was not a believer in Christ. Realizing Mr. B. would very soon be leaving this world, the chaplain desperately urged him to pray a sinner's prayer. Over and over again, my patient said he would really like to, but he simply could not. In consternation, the chaplain begged him to pray to receive Christ as his Savior, and each time Mr. B. would politely decline. He then lapsed into unconsciousness while the doctors were performing CPR and giving medications intravenously.

My nurse friend told me that this scene was surreal with everyone in the ER praying for Mr. B. as the resuscitation lasted for nearly an hour. Each time he awakened, other people also encouraged him to receive Christ. It was an unusual resuscitation because it lasted so long and because he regained consciousness so many times, but ultimately, he was placed on a ventilator and could no longer speak to the chaplain. When he occasionally awakened, he could only nod and squeeze the chaplain's hand. With many tears and loud urging over the noise and confusion in the emergency room and as multiple doctors and nurses were administering to my patient, the chaplain, kneeling on the floor at the head of his bed, implored Mr. B. to receive the Lord Jesus Christ before his life ebbed away. At this point, all he could do was shake his head indicating that he could not or would not.

Finally, it was determined by the doctors there was nothing more they could do to preserve his life, and all life-support measures were discontinued. Mr. B. slipped away into the next life, never having received the free gift of eternal life. A nurse friend told me there was great weeping in the emergency room that night from many of the nurses and technicians who witnessed this soul-wrenching drama. They realized their patient, whom they really didn't know, had just slipped into a Christ-less eternity. That was thirty years ago. I was not even there, yet I am weeping as I write these lines, weeping for the eternal, never-dying soul of my patient who had become my friend as so many of my patients do.

What happened in the ICU and later in the ER? I believe my friend had casually listened to J. Harold Smith present the gospel on the radio every day for forty years without ever responding to a gospel invitation. Over time, he hardened his heart to the voice of Holy Spirit calling out to him. He developed what the Scripture calls a "seared conscience" (1 Timothy 4:2), or a heart that is calloused to the subtle prompting of Holy Spirit. Sometime during those forty years, he had crossed the dividing line between God's mercy and God's wrath; even though he wanted to repent at the end of his days, he could not. As Paul describes in Romans 1:28, "God gave them over to a depraved mind." Tragically, there is a point of no return. God may eventually stop trying to bring the chronically rebellious to repentance and gives them over to their own way. No sinner knows when this point of no return is, so the better part of wisdom is timely repentance. The psalmist encouraged us to be

> *Over time, he hardened his heart to the voice of Holy Spirit calling out to him.*

timely, "Today, if you would hear his voice, do not harden your hearts" (Psalm 95:7b-8a). What happened to Mr. B. was a mystery to those of us who looked on. It was heartbreaking as well.

As I have shared this account with folks over the years, some have said to me, "Well, my God is not that way. He would never harden a person's heart or give up on them."

To which I respond, "Your God is obviously not the God of the Bible."

They then look at me like I'm an alien from another planet while I calmly explain, "You should ask the unrepentant sinners who beat on the door of Noah's ark before the flood took them away if, in fact, there is a line that can be crossed between God's mercy and God's wrath (Genesis 7:16). Or better yet, ask Pharaoh what happens when one hardens his heart against God's eternal plan so many times that God was the one who hardened Pharaoh's heart so 'he did not let the sons of Israel go out of his land' (Exodus 11:10b). Ask all the Egyptians who lost a firstborn son what the consequences are in a nation when their leader hardens his heart against God. Oh, yes, my friend, the God of the Bible is like that. He is a God of mercy and a God of wrath. He is not to be trifled with."

Postponing repentance not only leads to a hardening of our hearts, but it also leads to a forestalling of certain blessings from God that accrue to our spiritual accounts when we repent. By delaying repentance, we miss out on God's spiritual refreshment. "Repent, therefore, and return, that your sins may be wiped away, in order that times of refreshing may come from the presence of the Lord"

> *Postponing repentance not only leads to a hardening of our hearts, but it also leads to a forestalling of certain blessings from God.*

(Acts 3:19). In addition, we may not prosper. "He who conceals his transgressions will not prosper, but he who confesses and forsakes them will find compassion" (Proverbs 28:13).

My friend, if God is calling you to repent of your sins and receive the Lord Jesus Christ as your personal Savior, then I encourage you to fall on your knees this very moment. Cry out to Jesus, asking for forgiveness of your sins, and He will save your eternal, never-dying soul. Don't postpone. Don't procrastinate. Don't allow your heart to become hardened to the sweet invitation of Holy Spirit. It is a dangerous thing to say "no" to Holy Spirit repeatedly. We never know when our heart will become insensitive to the subtle and sweet invitation of our Lord Jesus Christ.

If you have friends who have been delaying their decision for Christ, then implore them to hasten their decision. Do not allow your friends to put off their decision indefinitely. Every day they postpone, their hearts become a little harder and a little more insensitive. "We are ambassadors for Christ, as though God were entreating through us; we beg you on behalf of Christ, be reconciled to God" (2 Corinthians 5:20). This is a matter of urgency. Why? "There is a line by human eyes unseen."

When I was a boy, the forest service conducted controlled burns of the pine forest around my home to clear out the small trees and briars inevitably growing underneath the tall pines. I used to go with my young friends and watch the forest service men set the fires and burn up the pine needles on the forest floor along with the briars and small trees. All of us adolescent boys were young arsonists at heart, so this spectacle thrilled us to no end. I noticed the fire would set old stumps aflame for a while, but they would usually turn black and burn out very quickly. Not only did they blacken, they also hardened. Whenever another controlled burn would be conducted a year or two later, the fire jumped over these old stumps. They were too hardened by previous fires to catch this time. When I was much older, I watched revival fires sweep through churches, catching many hearts on fire with Holy Spirit conviction of sin and bringing repentance and newness of life in Jesus Christ. I also observed hardened hearts — hardened by sin, hardened by years of saying "no" to Holy Spirit, being skipped over by that same revival fire. Those same folks would say things like, "What's the big deal? Why all the emotion? What's everybody so excited about?" They missed all the joy because the Giver of joy just jumped right over their hardened hearts.

Now, let me give you a word of caution here. None of us knows when someone else crosses that unseen line. Only God knows that. We can never assume someone has crossed that line. In fact, we should assume Holy Spirit is working in everybody's life and "beg them on Christ's behalf to be reconciled to God" until they take their last breath. We all know people who are born again on their deathbed. God still saves people at the last moment. It is true that God is gracious to us, and a person may be able to repent up until the day he dies, but we should not live presumptuously. I share this story not to deter us from evangelism but to encourage our friends and family not to procrastinate. "I tell you, now is the time of God's favor. Today is the day of salvation" (2 Corinthians 6:2, NIV). A quote attributed to D.L. Moody says, "If God's today is too soon for your repentance, then your tomorrow may be too late for God's acceptance."[2] I can put it no other way.

How about you, good friend? Have you postponed making a decision for Christ? Do you know in your heart of hearts that you have never been born again and that you have listened to a hundred gospel presentations without responding? You realize now what's happening, don't you? Just like Mr. B., you are developing a seared conscience — a calloused heart — that will very soon no longer be responsive to the voice of Holy Spirit. That's dangerous ground. "There is a line by human eye unseen that crosses every path." Make sure you don't cross it. Tomorrow may be over the line. If you wait too long, you can ask Mr. B.

STUDY QUESTIONS | Chapter 7

1. Who hardened Pharaoh's heart? Why? Is that fair?

2. Who hardened Mr. B's heart? How does this happen?

3. Have you ever made a fake decision for Christ? Do you know someone else who did before they were genuinely born again? How does this happen?

4. Why are people offended by this story, offended enough to declare, "My God is not that way"? Is God really like this? How does Scripture portray God? Look up references to God's compassion, patience, justice and wrath.

5. Why is this event in the life of the author an incentive to evangelism?

8

A NEIGHBOR

When we moved into our new house on Ryan Road, my wife asked me one day, "Have you noticed the gentleman in the house on the right as we drive in? He's often sitting on the picnic table under his carport all alone."

"Yes, ma'am. I have. His name is Buford."

"Oh, you've met him?"

"Yes, I have. Just about every Thursday on my afternoon off before I get home, I pull in his driveway and talk to him for a few minutes."

"I had no idea. Why didn't you tell me?"

"I can't tell you everything."

As she punched my shoulder, she asked, "Well, what's his story?"

"Hmm, let's see. He's retired on medical disability. He smokes two packs per day, and I suspect he drinks too much since I smell alcohol on his breath in the middle of the day."

"Not his medical story, doctor — his family. You know what I mean." She punched me again. This was becoming abusive.

"Okay, okay. This is his second marriage. His wife works in payroll at Kohler. She knows our good friend Dickie, who works there. All of his family members have died young due to an inherited blood-clotting disorder. He lost one of his legs below the knee due to the same disorder and has to take blood thinner every day. He's disabled because of the amputation and blood thinners."

"What's his spiritual life like?"

"He's not a believer and does not attend church anywhere right now, but he's not antagonistic toward the gospel. We've had a few interesting discussions already."

As soon as we moved onto Ryan Road, my wife and I tried to meet our new neighbors and began to pray for all of them. We believed it was foolishness to pray for lost people in the furthest parts of the globe if we weren't going to pray for our immediate neighbors and attempt to share the gospel with them.

Interestingly, one of my neighbors and his wife experienced a spiritual revival in their lives a few years after we moved there. They suddenly became active in their church. He became an outspoken evangelist. The joy of the Lord was evident in their lives every time we saw them. Only God knows if our prayers for our neighbors had anything to do with that. I would like to think so.

A few years after I had begun this new friendship with my neighbor who was named Buford, a close family friend and a pastor's wife died suddenly of a heart ailment, the consequence of chemotherapy for cancer. We were grieving the loss of this friend deeply when shortly thereafter I asked Buford if I could borrow his truck to haul trash to the county dump. He agreed, and I invited him to tag along.

As we were traveling, I shared with him what was so heavy on my heart. In our conversation he responded, "You know, Doc, all my family have died young from this blood-clotting disorder. I suspect I will, too."

"Buford, are you afraid of dying?"

After a long pause, he said very heavily, "I reckon I am. I've done a lot of things in my life that I'm not proud of."

I looked over and saw tears rolling down his cheeks. I remained silent for a while out of respect for his feelings; then I said, "Buford, there are a lot of things in my life that I'm not proud of. In fact, when I think about them, my face burns hot with shame. I'm not going to tell you about them, but God knows. Every sinful, prideful, arrogant thing you and I have ever done is sufficient to separate us from God and heaven forever. You understand that?"

Again, tears immediately welled up in both eyes and he simply nodded.

I continued, "The Bible says, 'For the wages of sin is death, but the free gift of God is eternal life in Christ Jesus our Lord' (Romans 6:23). God loved you and me enough that He sent Jesus, His only Son, to be our sin bearer on the cross. Buford, Jesus didn't die on the cross for anything He did wrong. He died to pay the penalty for your sin and mine. The Bible also says, 'But as many as received Him, to them He gave the right to become children of God, even to those who believe in His name' (John 1:12). You must confess your sins, repent of your sinful lifestyle, and receive Jesus as your sin bearer, your Savior. Otherwise, friend, you're going to bust hell wide open when you die. Is that what you want?"

He shook his head vigorously in the negative with more tears streaming down his cheeks; now he was snubbing.

"Buford, I've been praying for you since the first day I moved into our neighborhood. I've been praying that God would reach down and pluck you up from the miry clay and put your feet down on the solid rock. You know what you need to do. It's up to you."

I dropped by the next Thursday afternoon. As usual, he was outside, smoking a cigarette.

"Buford, I've been thinking. Would you be interested in a five-week Bible study — just you and me — about the life of Christ?"

He immediately lit up and said, "You know, I would like that. When?"

"How about my afternoons off at my house? We'll start today. Get in my truck and let's go."

We started a five-week study, and he listened intently each week. In the middle of the third week's lesson, he stopped me, and said, "I'm ready."

I knew what he meant, but I made him say it. "Ready for what?"

"I'm ready to receive Christ and become a believer."

"Are you sure?"

"Yes, I'm sure. Let's pray right now," he said with a great big smile.

So we did. We held hands and prayed a sinner's prayer. As the song goes, "Jesus gained a soul and Satan lost a good right arm"![1]

A week later, the transformation was totally complete. Whereas before he sported a tight curly perm haircut and a goatee, he now was clean-shaven with straight hair parted on one side. Nothing wrong with tight curls and a goatee, but this change represented publicly a transformation to a new life for him. I almost didn't recognize him. He said, "Doc, I've cut my smoking down to half a pack per day, and it's purt' near killing me," but he was proud of himself.

His wife, whom I had met only twice, called me two weeks later, weeping. "I don't know what you've done to my husband, but I want to thank you."

"What do you mean?"

"You may not know this, but he's been an alcoholic for years. Since meeting with you, he hasn't had a drop. He's hardly smoking at all. More than that, he used to go to all the little juke joints around here and hit on the women while he was drinking. Well, that's over with, too." Before she hung up, she wept again.

Buford began attending church with us regularly and decided he wanted to be baptized. Our church at that time baptized in a pool or the Pacolet River behind my home. Because of his artificial leg, he was terrified but determined.

We planned his baptism carefully. All of his extended family was invited. It was a beautiful springtime day with wild roses blooming on the opposite riverbank. We drove Buford out onto a sandbar in a lifted golf cart. He then walked into the water as far as he could with his four-post walker and on one leg. He left the artificial leg in the golf cart. Two strong men stood on either side of him because of the current to help him get out deep enough to be baptized. We took away the walker, and there he stood on one leg in a white shirt between the pastor and me. The pastor said a few words. I had the privilege of baptizing my new brother in the Lord while his family and friends stood on the riverbank watching. When we dunked him under, he lost his footing and his single good leg began floating downstream in the swift current. I saw his eyes pop wide open underwater in surprise. We quickly stood him upright on his one good leg; he took a deep breath, looked around, and said, "Hallelujah."

The pastor and I looked at each other with a sigh of relief, and whispered, "Yeah, hallelujah."

Everyone on the riverbank, none the wiser, began clapping.

The whole scene reminded me of the aforementioned song:

> *They baptized Jesse Taylor in Cedar Creek last Sunday.*
> *Jesus gained a soul and Satan lost a good right arm.*
> *They all cried, "Hallelujah" when Jesse's head went under*
> *Because this time he went under for the Lord.*[2]

Six months later, Buford was diagnosed with lung cancer; a few months later, he was gone — gone to Jesus.

What if I had not taken time to be his friend, to pray for him, and to plant the seed of the gospel in his heart? Would this story have ended well? I'm doubtful. Who else prayed for Buford? His mother, his grandmother, a previous coworker, a Sunday school teacher when he was a child? I'll bet I wasn't the only one to pray for Buford in his lifetime, but I had the privilege of leading him to Christ. First Corinthians 3:6 says, "I planted, Apollos watered, but God was causing the growth." What an infinite privilege with eternal consequences!

How many people are there like Buford in your life — on your street, in your neighborhood, and at your workplace? I am confident Buford's heart was prepared in advance by someone's prayers. May I encourage you to create a prayer list of the people in your circle of influence? Pray for their salvation daily and then make plans to be their friend. The closer you are to someone, the greater the influence you have in his or

The closer you are to someone, the greater the influence you have in his or her life.

her life. Back in the 1980s, we called this FRAN-gelism when we concentrated on reaching our **F**riends, **R**elatives, business **A**ssociates and **N**eighbors — in other words, our circles of influence. Can you imagine what would happen if every evangelical Christian in America took seriously the challenge to reach their own circle of influence (COI)?

Praying is good, being their friend is important, but you have to go speak to them about Jesus sometime. All right, let's get started.

STUDY QUESTIONS | Chapter 8

1. What is FRAN-gelism? What is the point of the acrostic?

2. Who are the lost people in your circle of influence?

3. Why was a rough character like Buford willing to connect and listen to the author?

4. Could you lead a five-week study on the life of Christ? Why or why not?

5. Have you ever led a friend or neighbor to faith in Christ? Can you describe this experience?

9

MA, GOOD DON'T GET IT!

I entered Exam Room Four to find Doug sitting with his elbows on his knees, face in his hands, and sweat dripping off his forehead onto the carpet. Nervous, afraid and sick, he was withdrawing from some kind of drug. He was only there at the insistence of his wife, Deb, a God-fearing Christian woman who had recently joined our church. She had taken him to drug rehab twice already, and he attended NA meetings weekly, all to no avail. She was desperate for help and afraid for his life. He was slowly selling off all their possessions to support his drug habit. This was my first acquaintance with Doug and Deb, who were both to become great friends.

I sat on my exam stool and looked at Doug, but he did not look up due to sickness and shame.

Deb spoke first. "Dr. Jackson, you've got to help Doug. He can't get free of cocaine. It's ruining his life and taking all of our money. It's driving us apart. It's like he has another woman in his life. Cocaine is more important to him than me or his job or anything else. I'm afraid he's going to go to prison or get killed!"

Doug never moved, never looked up, never spoke. He just shivered a little and dripped sweat while clutching his head.

I pondered this a moment, then responded, "Doug, I can't help you. I don't think another round of rehab will help you either. You've already tried that twice. What you need is a source of strength outside of yourself and greater than yourself to come inside of you and radically change your heart. Isn't that what you talk about in NA meetings?"

He imperceptibly nodded his head.

"Well, I'm here to tell you that source of strength is Jesus. Doug, you need Jesus to come into your life to radically transform your heart from the inside out. I'm challenging you today to confess your sin, repent of your sin, and receive Jesus Christ as your only Savior — not because you need to be delivered from drugs, but because you need to be delivered from hell. Doug, your sins are going to send you to hell forever. You need Jesus to save you from your sins and the penalty of sin — to be forever separated away from God in a place called hell. Do you understand that?"

Another shiver and an imperceptible nod.

"I can't guarantee it, but if God is merciful to you, He may set you free from your drug habit, but you certainly can't do it on your own. I can guarantee that He has the power to deliver you from your sin, and He may deliver you from your drug habit."

By this time, I was kneeling down on the floor and looking up at his face so I could see him and he could see me. Tears were streaming down his face and joining the sweat drops on their way to the floor. His face was flushed red from drug withdrawal and shame.

"Doug, I want you to think carefully about everything I've said. I encourage you to go home, kneel down by your bed, and talk to God about your sin and your soul."

I then prayed for him and for Deb, and they were gone. To my surprise, I saw Doug walk the aisle at our church the next Sunday morning, wearing a white shirt and a thin black tie, to make a profession of faith in Christ. Deb was so excited, she was beside herself! Doug was a changed man.

"If any man is in Christ, he is a new creature" (2 Corinthians 5:17). He began to attend a discipleship group with me and three other men called the Biscuit Busters Discipleship Group (BBDG), because we always ate sausage biscuits before we began our 6:00 a.m. Sunday meetings. (If you feed them, they will come!) Doug grew in the Lord and prospered spiritually the entire time he was a part of our BBDG. His spiritual journey was tumultuous, but he did well as long as he stayed connected to our discipleship group. Whenever he was disconnected, he tended to stray.

On one occasion, I was at his home when he was talking to his mother on the phone. He was excitedly describing his newfound faith in Christ. You have to understand that Doug's mom operated a saloon all of her life, where she raised Doug and his brothers in the back of the saloon. He was around alcohol and drunks all of his life. His mother chain-smoked and drank booze excessively; plus, she had an endless succession of men in her life.

I was listening to Doug's side of the conversation and could tell he was getting frustrated with his mom. Doug kept talking about sin and the consequences of sin. His mom, who was pretty loud and could easily be heard through the phone, kept protesting that she was a good woman (which made me laugh).

Finally, in frustration, Doug said sternly into the phone, "Ma, good don't get it; don't you understand? You have to have the righteousness of Jesus."

That stopped his mom cold in her tracks. She had no comeback for that. I smiled. My disciple was now an evangelist and a budding young theologian!

Doug's mom is not the only one who doesn't get it. I live in the South, and a "works type of righteousness" prevails round these here parts. What do I mean by this? Well, I've been asking my patients for years, "If you die tonight and stand before God, and He asks you, 'Why should I let you into my heaven?' what would you say?"

Most "works type of righteousness" folks say something like this:

"Dr. Jackson, I go to church. I pay my tithe. I sing in the choir. I read my Bible. I pay my taxes." That's a list of good things that they do, as well as, "I don't lie or cheat or steal. I don't drink or do drugs. I quit smoking a long time ago. I don't fool around." That's a list of bad things they don't do.

> *I live in the South, and a 'works type of righteousness' prevails round these here parts.*

Then I look at them and say, "So you're counting on the good to outweigh the bad on the scales of justice so God will let you in?"

Usually, they confidently smile and nod.

I reply, "The only problem is, God is holy, and the Bible says, 'Thine eyes are too pure to approve evil, and Thou canst not look on wickedness with favor' (Habakkuk 1:13). What are you going to do to erase your sin? Jesus said, 'Unless your righteousness surpasses that of the scribes and Pharisees, you shall not enter the kingdom of heaven' (Matthew 5:20). He also said, 'You must be born again' (John 3:7). You see, getting into heaven is all or nothing. It's like the quiz in high school when you made 100 or 0. You were all right or all wrong. Either you have Jesus, or you don't. You're either black or white, sheep or goat, in or out; you're either a saint, or you ain't. Got it?"

My patients will then look at me sideways like my beagle does when I make cat sounds, completely bewildered. I usually have to explain further, "The Bible says, 'The person who sins will die' (Ezekiel 18:20), and 'He will by no means leave the guilty unpunished' (Exodus 34:7). Do you think that your little bit of goodness will excuse your sin and satisfy God's justice?"

Further confusion is seen on my patients' faces. Then I help them out a bit. "What about the blood of Jesus?"

"Oh, yeah, Doc, I trust in the blood. I'm a Christian."

"But that's not what you just told me. You told me you were trusting in your good works. You didn't mention Jesus at all, and, remember, you were talking to God at the gates of heaven, not me."

My patient is really squirming now.

"Do you know what you are like? You are like the man standing with one foot on the solid Rock, which is Jesus, and one foot on the quicksand, which is your good works. What will happen to that man? He's going to sink right into hell because he's a double-minded man. The Bible teaches that a double-minded man is unstable in all his ways."

Now, Reader, pay close attention. What was the Protestant Reformation all about? The protestors — the Protestants — took a stand against the Roman Catholic Church's teaching (doctrine) that people could be made right with God (or saved) by various sacraments. In fact, the Catholic Church taught one could not be saved unless he believed in Jesus Christ, demonstrated "good works" *and* practiced the Seven Sacraments of the Catholic Church.[1] This amounted to a faith-plus-works type of salvation that the Protestants rejected as unbiblical. Their contention was that the Bible taught salvation through faith plus nothing. Their rallying cry was *sola gratia* (grace alone) and *solus Christus* (Christ alone).

I speak to folks who sit in Protestant churches every Sunday, the heirs of the Protestant reformers who gave their life blood to overcome the doctrinal error of their day, and guess what? I hear these people tell me the same doggone thing that the faith-and-works heretics of a previous generation tried to force on the Protestant reformers. The progeny of the Protestant reformers is unwittingly accepting and repeating that dogma without any duress. They say to me, "I'm a good person, Dr. Jackson. I go to church. I pay my tithe and, my granddaddy was a Baptist preacher. Oh! And I believe in Jesus!" Well, which is it? Are you trusting in Jesus alone, or are you trusting in your church attendance? Or are you hoping to get into heaven on your grandfather's coattails? You know God has no grandchildren. Am I hurting anybody's feelings? Have I offended your tender sensibilities?

I must disabuse you of false notions and false thinking that may delude you into thinking that your relationship with God is up to snuff when, in fact, He is going to say, "Depart from me, I never knew you." Many of you will have friends say these same things, and you can't allow them to go through life with double-minded thinking. It's our responsibility to help them clarify their thinking about what and in whom they trust.

> *Many of you will have friends say these same things, and you can't allow them to go through life with double-minded thinking.*

Doug was a baby Christian, yet he already knew enough to correct his mother's theology by saying, "Ma, good don't get it!" If you delve a little deeper, you will find that many of your so-called Christian friends are deceived by false theology. They labor under a "works type of righteousness" doctrine of salvation. If you don't believe me, ask ten of your friends the diagnostic question: "If you die tonight and God stands at the door of heaven and asks, 'Why should I allow you into my heaven?' what would you say?" The answers you receive may be surprising, shocking and revealing. It may also give you a chance to do some real evangelism with some folks who you didn't think needed it. Be gentle, though; they may be as surprised and as upset as you. Remember also: Jesus is the one who set the standard. It was Jesus, not Doug, who said, "Good don't get it."

STUDY QUESTIONS | Chapter 9

1. Why is being good not enough to satisfy God?

2. What did Jesus mean when He told the disciples, "Unless your righteousness exceeds that of the Pharisees, you cannot enter the kingdom of heaven"?

3. What did the Protestant reformers mean by *solus Christus* and *sola gratia*? Why were they called Protestants?

4. Why was drug rehab not helping Doug? Can you confidently look your alcoholic or drug-addicted friend in the eyes and say, "Jesus can set you free"? Do you really believe that?

5. Is there anybody whose life situation is so complex or so difficult that Jesus cannot deliver them?

6. Of whom would you be willing to ask the diagnostic questions? Write down their names, pray first, and then ask them this week.

10

THE MEANEST MAN ALIVE

A serious deer hunter from Laurens, South Carolina — my friend, Mark Hardin — was riding to his hunt club with the club manager, Pee Wee Coates, when suddenly a hunter in camouflage emerged from the woods on the side of the road right next to a "Posted — No Trespassing" sign that Pee Wee had posted himself. Pee Wee immediately knew this hunter was trespassing and not a member of the club. Flying into a rage, he slammed on the brakes, sliding sideways on the country road, blue smoke boiling up from the mud-gripper tires. Mark threw his hands up to avoid hitting the dashboard as profanity turned the air in the truck cab blue. Mark winced as his spirit was wounded deeply by the foul language erupting from his hunting buddy.

Before the truck had fully stopped rocking, Pee Wee was out the door and running toward the hapless trespasser. Even though the trespasser was fully armed and Pee Wee was, as his name implied, only five foot two in stature, he was on the intruder like a wild dog on a bone. Ten minutes later, he was still yelling, cursing and gesticulating without taking a breath. It was the Tasmanian devil in camouflage. The trespasser couldn't even say, "I'm sorry," or "I was lost." He couldn't squeeze an apology in edgewise. Mark sat in shocked amazement and watched this unfold from the truck's cab. Now he understood full well why everyone called Pee Wee "the meanest man alive."

Pee Wee managed a 10,000-acre hunt club with 100 members located in Laurens County. He ruled the club with an iron fist. His word was law. He operated the club like a dictator. If anyone contradicted him, he cursed him like a dog, then expelled him from the club. It was his club, and it did not operate like a democracy. There were no meetings and no votes. He made all the decisions. He constantly patrolled, looking for trespassers and poachers. Pity the poacher who fell into the grasp of Pee Wee Coates — the meanest man, the most profane man alive, who would threaten to shoot them on the spot. In his fury, many believed he might just do it. Better to fall into the hands of a game warden than Pee Wee Coates any day.

Interestingly, Pee Wee's mom took him to a Methodist church until he was six years old, at which time he decided he was old enough to fish and hunt with his uncles. He no longer needed Jesus or church. That was the last contact he had with religion for fifty-nine years, except to take God's name in vain on a daily basis.

Then along came Mark, a new member of the hunt club. Mark was a valued member because he brought with him several additional paying members. The only problem was that Mark was a Christian man — not just a Christian in name, but an outspoken Christian man who lived out his faith. He began to pray for Pee Wee.

Knowing Pee Wee would be unlikely to go to a regular Sunday morning church service (lost people avoid church like the plague), he invited him to a wildlife dinner at a local church in Laurens. "Pee Wee, why don't you come hear Bobby Richardson speak and eat a wildlife meal at my church on Friday night?"

"Mark, I know you are a godly man and a church-going man, but that's not for me. I don't need none of that."

Mark was disappointed but not discouraged. He began to pray for his friend even harder. He even recruited some of his friends at church to pray as well. Three years went by. Every year, Mark invited Pee Wee to a wildlife supper. Each time the response was the same: "I don't need none of that."

Although a little discouraged, Mark did not give up. He recruited others to join him in praying for Pee Wee. He continued to invite him each consecutive year for four years. Each year, the response was the same: "Mark, I don't need none of that," usually accompanied by vile cursing. Finally, after four years of praying, the wildlife committee invited Bobby and Tommy Bowden, the famous football coaches, to speak on consecutive nights. Over 750 men attended each night. I remember because I was there myself the second night to hear Tommy speak. He did an excellent job telling stories and presenting the gospel message.

Each year, the response was the same: 'Mark, I don't need none of that,' usually accompanied by vile cursing.

Mark invited Pee Wee again, expecting the same response, but this time he said, "You know, Mark, I'd like to hear those football coaches speak." So he came and ate a wildlife dinner with all of those men at North Spartanburg First Baptist Church. He heard a powerful gospel presentation, and at the end tears streamed down his cheeks. Mark noticed that he was actually sobbing.

Mark asked, "Pee Wee, are you okay?"

"I'm good, Mark, I … I just got saved! I haven't felt this good since I was in church with my mama when I was six years old."

Mark got a call from a member of the hunt club two weeks later to tell him Pee Wee had died suddenly of a massive heart attack!

Well, the meanest man alive was now good. He had just been saved two weeks prior. His goodness was not his own. It was the righteousness of Jesus Christ that was gifted to him freely at a wildlife banquet when a football coach preached. Isn't that an amazing turn of events? God is good!

Now let's dissect this entire scenario. I'm a doctor. We physicians delight in dissections. We call it a postmortem when we perform an autopsy to discern what occurred before a patient's demise. In this case, what happened before the death of Mr. Coates' old man and before he was resurrected to newness of life?

He had just been saved two weeks prior.

1) We see the power of a carefully planned and executed evangelistic event. There is no doubt that God uses evangelistic events like outdoor crusades and wildlife banquets, involving evangelists, musicians, illusionists, power teams, etc., to bring many people into His kingdom. Never minimize the power of evangelistic events to reach lost people. The event attracts people, often people who would not ordinarily come to a regular church service — but, remember, the power is in the gospel message and the presence of Holy Spirit, not in the event itself.

2) We see the power of persistent prayer, especially the prayer of a close, personal friend. There is no doubt in my mind that Pee Wee Coates is in heaven because of the persistent prayers of his friend Mark Hardin. Do you remember the parable of the unjust judge? Do you remember what Jesus said about him? Although he feared not God nor man, he gave the widow her request. Why? Her persistent begging stirred him. God honors perseverance in prayer. He honors persistent prayer. The devil tells us not to bother God the Father with repeated prayer requests, and we sadly and foolishly listen to him. We believe the lie that we are a bother to God when, in fact, He is the One who encourages us to prevail with prayer over time. Do you have hard-hearted friends like Mr. Coates? Do you think they will never soften to

the gospel? Remember: Your praying and the power of Holy Spirit is stronger than their hardened hearts. Pray on, my friend, pray on.

3) We also see the power of repeated invitations. Mark invited Pee Wee multiple times over three to four years to a wildlife banquet before he responded. Mark told me he almost didn't invite Pee Wee the last time for fear he would refuse yet again and with cursing. Nevertheless, he invited him one last time, and we see the eternal results in Mr. Coates' life. Jesus told a parable of a nobleman who threw a party, but none of the invited guests showed up. So, he sent his servants out to invite whomever they could find, and he told his servants to compel them to come in so that his banquet hall might be full. The nobleman was quite insistent. He wanted his banquet hall to be full. So does God the Father. In like manner, we want all our friends and family to attend the marriage supper of the Lamb.

Eternity hung in the balance for Pee Wee. Your friends' or family members' eternal, never-dying souls hang in the balance. Invite them repeatedly. Never give up on their immortal souls. Compel them to come in, because God's banquet hall still has plenty of open seats. We never know when our prayers and the ministry of Holy Spirit will combine to prepare their hearts to say yes to our invitation just like Pee Wee Coates — once the meanest man alive, but now made righteous by the blood of the Lamb — and just in the nick of time!

STUDY QUESTIONS | Chapter 10

1. Why do we conduct outreach events? What is our responsibility prior to, during, and after these events?

2. Why do outreach events work? Do they still work?

3. Why did Pee Wee Coates eventually come?

4. Who is like Pee Wee in your life? Would you be willing to pray for them and invite them to church or an event? Repeatedly?

5. Discuss the meaning of Romans 1:16.

6. If the gospel is powerful to save, then why do some people get saved and others do not?

11

WHAT'S IN YOU?

My first patient in medical school was named Mrs. Brown from Myrtle Beach, South Carolina. She was very patient with me because my interviewing and examination skills were quite rudimentary, but we connected quickly. We connected because we realized early on in my slow and meticulous exam that we both loved Jesus. She confided that she had been ill for a long time with ITP (idiopathic thrombocytopenic purpura). I don't know why I remember that after thirty-eight years. She had been referred to the Medical University of South Carolina because her local doctors could find no etiology for this condition, which caused low platelets and constant big-time bruising. She told me she often put her hand on the radio when Oral Roberts prayed for his listeners, trusting God that she would be healed. We both shared our testimonies of how we came to Christ, and when I finished my exam, I offered to pray for her. She responded with a statement that has stuck with me ever since, "Well, young man, that is very kind of you. None of my doctors have ever offered to pray for me, and I have had a dozen of them." I made a commitment in my heart right then to be a doctor who would pray for his patients.

About that time, a female voice on the other side of a curtain in that two-bed ward piped up, and said, "Please pray for me, too." Evidently, someone had been listening in.

"Ma'am, what's your name?" I asked. "We will be glad to pray for you." So right there at the beginning of my medical career with my very first patient, I had the opportunity to share my testimony and to pray with not one but two patients. Why is that? Because what's in you is what comes out of you. If you squeeze a lemon, you'll get lemon juice. If you squeeze a Spirit-filled Christian, you get Jesus. Really, you don't have to squeeze them. They emanate the aroma of Christ wherever they go. The light of Christ shines out of a Spirit-controlled Christian. The cool, clear water of life flows up and out of the well and splashes on everybody around them. They can't help it; it just happens.

The popular TV credit card commercial asks the question, "What's in your wallet?" The implication is that if you have the right credit card, all of your travel and financial difficulties will be solved.

Well, let me ask you: Who is in your heart? The better question is: Who is in control of your heart? For, you see, every day in a Christian's life is a struggle for control. Will you sit on the throne of your heart as the master of all decisions, or will you die to self/sin and allow Holy Spirit who lives in you to sit in His proper place on the throne as the King in your life, making all the decisions and choices? In other words, will you be "alive unto Christ"? It is only as we daily abide in the Word of God and in prayer and conscientiously put to death the flesh in us that we begin to achieve victory in this area of our lives. Then people begin to see Jesus in us. Slowly over time, we begin to think the thoughts of God, speak the words of God, walk like Jesus, and talk like Jesus.

The better question is: Who is in control of your heart?

When I was in my third year of medical school, I was in a psychiatry rotation. I was called on a Sunday morning to consult with a depressed patient whom the nurses considered to be suicidal. I arrived at her room about 1:00 p.m. and found a 101-year-old black woman who was blind from diabetes and had suffered the amputation of both legs above the knees from diabetic ulcers. Despite her age, she was a big woman, quite robust, quite talkative, and anything but depressed. She had her white Sunday go-to-meeting hat on her head and her Bible on her lap (even though she couldn't read due to blindness from her diabetes). This centenarian was the matriarch of a huge family. She had nine children, scads of grandchildren, and a gazillion great- and great-great-grands, which she proceeded to tell me all about. She was sitting bolt upright in the bed with a mountain of pillows all around her to support her. She had three daughters there that she commanded like a general on the battlefield, which was a little odd because her daughters were the age of my grandmother. Her mind was as sharp as a tack with no evidence of dementia whatsoever. In five minutes flat, we were sharing testimonies and praising the Lord together. What's in you is what comes out of you!

I asked her all the routine questions about depression. All of her answers were in the negative for depression, so I finally asked, "Ma'am, why do the nurses think you are depressed?"

"Lord, doctor, I don't know. I suppose it is because I told them I am ready to go see Jesus. I am 101 years old. I can't see. I can't walk. I am tired of being a burden to my children. Doctor, I'm ready to go see Jesus. I've been ready ever since my husband left me twenty years ago. That is the only reason I can think of. What do you think?"

"I think you are mighty perceptive."

About that time, a dozen of her grandchildren came in the door straight from church dressed in their Sunday best. You should have seen her face light up when she realized they were there. She was like a queen holding court. She knew everyone's name and where they worked or went to school. It was amazing. Then the second shift came in from another church. Soon, about thirty children, grandchildren and great-grandchildren filled the room. It started to get hot and stuffy.

Then she quieted everyone down, pointed to me, and spoke, "Y'all, look-a-here. This is my little Dr. Jackson. He is a fine young fellow. He is a Christian, too. Dr. Jackson, tell them how you got saved."

Well, that was like asking Billy Graham if he would like to preach. I smiled broadly and launched into my testimony. The entire room started swaying back and forth, and folks started saying, "Amen." A few arms went up into the air.

Suddenly, a young nurse appeared in the doorway; a frown appeared on her face. She put her hands on her hips, surveyed the room, spied me in the middle, and then stomped off. I had a premonition that trouble was coming; nevertheless, I finished my testimony and was hugged by about thirty people. My patient was delighted. I excused myself and wrote up my consultation: Patient is not depressed; nursing staff misinterpreted her comments; she is ready to go to her ultimate reward due to her medical conditions.

One week later, I was summoned to appear before the psychiatry department.

"Robert Jackson, a complaint has been filed against you, alleging that you have been unduly influencing a patient with your religion."

'Robert Jackson, a complaint has been filed against you, alleging that you have been unduly influencing a patient with your religion.'

I laughed inside but kept it to myself as I recalled that jubilant scenario. "May I ask who has filed that complaint?"

"You may not."

"So I don't get to appear before my accuser?"

"That will remain anonymous. This is not a court of law."

"Then I am free to leave and ignore the complaint?"

"No, sir, you are not."

I explained the circumstances and how difficult it was for a respectful young man like me to refuse the request of a 101-year-old matriarch/ general who requested/commanded me to share my testimony. "Besides, why would I not share my testimony? This is America, and it is my right and privilege to do so whenever and wherever I please. Is that not correct, sir?"

He sat back in his chair and rubbed the top of his completely bald head but did not answer my question. He merely said, "You will have to appear before the entire department of psychiatry in one week to make a statement."

My Christian friends and I prayed hard all week, because he made it plain that my continuing in medical school depended on the decision of the psychiatry department hearing. Now isn't that bizarre that in the buckle of the Bible belt in Charleston, South Carolina, in 1979, a medical student could be kicked out of medical school for sharing the gospel with a patient at the patient's request? I was quite bumfuzzled. I wasn't in Russia or China. I was in America. Looking back on it, I think the enemy didn't want me to graduate from medical school. He knew the damage I might do to his kingdom as a medical professional (this was one of two attempts old Slewfoot made to kick me out of medical school).

The next week, I appeared before the entire department of psychiatry. About twenty medical doctors sat at a huge round table (like the knights of the round table) with their attention focused on me, a third-year medical student. I rehearsed the entire story for them, being careful to include a clear presentation of the gospel (like Stephen before the Sanhedrin!). Thankfully, no one tore their clothes or gnashed their teeth, but they did sit in stone-cold silence; then they excused me to sit in the hallway while they deliberated. There was a stool in the hallway on which I sat for two hours while they considered my future. I felt like a bad- behaving school child sitting outside the principal's office. All I needed was a dunce cap!

After two hours, they called me back into the room to deliver their verdict. The head of the psychiatry department looked at me and said, "Robert, although the circumstances of the case are highly unusual, we concede it is culturally acceptable in the South for people to talk about their religion."

Then there was silence. Nobody moved, smiled or nodded in affirmation. They just stared at me.

I raised my hand. "Does that mean I get to stay in medical school?"

"Yes, sir, it does."

"Thank you kindly."

"You may go now."

I stood and nodded at the entire circle of psychiatrists and said, "You gentlemen have a nice day and may the Lord bless you all." What is in you is what comes out of you. If Jesus is not coming out of you regularly, then you need to reconsider who is in you or who is in control? Just saying!

◆   ◆   ◆   ◆   ◆

Jesus said, "Remember the word that I said to you, 'A slave is not greater than his master.' If they persecuted me, they will also persecute you" (John 15:20a). It is a common occurrence for those with a secular perspective in positions of authority to deal harshly with Christians under their authority, whether they be in the government, the military, or in a school system. We are accustomed to hearing about our brothers and sisters being persecuted by tyrant dictators in third world countries. We assume these non-Christian, backwater dictatorships will behave that way. We expect this to happen in those kind of countries, but we are inflamed when a school teacher takes a Bible away from an elementary school kid, or a professor gives a failing grade to a Christian student who refuses to capitulate on evolutionary dogma in his class, or when a medical student is threatened with dismissal for sharing the gospel with a patient. Our culture in America is just as secular and pagan as the third world countries; the tyrants just don't have absolute power yet, thanks to our Constitution. The secularists hate God and His people today as much as they hated Jesus in His day. Paul told Timothy, "All who live godly in Christ Jesus shall suffer persecution" (2 Timothy 3:12). If

> *The secularists hate God and His people today as much as they hated Jesus in His day.*

you don't believe me, just take a strong, public, principled stand on any moral or ethical issue and watch what happens! The God-haters will find you and bash you. Better yet, start writing editorials to the local paper on ethical issues and see what happens. Opposition and persecution will follow; this is a good thing. Jesus said, "Blessed are you when people insult you, persecute you" (Matthew 5:11-12). If nobody is opposing or persecuting us, perhaps we are not living a godly enough life. Maybe we aren't enough like Jesus to stir up any opposition — just something to think about. Oh, and one more question: What's in you?

STUDY QUESTIONS | Chapter 11

1. Finish this sentence: "If you squeeze a Spirit-filled Christian, you get
   _____"?

2. Has life ever squeezed you? What came out?

3. Have you ever been persecuted for your faith or the expression of
   your faith?

4. What does it mean to "live godly in Christ Jesus"? Does persecution
   inevitably follow?

5. Who do you pray for? Do you pray for lost people? Do you pray for
   their personal concerns in their presence? Why is prayer a ministry?

6. What does it mean to be "the priest" in someone's life?

7. What do we have to do to let Jesus in us shine out of us?

12

THE FRIEND OF SINNERS

Devonte presented to my office covered with infected sores from head to toe. The sores were draining and weeping corruption, which reminded me of Job — except Job was a righteous man who eschewed evil. Devonte was not.

The look of desperation was obvious in his eyes. "Dr. Jackson, you've got to help me. What is wrong with me? These sores popped up a week ago, and now they are all over me. Please help me. I feel like a leper!"

Indeed, the purulent drainage was so copious, it was seeping through his clothes. From across the room, I observed enlarged lymph nodes in his neck. I asked, "Have you had any fever?"

"No, sir, but I've had night sweats."

"Are you losing weight?"

"Yes, sir, about thirty pounds in the last six months."

"Do you use illicit IV drugs?"

"Oh, no, sir, I would never do that," he answered indignantly.

"Are you involved in any homosexual activity?"

His face fell, and he looked at the floor for a long moment. "My friend-boy left me when these sores showed up. He said he would come back when I got well."

"Have you ever been tested for AIDS?" (This was in the early '80s;

now we use the term HIV.)

"No, sir."

"All right then. Let me prescribe some antibiotics, and we'll draw some blood tests. Come back in a week, and we'll discuss the results."

This conversation took place at a time when treatment for advanced HIV was rudimentary and required a three-drug regimen.

Devonte returned in one week, completely free of the skin lesions. He was smiling from ear to ear until I told him that his HIV test was positive. His smile disappeared; the tears began to flow. After he regained his composure, he told me two of his friends had recently died a slow death from HIV, and he was terrified of a similar fate. Then he began to sob great, heaving sobs that shook his whole body. I put my arms around his shoulders and just held him tight until he cried it all out.

"Devonte, I'm going to refer you to an infectious disease doctor, but you already know where this may be headed." He nodded glumly. "There's nothing I can do to change that. So, talk to me about your spiritual life."

He continued to stare at the floor, then responded without looking up, "My grandma prays for me every day."

"Why does she do that?"

"She says I need to be saved."

"Saved from what?"

"From my sins."

"Do you know what it means to be saved from your sins?" Now he was looking at me instead of the floor. He just shook his head in the negative. "Devonte, your sin is everything you've done or thought that offends Holy God. You already know what that is, don't you?"

He nodded affirmatively.

I continued, "The Bible says, 'The wages (or penalty) of sin is death,' which means eternal separation away from God in a place called hell. Is that where you want to go?"

He shook his head negatively.

"God loved you and me so much that He sent Jesus, His only Son, to live a perfect life and then give His life on the cross in our place as our substitute, taking the penalty for our sins. In other words, He died our death and paid our sin debt to God. You with me?"

He nodded affirmatively.

"Knowing that does not make you a Christian. You have to do something about it. The Bible says, 'As many as receive Him, to those He gives the right to become the sons of God' (John 1:12). Devonte, you have to confess your sins to God, repent of your sins, and receive Jesus Christ as your Savior and Lord of your life. When you do this, God imparts His life to you and gives you the righteousness of Jesus Christ. He washes away all your sin and makes you as white as snow. Does that make sense?"

He nodded again.

"Is this something you would like to do?"

He spoke for the first time. "I need to think about it."

"All right, can I pray for you?"

He nodded, and I prayed over him before he left.

Devonte returned two weeks later a changed man. When I opened the exam room door, he jumped to his feet and clasped my hands with a broad smile on his face, and said, "Thank you, Dr. Jackson." Three times in a row, he said, "Thank you." I could tell something had happened; I just didn't know what.

I sat down, looked at his smiling face, and said, "Tell me. What has happened?"

"Well, Dr. Jackson. I left here and went home. I thought about everything you said. Then I got down on my knees and confessed all the sin in my life to God. That took some time," he said with a smile. "I asked God to forgive me and asked Jesus to save me. He did. I'm a new man, Dr. Jackson. I told my grandmother first; then I went to church with her and joined the church and the choir. I'm going to be baptized next Sunday." He clasped his hands together in front of his chest and smiled even broader. "I told my friend-boy we were through and don't ever call me back!" Then he laughed out loud.

What an amazing transformation in Devonte's life. I saw him twice more over the next year as he was primarily cared for by the infectious disease physician. Each time I saw him, he was progressing nicely in his newfound faith in Christ.

If you noticed, I did not mention Devonte's lifestyle to him in my presentation of the gospel. I usually don't. It doesn't matter whether I'm talking to a drug addict, an alcoholic, a nicotine addict, or a sexual addict. The issue for all of them is the same — their underlying sin. Their addictions are just a superficial manifestation of the root problem, which is sin. "The heart of man is deceitful above all things and desperately wicked; who can know it" (Jeremiah 17:9). My patients already know their addictions are wrong/sinful and ruining their lives/health. The Holy Spirit convicts them of this. This is His ministry, His responsibility — not mine.

> *Their addictions are just a superficial manifestation of the root problem, which is sin.*

When I begin to talk about sin, people automatically know what areas of their lives are deficient without me explaining it to them. Holy Spirit makes certain of that. Isn't this true in your life? When the preacher starts preaching about sin, the sin in your life automatically pops into your mind. How does that happen? Is it just a guilty conscience, or is the Spirit of God fulfilling His ministry, "convicting of sin, and righteousness, and judgment" (John 16:8)? It's a good indication that your heart is still sensitive to the influence of Holy Spirit, which is a good prospect for future spiritual growth and prosperity.

However, on the other hand, if no awareness of personal sin comes into your personal conscience upon hearing the preaching of the gospel, you may have what the Scriptures call a "seared conscience." That means, a conscience that is insensitive or calloused to the subtle prompting of Holy Spirit when He convicts of sin. If that is you, my friend, you are in big trouble.

Now, let me ask you. Did you detect any hostility in my heart or conversation toward Devonte? Why, of course not! I treated him the same way I treat all of my patients. I am no respecter of persons. By this, I mean that I treat all people with the same degree of compassion and respectfulness. All of my patients have sin in their lives, same as I do. The flavors may be different, but we all need Jesus. God puts love and compassion in my heart for all of my patients regardless of the sexual orientation, addictions, abusiveness, immorality or irresponsibility. I remind myself, "But for the grace of God, there go I."

For their book *unChristian*, David Kinnaman (president of Barna Group, a leading research organization) and Gabe Lyons spent three years interviewing unchurched young people, aged eighteen to twenty-nine. They found that the most common belief about Bible-believing Christians today is that we are homophobic, anti-gay bigots.[1] Why would the under-thirty crowd view Christians this way? Are Christian people really like that toward homosexuals? I find it confusing because I am not that way, and almost all the Christian people I know are not that way toward sinners of any stripe. We treat gay people respectfully. We treat alcoholics and drug addicts

> *They found that the most common belief about Bible-believing Christians today is that we are homophobic, anti-gay bigots.*

respectfully. We treat our loud, brash, know-it-all back door neighbor respectfully, even though he drives us crazy, because that is what Jesus would do. In fact, He would go visit them, invite them over for a meal, and take them homemade strawberry jam (that's what we do at the Jackson household). It's called Christian hospitality!

So why do young Americans under thirty almost universally view us as homophobic, anti-gay bigots? You already know the answer to that. It's because the media portrays us that way. The under-thirty demographic is increasingly unchurched.[2] They don't know you and me unless they live next door or work with you or are in your extended family. Unless you talk to them reasonably and dispassionately about ethical issues and demonstrate how you love sinners yet hate their sin and how you personally minister to sinners like Jesus did, then they will lump you in with the TV media portrayal of all Christians. They will think you are like the Westboro Baptist Church crowd that shows up to protest at military funerals, or you are like Christians who protest at gay pride marches. Tell me honestly, who makes any friends at a gay pride march holding up a sign declaring homosexuality is a sin? Sinners know that they sin (unless they have a seared conscience). It's more productive to make friends with sinners. Isn't that what Jesus was called, "the friend of sinners"?

What's that, you say? You don't have any friends who are gay? What about drug addicts or alcoholics? Surely there is someone in your life that has serious issues. You can't really be like Jesus if you are not a friend of sinners and visit with them, eat with them, socialize with them, and be their friend. Why do you have to be their friend? It is because the closer you are to people, the greater the influence you can have on their lives. They trust you and receive your message. They reject the fake news portrayal of Christianity by the media and accept you as their friend. Then they learn what a Christian is really like.

For a long time, I've been telling my Christian friends that every

Christian should be a minister and that every Christian should have a ministry. What I mean by that is that every Christian should view himself as empowered by Holy Spirit to minister to his family and his circle of influence. Paul reminds us in 2 Corinthians 5:18-20:

> *All this is from God, who reconciled us to himself through Christ and gave us the ministry of reconciliation: that God was reconciling the world to himself in Christ, not counting people's sins against them. And he has committed to us the message of reconciliation. We are therefore Christ's ambassadors, as though God were making his appeal through us. We implore you on Christ's behalf: be reconciled to God (NIV).*

Did you notice that God gave all of us the ministry of reconciliation? Not just pastors or church staff. We are all Christ's ambassadors, His representatives. We beg the people in our circle of influence to be reconciled to God. But you will never do that if you don't have a vision of yourself as a minister of the gospel — not in the same way as a pastor who shepherds a church family, but as the shepherd of your circle of influence. You have to assume personal responsibility for the lost in your circle and be their minister, their shepherd. Why? You may be the only representative of God that they know. You may be God's ambassador in their life. That's why I say every church member should be a minister, and every member should have a ministry.

More than that, I think every Christian family should have a ministry project going on at all times. "Now, doctor, there is no end to you; whatever in the world are you talking about?" (That's what my grandmother's housekeeper, Lillie Mae, used to say to me when I was a child and I tried to explain to her how far the sun was from planet earth.

When I would excitedly finish my dissertation, she would cock her head to one side and say, "Robbie, there is no end to you. Whatever in the world are you talking about?") Let me illustrate with a story.

When I was in the Greenville County Detention Center for rescuing at the abortion clinic, I met a man named Nathaniel (Nate). Nate had been in and out of prison for most of his life. He was in this particular time for domestic violence and destruction of property (he had torn up a screen door at his girlfriend's house in a fit of anger). Most of his woes over time were due to alcohol abuse. Interestingly, he had been raised in church and knew a fair amount of Scripture. Unfortunately, his biblical instruction just did not affect his daily life like a lot of other so-called Christians that I know. He could point to a definite time when he had committed his life to Christ, but there had been no formal discipleship in his life ever. We became fast friends that week when I was in the slammer. When he got out several weeks later, I requested that he come to Spartanburg to get away from the negative influences in Greenville where he lived, and he agreed. He began to attend our small church. I got him a construction job and found him a place to live, all with the help of other Christian friends in the body of Christ, the Church. Nate became our family ministry project for many years. The day he got out of jail, he went with us on our first family camping trip. Our entire family fell in love with Nate.

My children instantly became very attached to Nate, and he fell in love with them. Did I tell you he was a fairly handsome black man with a goatee, a radiant smile, and refined manners? He had once served as the maître d' at the most upscale restaurant in Greenville. Nate frequently ate meals with us. He became a member of my Sunday morning Biscuit Busters Men's Discipleship Group, and he began to prosper spiritually. Our family bought him a used car after he paid off his DUI charges and was able to purchase his own very expensive insurance. Eventually, our church helped to purchase a used mobile home that he could call all his own. All he had to do was pay the lot fee and utilities. He was happy as a clam!

Fifteen years later, Nate has become independent. He attends church regularly, he has a new set of friends, he has had no further run-ins with the law, and he has a metal recycling business that is fairly profitable. You see what I mean by having a family project? What if every Christian family in your church would take seriously the challenge to be a minister and have a ministry? What if every Christian family had a ministry project? What if we Christians took in all the foster kids in our counties so that they all had a home? What if every international student in every college had a Christian family ready to adopt them during the academic year? You catch my drift? The opportunities are endless; you just have to find your niche and seize the opportunity that comes your way. Put down the remote control, turn off the TV, and begin looking for your ministry project. Remember: Every member is a minister, and every family has a ministry. What's yours?

If every Christian family had a ministry, it would be hard for the media to portray us as haters and bigots, because everyone would know it was a lie. We would be known as the friend of sinners across the board (Matthew 11:19). We would have a new designation. The millennials have a reputation for being impressed, not with big buildings, but with effective ministries. Here's what one millennial said in his blog:

> Millennials, more than any other generation, don't trust institutions, for we have witnessed over and over how corrupt and self-serving they can be. Why should thousands of our hard-earned dollars go toward a mortgage on a multi-million dollar building that isn't being utilized to serve the community or to

pay for another celebratory bouncy castle when that same cash-money could provide food, clean water and shelter for someone in need?[3]

If they knew that every family in your church had a ministry and was actively ministering in Jesus' name, it would change their perception of Christians and the church in a big, fat hurry!

That means the salt has to get out of the saltshaker and into the world. That means you have to meet and become friends with people you wouldn't ordinarily invite to supper. Nate was an alcohol abuser, a drug abuser, and a chronic offender. He had spent more time in jail than out. We were white folks; he was a black man. Our worlds did not naturally coincide, but we became great friends. He needed to be rescued, and our family was his lifeline. His rescue took over ten years. It wasn't easy or inexpensive. We also inherited his thirty-two-year-old son when he got out of prison after sixteen years of incarceration. He also became a part of the Jackson family ministry. That is another long, long story. But when you start, you can't stop. It's root, hog, or die. We commit for the long haul until spiritual maturity and victory come, and, guess what, everybody else in their family comes along also.

Are you a friend of sinners? Name one. What do you do with them or for them? Does your family have a ministry? Does your salt get out of the saltshaker and into the world?

STUDY QUESTIONS | Chapter 12

1. Are you a friend of any sinners? Name one. In what way are you their friend? Casual acquaintance or active ministry?

2. What is hospitality ministry? Is that a lost art?

3. Are any of society's outcasts in your circle of influence? Have you ever visited anyone in prison? Volunteered in a homeless center or soup kitchen? Why not?

4. Could you confidently look at a patient dying from HIV and say, "Jesus can help you"?

5. What does "every member a minister" mean to you?

6. Has your family ever had a ministry project? Was it short-term or long-term? What does the phrase "root, hog, or die" mean in regard to personal ministry?

13

A SIMPLE INVITATION

I sat on a bed in a dorm room at Clemson University looking at two wide-eyed freshmen on a Saturday afternoon, sharing the gospel for the first time in my life. My evangelism trainer, Bob, sat a little behind those two freshmen. He slowly shook his head back and forth and tried to get my attention, but I was too excited about telling someone about Jesus for the first time. I didn't pay him a lick of attention. Bubbling over with enthusiasm, I plowed right ahead with my first-ever gospel presentation.

I had attended a two-day seminar on evangelism training sponsored by Campus Crusade for Christ and conducted solely by college students. They did an excellent job on the training, teaching us students how to use gospel tracts effectively, how to maintain proper attitudes, how to answer common questions, and how to avoid specific issues. Mostly, they taught us to pray, pray, pray and rely on Holy Spirit.

Well, I was prayed up, full of Holy Spirit and totally ignorant. That's why my trainer, Bob, sat shaking his head. I quickly violated all of the rules we were taught to observe, rules such as sticking to the script in the gospel tract and not deviating. That was too simple for me. In my evangelistic fervor, I gave them all manner of brilliant illustrations along the way. A budding young evangelist was being born right there in Johnstone Hall while Bob rolled his eyes in exasperation!

Taught plainly to give a positive invitation at the end, I said, "You boys wouldn't want to pray and invite Jesus into your heart, would you?" as I wrapped up my brilliant presentation, drawing the net as every good evangelist would! Bob just about fell backwards out of his chair.

The two college boys looked at me, they looked at each other, then one of them said, "Sure, I would. How about you?"

The other student said, "Yes, me, too."

I then said, "Well, let's all kneel right here by your bed and we'll pray together!"

Another rule violation! Bob's head popped off. So we all got on our knees, and I led them in this long prayer they had no way of remembering. They taught us to use the short, printed sinner's prayer in the gospel tract, but, in my excitement, I clean forgot about that. Bob rescued them. After I eloquently prayed, he led them in the sinner's prayer in the tract, and, *bam!* it was done!

I was on cloud nine for a week. I had personally led two college boys to faith in Christ. I called home to tell my parents. I called to tell my pastor. Bob was all smiles. So proud of his new evangelist, he couldn't stop talking about me. I really think he and his more experienced Christian friends split their bellies laughing about me just like you are right now.

Here's the deal: When Jesus healed people in the New Testament, what did He do? He often told them to go immediately and present themselves to the religious leaders. Now, ostensibly, this fulfilled the requirements of the law, but it also compelled them to tell somebody. He told the Gadarene demoniac to stay home and tell everybody what happened to him. Did He put them in an evangelistic training class first? No, they just had to tell what had happened to them. Did they have to answer any questions people asked? No, the man blind from birth told the Pharisees, "Whether He is a sinner, I do not know; one thing I do know, that, whereas I was blind, now I see" (John 9:25).

I didn't know much either, but I did know Jesus. I couldn't answer many questions, but I had Holy Spirit and an abundance of enthusiasm. I led a fair number of students to faith in Christ as a college student with a little knowledge and a lot of Holy Spirit. That's not a bad combination!

The Results of a Simple Invitation

As senior students at Clemson, my college roommate and I noticed a guy on our floor named Kenny who always seemed out of sorts, really out of sorts. We lived on the ninth floor of a male dormitory. The elevator often did not work, so we had to hike down the stairs. Not Kenny — he would just turn around and go back to bed. Once, he slung his books against the wall and went back to bed for three days. We knew how long it was because his books lay against the wall for an entire three days. On another occasion, I saw Kenny sling his food tray across the cafeteria. He was infuriated because his bacon was limp. He liked crispy bacon. The entire cafeteria stared in silence as he stomped out of the cafeteria and up to our dorm. I didn't see him for three days once again. He was a volatile and tempestuous young man. He really spooked the rest of us living on the same floor with him. We would greet him in the mornings, but his responses — either none, or a grunt — reminded me of Boo Radley's responses to Scout in *To Kill a Mockingbird*. Scout was always afraid Boo would do something bizarre like stick a pair of scissors in her thigh.

Well, my roommate Barry and I decided to pray for Kenny, which we did for months. I used a quiet, little study hall on our floor to get away from everyone. Well, guess who started showing up? You got it: Boo Radley! (Just kidding. It was Kenny!) He never said a word. Neither did I. I was afraid he might "stick a pair of scissors in my thigh" or something terrible like that. I couldn't study for watching him out of the corner of my eye.

One day while sitting together in the study hall, him studying and me carefully watching my back, I just blurted out, "Kenny, how would you like to do a five-week Bible study on the life of Jesus?" *Bam!* Just like that! Only conversation I had ever had with him other than a "Good morning." I felt like an idiot. Why would I ask a question like that? He turned slowly around and stared at me. I watched for the scissors.

With an eerie look on his face, he asked, "How did you know?"

I looked around. "Know what?"

"That I was interested in the life of Jesus."

I shrugged nervously, thinking he might be paranoid or something. "I didn't know, Kenny. I was just asking."

"Well, then, I would be glad to."

It turns out Kenny had been on a spiritual journey for months. He had been reading books about major religions and religious personalities in a search for what was the truth. When I offered the Bible study, it was just what he was looking for. Who knew?

He and I met for five weeks. He devoured the information and asked tons of great questions. I couldn't answer all of his questions. Remember, I was just a college kid. I was only one step ahead of the dogs, but they were the same questions I had asked myself, so I had some answers.

On week four, we met to do a lesson on why Jesus had to die. Before I started the lesson, he looked at me and said, "I think I'm ready."

Caught a little off guard, I asked, "Ready for what?"

"I'm ready to pray and receive Christ."

We were not finished with the five-week Bible study, so I wasn't ready for him to be ready. After all I needed to follow the script! I looked at him and asked, "Are you sure?"

It turns out he had been talking to some other Christians he knew besides just me. They had been answering his questions as well. We got on our knees in his dorm room, and Kenny prayed to receive Christ that day. I was elated, and he was overjoyed. Who knew a simple invitation to a five-week Bible study would end up with him praying to receive Christ.

Over the next few months, God changed Kenny. Gone was the irritable, unpredictable, tempestuous young man who made people shy away from him. He became friendly and talkative; Boo Radley disappeared. He began attending Bible study with some Christian friends

> *Who knew a simple invitation to a five-week Bible study would end up with him praying to receive Christ.*

in downtown Clemson who operated a bicycle shop. He started passing out gospel tracts to everyone he met!

One day as my roommate Barry and I left the cafeteria and headed back to our dorm, we looked up and noticed a student standing on the very edge of the parapet surrounding the top of our ten-story dorm. Barry exclaimed, "Oh, no, we've got a jumper!"

I looked up, squinted, and quickly responded, "Barry, that's Kenny!"

We took off in a sprint. True to form, the elevator was nonfunctional, so we ran up ten flights of stairs to get to the roof. We stopped at the top to get our breath and slowly opened the rooftop door. Twenty paces away was Kenny with his arms up in the air, standing on the edge of the dorm parapet, facing Lake Hartwell and the sun setting on the Blue Ridge Mountains in the west. He was praising God for all he was worth. Barry and I looked at each other, smiled sheepishly, and shut the door quietly. There was a changed man, just as the verse says, "Therefore if any man is in Christ, he is a new creature; the old things passed away; behold, new things have come" (2 Corinthians 5:17).

I lost touch with Kenny after three months when I graduated from college. I often wondered what became of him. Over twenty years later, I was attending a Christian concert at the new BI-LO Center (now Bon Secours Wellness Arena) in Greenville, South Carolina. Seated in the nosebleed section with our church group, I looked down twenty rows in front of me and said to myself, "I recognize the back of that head. Who is that?"

I couldn't pay attention to the concert for trying to figure out who it was. I asked my wife if she recognized who it was, but she did not. I kept saying to myself, "I recognize him. Who is it?" Then suddenly, it came to me. "It's Kenny. That's Kenny. I can't believe it." I wasn't 100 percent sure so I waited until the concert ended to say anything. Sure enough, when he stood up and turned around, it was Kenny. I shouted his name, but people had started talking and leaving, and he never heard me. Terribly disappointed because he got away, I was nevertheless greatly encouraged to know that years later he was still faithful to the Lord.

Where did all that start in Kenny's life? Well, obviously, Kenny was seeking spiritual truth. Although he was a depressed, angry young man, he was still a sincere seeker. "Seek the Lord while He may be found; call upon Him while He is near" (Isaiah 55:6). So many people around you and me are sincere seekers. We just don't know it until we inquire.

Two college boys prayed for Kenny for months. His temper was intimidating, and other people wrote him off. Barry and I took him on as a personal project. We made a point to try to be his friend, which was a little scary and difficult. We also committed to pray for him. Who knows what spiritual obstacles in his life came tumbling down because of the spiritual battle waged on his behalf. You see, he was reading books on the occult while we were praying. Who else was praying for him? I don't know — perhaps his mom or grandfather or a Sunday school teacher from childhood. I don't know those answers, but I'm certain prayer prepared his heart and perhaps protected him from a lifetime of involvement in the occult.

Then there was an invitation. Somebody invited him to investigate the life of Christ. This invitation came at just the right time. It was a God-inspired invitation. I admit I was frightened at the prospect of dealing with Kenny in any way. It is said, "Courage is not the absence of fear, but the capacity for action despite our fears."[1] When we care about people, we do the right thing even in scary situations. I'm really glad God gave me courage enough to invite Boo Radley — I mean Kenny — to a Bible study; it changed his life for eternity.

Who in your life intimidates you? What kind of invitation do they need? Are you praying in preparation for the invitation?

STUDY QUESTIONS | Chapter 13

1. Who is the lost person in your life who intimidates you? Why do they intimidate you? Has God burdened your heart for their salvation?

2. What is the connection between fear and obedience?

3. Do you have to say everything correctly to win a friend to faith in Christ? Do you have to have all of the answers?

4. What happens if you wait until you learn all the answers to all the questions before you start sharing the gospel?

5. Are we saying that training is not important or valuable?

6. Will all invitations be greeted with a positive response?

14

THE FULLER BRUSH MAN

When I was elementary school age, the Fuller Brush salesman would come by our home to make his sales pitch once a year. I learned a lot by simple observation. For starters, he was dressed in a suit and tie with highly polished shoes. He was very friendly and knew a lot about our family. His presentation was well rehearsed.

"Howdy do, Mrs. Jackson, the top of the morning to you. I believe these are Robert and Miss Anne. Y'all call them Robin and Sugar. Am I correct?"

My mother was beaming that he had remembered not just our names but our nicknames. He then surveyed the den and kitchen of our home for a moment before observing, "I see that you have a new set of drapes since I was here last year. I like your decorating touch."

My mother was totally impressed that he would notice the difference from one year to the next. He then inquired about her parents, whom he seemed to know, and made some small talk for a few minutes.

Then what to my wondering eyes did appear? A jolly old elf and eight tiny reindeer? No, not quite! He opened his black case of brushes and laid out a black velour cloth on my mom's coffee table in front of her sofa where we all sat. My little eyes popped as he began to set out little shiny brushes on the black cloth. As a little boy, I thought they were like diamonds in a jewelry store. Starting with the smallest, most unique brushes, he explained their particular uses with a flourish.

He then explained the special deal of the day and the free brush that went with it. He put those in my mom's hand and then pulled out his order book, leaned in close, looked my mom in the eye, and said, "Mrs. Jackson, which one of these excellent Fuller brushes can I order for you today?"

Then he stared at her expectantly and didn't say another word. The uncomfortable silence hung in the air. My mom sighed and we all stared at her. Finally, not being able to resist a sales pitch then or now, I said, "Mama, I think you need those three right there for sure."

The Fuller Brush man smiled knowingly. My sister, Anne, piped up in her eight-year-old southern drawl, "Now Mama, y'all know you haven't touched the brushes you bought last year."

The brush man shot daggers at her with his eyes. That quieted her right down. My mom — knowing she was a doctor's wife, knowing she would never use the brushes, and knowing this was his livelihood — said, "I'm pretty sure I could use these brushes right here." She pointed out several brushes.

The brush man smiled appreciatively, threw in a free useless brush that I used later to wash my beagle, and departed a happy man.

Let's contrast that with the next salesman who showed up later the same summer. He was a college kid selling the *Encyclopedia Britannica*, probably just a summer job for him. He pulled up our driveway in a Volkswagen van with anti-war stickers all over. I immediately thought to myself, "He better be glad my Vietnam vet father is not here. If Dad comes home for lunch, it will be spectacular. Maybe I should call him. I imagined saying, 'Hey, Dad, there's a long-haired hippie war protester here at the house harassing Mom. What should I do?'" I'm still laughing just thinking about it. My dad would have probably gone to jail for a long time. It would have been worth it though — another chapter in another book!

It started off badly for him. My sister invited him in. Mom walked in the door in her housecoat and slippers with curlers in her hair and found this college kid sitting on the couch with long unkempt hair, trying to grow sideburns and a goatee and failing miserably. He had on blue jeans and sandals and no socks — very unprofessional. He began by apologizing for taking up our time. Then he started telling us how hard the job was and that no one wanted to buy any books. Then he commenced to speaking poorly of several of the neighbors who treated him rudely, or so he said. Unfortunately for him, all of those neighbors were in my mom's bridge club. He hadn't even started yet, and he was sinking like a rock.

Then he asked us all to sit on the couch, which we did. He smelled so badly that my sister and I got up and sat elsewhere. My mom was too polite, so she stuck it out. She should have gotten hazardous duty pay, but I guess she was used to my brothers and me.

He opened his presentation by saying, "These are the hardest encyclopedias to sell. It seems that everybody around here has a set of *World Book Encyclopedias*, which are quite inferior to *Encyclopedia Britannica*."

I glanced over at our set of *World Books*, which we bought from a door-to-door salesman a year before. I loved them, and here he was throwing off on my favorite encyclopedias. I was ready to call my dad.

He went through his presentation slowly and arduously with frequent grammar mistakes, which my mom felt compelled to correct. My mom is the original grammar nazi. She graduated from college with a degree in English after raising four children. She then taught (you guessed it) English grammar in high school. Each time she corrected him, he would stop and stare at her. My sister would giggle, which would throw him off even more. I could tell he was rehearsing his lines mentally in order to pick back up his presentation where he left off. On one occasion, he went all the way back to the start, went through all of his lines under his breath quickly, and started back where he left off. We all just rolled our eyes and sighed.

This cycle persisted with me urging him on mentally. Finally, I grabbed my mama's arm as she started to correct him for the fifth time and shook my head; she caught on. This would take all day.

When he finished with a broad smile and a sigh of relief, we all smiled and sighed as well. I was ready to cry or scream. He then said, "Mrs. Johnson, you wouldn't want to buy a set of these excellent encyclopedias, would you?"

"Jackson."

He just stared.

"Jackson. My name is Mrs. Jackson and, no, I wouldn't like to buy a set of *Encyclopedia Britannica*. I have an excellent set of *World Book Encyclopedias* with which we are perfectly pleased. We appreciate your time, and, young man, you need to desperately work on your grammar. My son will see you to the door."

What lessons do we learn from the tale of these two salesmen? First, don't be too hard on the college kid. He was just learning the trade. The Fuller Brush man was a seasoned professional and had been at it for a long time.

— The Fuller Brush man was neat in his appearance; there was nothing about him that was offensive. As Christians, we should be careful that our language, conduct and appearance are not offensive. The preaching of the gospel is offensive enough. Why add to it?

— He was also quite friendly. He connected with my mom, asking about her family. We should always be showing ourselves to be friendly and be in the process of making new friends. Every time you make a new friend, you expand your potential influence for the kingdom of God. Remember, Jesus was called "the friend of sinners." The closer we are to people, the greater the opportunity to influence their lives.

— His presentation was well-rehearsed and well-practiced. We should all know a gospel presentation by heart. We never know when we will have the opportunity to share Christ with a neighbor, a friend or coworker. More than that, a well-rehearsed three-minute testimony should be a part of our spiritual armamentarium. We never know when we will have the opportunity to share with people briefly how we came to know the Lord (1 Peter 3:15).

— He knew how to close his presentation. Evangelists call this "drawing the net." He was not apologetic. He was very confident as he invited my mom to purchase his excellent brushes. No salesman worth his salt concludes without giving an invitation to make a purchase. The pharmaceutical reps at my office often say hokey things like, "Dr. Jackson, will you commit to trying our fantastic diabetes drug on your next ten diabetics?"

Seeing through their sales ploy, I just smile and nod, "I'll remember your product." They have fulfilled their sales responsibility. In like manner, we Christians shouldn't be afraid to ask people if they would like to receive Christ right now. You would be surprised how often that is all that some folks need to make a commitment to Christ — a simple invitation.

You would be surprised how often that is all that some folks need to make a commitment to Christ — a simple invitation.

— Good sales people make a lot of presentations. Every salesman knows that if you throw enough mud against the wall, some of it will stick. If you make enough sales presentations, you will sell some product, maybe a lot of product. If you talk to enough people about Jesus, you will lead a lot of people to faith in Christ. Most of us just don't make enough sales presentations — I mean gospel presentations.

What was the college boy's frustration in my illustration above? Somebody had been through the neighborhood ahead of him selling *World Book Encyclopedias*. They had made a lot of sales presentations before him. They had beat him to the punch. All he got was the leftover gleaning after the harvesters went through. That's what happens to us when we allow television, movies and the world system to sell a secular product to our children, grand-children, friends and neighbors before we get there with the best product of all — the good news of Jesus Christ. All we get is the leftovers.

> *If you talk to enough people about Jesus, you will lead a lot of people to faith in Christ. Most of us just don't make enough sales presentations — I mean gospel presentations.*

Twenty-plus years ago, the South Carolina Baptist Pastors Conference had an evangelistic speaker who challenged all the attending Baptist pastors to attempt to lead at least one person to Christ per week for one year. My high school Bible teacher, Rev. David Dinkins, had become pastor of Doctors Creek Baptist Church in Walterboro, South Carolina. He gladly accepted that challenge. I talked to him about twenty weeks into the process. He was both excited and amazed at the same time. He was excited because he was ahead of schedule, God having blessed his efforts and allowing him to lead more than one person per week to faith in Christ — not from the pulpit, but from one-on-one evangelism.

"Brother David, what about the process has been most surprising?"

"The surprising thing has been how many people I have needed to talk to in order to lead just one person to faith in Christ. I estimate on average I have to talk to ten people in order to lead one person to faith. When I say talk to ten people, I mean making a full presentation of the gospel and giving them an invitation to receive Christ. This is an enjoyable ministry, but at the same time it requires a significant investment of time. I realize my parishioners do not have the time to do this, but as a minister I have the luxury and the privilege to invest this kind of time into evangelism."

"You mentioned that you were amazed by the process as well. What did you mean by that?"

"To put it bluntly, I have been amazed by the unorthodox theology that so many people in this community possess. I have spent a great deal of time correcting inaccurate theology and teaching true biblical doctrine. For me, this has been a delightful process."

"How has your church responded to all of this?"

"Well, since we have baptized more new believers in the first five months of this year than in many previous years put together, they are excited and challenged at the same time."

My friend Reverend Dinkins threw a lot of mud against the wall. He made a lot of gospel presentations and saw a lot of good results. What's it going to take to win one person to Christ? We will have to share the gospel with a lot more people.

"Well, shoot dog, doctor. Who has time for that?"

It all begins with gospel conversations. Please read on.

STUDY QUESTIONS | Chapter 14

1. What are the elements of a good sales presentation?

2. What detracts from a good sales presentation?

3. What are the elements of a good gospel presentation? What detracts?

4. What do we contend with in gospel presentations that is usually not a factor in sales presentations?

5. What does it mean to "draw the net"?

6. Have you ever made ten gospel presentations start to finish? Why ten?

15

SPRING BREAK BREAKTHROUGH

It was spring break, April 1976 — time for the annual pilgrimage to the college mecca of Florida — Daytona Beach. College kids from around the country covered the sand like the locusts covered Egypt. Most were there to bask in the sun and have fun. However, a certain subset determined to drink themselves into oblivion with alcohol, succeeding in doing so with reckless abandon. The first hour after I arrived, I observed completely intoxicated and completely nude guys and gals jumping into the motel swimming pool. Their unruly behavior continued unabated all week long.

My purpose for being in Daytona wasn't quite the same, as I was one of 1,500 Christian college students determined to share the gospel during the daytime on the beach when most people were sober. We attended praise and worship sessions in the early morning followed by intensive Bible study until noon. The atmosphere was electric. Can you imagine 1,500 college kids praising God all at the same time in a high-arched, Gothic-appearing sanctuary? It was inspiring! The contrast between the party animals on the beach and the God worshipers in that sanctuary could not have been starker.

In the afternoon, we went out two-by-two on the beach to find anyone who would be interested in a spiritual conversation. Many reported college kids meeting Jesus on the beach that week. I spoke to thirty-six people myself, but guess what? Everyone listened politely, but no one prayed to receive Christ. I was pretty bummed. Now don't get me wrong. I understand the importance of being a seed planter. I also understand Holy Spirit is the one who convicts and regenerates, but I had really hoped to lead someone to faith in Christ.

I prayed with urgency on Friday, our last day in Daytona. I honestly expressed my frustration to the Lord and specifically asked Him to allow me to lead to faith in Christ everyone with whom I shared the gospel that day. The worship this particular morning was fabulous because we all knew it was the last day. We sang with extra gusto — so much so, the memory is still with me even now, forty years later. It was emotional, encouraging and challenging. As they say, "It still warms the cockles of my heart."

That afternoon, my partner was my college roommate Barry. We walked down the beach and spied two college boys sitting on a towel. We introduced ourselves and said, "We are talking to college students about their spiritual lives. Would you be willing to take a few minutes to talk about yours, and may we share with you about the 'Four Spiritual Laws'? Have you heard about them?"

They looked at us like we had two heads, then looked at each other. Finally, one grunted, "Sure." The other guy looked disgusted, but we ignored him, plopped down on the sand and began asking questions. Turns out they had driven to Myrtle Beach from Ohio for spring break, but Myrtle Beach was too cold in April, so they decided to drive down to Daytona. They only had one hour to spend on the beach before they had to drive back to Ohio. No wonder he looked disgusted; we were taking up his one hour. Oh, well, we were committed.

Barry read through the gospel tract, and I shared my three-minute testimony. It was obvious they were paying close attention despite the wind and waves and pretty girls walking by. They both asked a few good questions; then I asked, "Is there any reason you would not want to ask

Christ to be your Lord and Savior right now?"

They were good friends, so they seemed to know what the other was thinking. They looked at each other and nodded; then one of them said, "It seems to me we have driven all the way from Ohio just to become Christians." They both laughed. Then we all bowed our heads on the beach, and Barry led them in a sinner's prayer. A few minutes later, they collected their belongings and headed back to Ohio as new believers in Christ. We got their phone numbers and connected them with some Christian college staff we knew on their college campus.

Later that evening, I stood on the balcony of our motel with another student from my college named Susan. We were observing all the last-minute partying going on around us. We were both grieved in our spirits by the amount of sinful behavior we saw. Finally, I said, "Susan, we still have several hours left in this day. I prayed this morning that God would allow me to lead to faith in Christ everyone I spoke to today. You want to go on an adventure?"

She smiled broadly and said, "Sure." So off we went.

We walked around the motel looking for open doors. We found one with four college kids sitting on beds, watching TV, and drinking beer. It was obvious they were not intoxicated, so I stuck my head in the door and said, "Hi, my name is Robert, and this is Susan. We are going around talking to folks about their spiritual lives and how they can know Jesus in a personal relationship. Y'all interested in a little dialogue?"

They all stared at me slack-jawed for about thirty seconds. I knew better than to say anything. I just stared back at them unblinking like a coon in a tree. Finally, one of the girls broke the silence with, "Sure, come on in." The other three looked seriously grieved. I smiled broadly and walked in, switching off the TV as I went by. Susan handed everyone a gospel tract and sat down between the two girls while I sat down between the two guys. Seeing Susan, the guys were all in.

I have to back up and explain something here. Tall, blue-eyed and blonde, Susan created a sensation wherever she went. She was usually the center of attention at all of our Christian gatherings — the guys' attention, I mean. She always dressed modestly as Christian college girls should, but her appearance was too striking to go unnoticed. She would have had to wear a Middle Eastern burka covering her from head to toe for guys not to notice her.

Now you understand why the two guys were all in. They kept cutting their eyes over toward Susan while I read from the gospel tract. I asked them questions periodically to make sure they were tracking with me. When I got to the part about the blood of Jesus and the cross, the devil showed up — not literally, but figuratively. Two fully intoxicated guys walked into the open door of the motel room.

The first one in the door spied Susan and immediately grabbed her arm, lifting her up as if to dance. He put his arm around her waist and began to make lewd comments. My mind began to race. I was thinking, "Oh, no, am I gonna have to fight this drunk guy to protect Susan's honor in front of these people with whom I've been sharing the gospel? What kind of testimony would that be? Then again, I can't let this guy take advantage of her." The air in the room was filled with tension.

Praise Jesus, Susan was way ahead of me. She turned on this million-dollar smile, lighting up the entire room, and then she said, "Praise the Lord! Hallelujah! Jesus is in this place right now. Do you fellas want to hear the rest of our gospel presentation?"

The guy who had his arm around Susan looked like he'd been sucker-punched. He dropped his beer can on the floor and staggered backwards right out the door he had just come in. He and his friend took off running down the balcony. Still smiling that radiant smile, Susan asked, "Isn't God good?" Then she sat back down like nothing had happened. Maybe this happened to her all the time? I never asked.

At first, the four college kids in the room began to laugh nervously, then harder and harder, until tears flowed down their cheeks. However, they eventually controlled themselves and began to pay attention to the rest of my presentation, and all four of them prayed to receive Christ. Like she said, Jesus was definitely in the room, and God was good!

I learned a big lesson that day: Don't go witnessing with movie star blondes! (No, that's not it!) I learned a valuable lesson about the power of genuine praise. Do you remember what King Jehoshaphat did when he was confronted with a much larger military force than he had at his disposal? He put the choir up in front of the soldiers and instructed them to praise Yahweh Adonai, the Lord God Almighty. Jehoshaphat understood the power of praise (2 Chronicles 20:21-22). He understood that Satan and his minions are allergic to praise, that they go into anaphylactic shock when they are in the presence of God's people praising their God. The praises of God and the presence of Satan are mutually exclusive. Satan is rendered weak and powerless in the presence of God's people worshiping God. Why? It is because God inhabits the praise of His people. The praise of God's people and the presence of God's power are mutually inclusive. Where you find one, you'll find the other. Where you find God, you won't find the enemy of your soul or opposition to your spiritual ministry.

> *The praises of God and the presence of Satan are mutually exclusive.*

Susan understood this clearly. She comprehended spiritual warfare as described in Ephesians 6:12: "For our struggle is not against flesh and blood, but against the rulers, against the powers, against the world forces of this darkness, against the spiritual forces of wickedness in the heavenly places." I did not need to grapple with the drunken intruder to protect my female friend. I just needed to understand the power of praise to drive away the enemy and his minions.

Why do we begin every church service with worship and praise? Why, of course, it is to drive away the enemy and to welcome Him who inhabits the praise of His people.

The praise of God's people and the presence of God's power are mutually inclusive.

Subsequently, the preaching of the Word is uncontested by our adversary, old Slewfoot. Why do we begin every day in prayer worshiping our Creator, Sustainer and Redeemer? Why, of course, to bind the enemy who "roams about like a roaring lion seeking whom he may devour" and to engage the presence of Him who is worthy of our soul's best songs!

I have to admit, I wasn't good at this until one of my pastors, Ron Jackson at Rock Hill Baptist Church in Inman, South Carolina, challenged the congregation to do two things. First, he challenged us to memorize Scripture verses pertaining to the attributes of God and to pray these verses back to God in our quiet time, which I began to do slowly over months of time. Second, he challenged us to practice Psalm 119:164: "Seven times a day I will praise Thee, because of Thy righteous ordinances." He asked us to write a reminder on our hands for one week, and to not listen to our car radios but rather to praise God instead.

I actually did this for one week. It was so much fun, it turned into a habit. I learned to take every still moment — at a stop light, at an elevator, at night before falling asleep, and in my car while driving to work — as an opportunity to praise the Lord. I discovered I needed more verses to pray, so I memorized more verses about the attributes of God, the names of God, the names of Jesus, etc. Now, spending time alone worshiping the Lord is one of my favorite pastimes. Guess what else? It gives power in prayer and in witnessing.

Well, Daytona was not a bust after all. I shared the gospel with forty-two people in one week. Six people were born again into God's kingdom on the last day, in answer to my specific prayer request. I learned an important lesson about prayer warfare from my friend Susan. I also learned that Satan always interrupts when we talk about the blood of Jesus and the need for repentance. We must learn the art of praise and worship to block him from intruding at that point or any other place in our ministry.

I also learned that if you talk to enough people, somebody will get saved. Remember my friend, David Dinkins, estimated that if he talked to ten people about Jesus, one or two will make a commitment. At some point I heard this statement elsewhere, but I cannot document it; however, I suspect it may be true. I also believe this explains why most of us never lead anybody to faith in Christ. We don't talk to enough people.

What if we all responded to a challenge from the former president of the South Carolina Baptist Convention, Keith Shorter, who serves as pastor of Mt. Airy Baptist Church in Easley, South Carolina? In an article he wrote for *The Courier* in August 2017, he described an epiphany he had one day while walking his dog and reading Twitter "to pass the time." He read a post from Kevin Ezell, which stated, "16.7 million … the number of gospel conversations if all 46,000 SBC churches would share with one person each day for a year."[1] His mind went into a whirl contemplating the possibilities. The result? A proposal called the 365 Challenge, calling churches in South Carolina to "average one gospel conversation a day for a year."[2] What if we did this, in just Southern Baptist churches around the country?

If what I suspect is true in the previous paragraph that at least one conversion results from ten conversations, then 1,670,000 people would come to Christ in the entire country in a year. Let's break this down for my home state, South Carolina, which has 2,149 churches and missions, according to the 2016 Statistical Summary for the South Carolina Baptist Convention.[3] So what if one person from each of these churches had one gospel conversation per day for an entire year? This would be a total of 784,385 gospel conversations, which would lead to 78,438 conversions in the course of a year, instead of just the 16,671 baptisms recorded in the same statistical summary.[4] We realize not all salvations result in baptism in a South Carolina Baptist church, so this number could be more and may not accurately reflect the evangelistic efforts of South Carolina Baptists, but we believe the number could be dramatically higher if more people talked about Jesus in their daily conversations with lost people.

What's the difference between a gospel conversation and a gospel presentation? A gospel conversation involves mentioning Jesus or something Jesus said or a biblical principle in our everyday conversation, and planting a seed in the heart of our friend or family member. It will be up to them to follow up on the comment. A gospel presentation involves a full explanation of the gospel message with Scripture and an invitation to accept Christ. That's what comes to mind for most of us when we think about sharing the gospel. However, that is not always possible or suitable. It depends on the situation, the time

> *A gospel conversation involves mentioning Jesus or something Jesus said or a biblical principle in our everyday conversation.*

available, and the openness of the person involved. Sometimes a brief gospel conversation (a word seasoned with salt) is all that is appropriate. Our friend will bring it up later after Holy Spirit waters the seed we have planted. Another Christian in the person's life may get to harvest the fruit of the seed we plant. "I planted, Apollos watered, but God was causing the growth," said Paul in 1 Corinthians 3:6. For his book *Abandoned Faith,* Alex McFarland interviewed Ed Stetzer, executive director of the Billy Graham Center for Evangelism and executive editor of *Facts and Trends Magazine*. Dr. Stetzer described many shifts in our culture today, including spiritual, but noted that surveys "have shown that 89 percent of the unchurched are willing to have a conversation with a friend about Christianity."[5] What an encouraging thought as we ponder planting the seed of the gospel with gospel conversations.

Many people have become believers over the years as a consequence of cold contact evangelism like we conducted on the beach at Daytona or door-to-door evangelism like many churches still conduct in their neighborhoods. This sort of outreach is hard and poorly received most of the time. Warm contact evangelism involves planting the seed of the gospel in the heart of people close to us in our circle of influence. We start the process with friends, relatives, business associates, and neighbors using gospel conversations, eventually leading to gospel presentations. This approach is received much more favorably. It's also much easier on most Christians who aren't gifted as evangelists. Cold contact evangelism is emotionally difficult, and it is the rare individual who enjoys it.

Here's the deal. I don't think God holds you and me responsible for the entire lost world. He does hold me accountable for my circle of influence. We need to have an epiphany like Keith Shorter did. His vision was for Southern Baptists in South Carolina impacting their state. You and I need a vision for reaching our network of family, friends, neighbors and coworkers. If every Christian did this, starting with gospel conversations, our entire country would be changed. Perhaps the revival we've prayed for so long would finally come. Revival always starts in your heart and mine. The overflow of a revived heart is always telling people what Jesus has done for them. This is where gospel conversations begin.

STUDY QUESTIONS | Chapter 15

1. What's the connection between worship and evangelism? Why should worship precede and undergird evangelistic efforts?

2. Have you ever participated in beach evangelism or door-to-door evangelism? Would it be hard for you? Is it effective? What is more effective?

3. What does it mean for God to "inhabit the praise of His people"? Did it make any logical sense for Jehoshaphat to put the choir in front of his enemy?

4. Would you be willing to take the challenge to praise God seven times a day for one week and memorize verses pertaining to the attributes of God to use in your worship time? Take the dare!

5. Would you be willing to be one of the Christians involved in the gospel conversations all around the United States? What is the difference between a gospel conversation and a gospel presentation?

16

Abandoned at Birth
First Base: Assurance

On February 4, 2011, either a desperate (or confused) twenty-four-year-old woman gave birth to a six-pound boy in the bathroom at what was then called the BI-LO Center in Greenville, South Carolina, during a Ringling Brothers and Barnum & Bailey Circus show. Hearing what sounded like a baby, a custodian found him, cold but alive, about an hour later, dangling in the toilet water with no mother around. Of course, the story made national news, with the media and everyone else in a frenzy over a mom abandoning her child in a toilet.[1]

How many times have you known folks to be excited about someone's public decision for Christ at church or at an evangelistic event, but in three months' time that person can't be found? The person is not in church. His life has not changed, and he is running with the same rough crowd. You know what I mean. There is a disconnect somewhere. Either they were never truly born again, or they were born again but abandoned at birth.

What do I mean by "born again but abandoned at birth"? I believe that just as much as parents have a responsibility to nurture and protect newborn babies, the church has a responsibility to nurture baby Christians. It doesn't matter whether we call it follow-up or discipleship, there are certain basic truths every new believer needs to grasp if he is to succeed in the Christian life.

I believe that just as much as parents have a responsibility to nurture and protect newborn babies, the church has a responsibility to nurture baby Christians.

If I personally lead someone to faith in Christ, I always take it upon myself to attempt to meet with him personally for several visits to help establish him in the basic disciplines of the Christian life. If I am the first assistant when Holy Spirit births someone into the kingdom of God, then I should help him take his first steps. If that's not possible, I point him to a local church near where he lives or invite him to my church. Involving him in a small group Bible study like Sunday school or a home group is essential to long-term success in the Christian life.

What are the basic concepts I try to communicate during my follow-up sessions? Let me illustrate them with a baseball diamond to make it easier to remember.

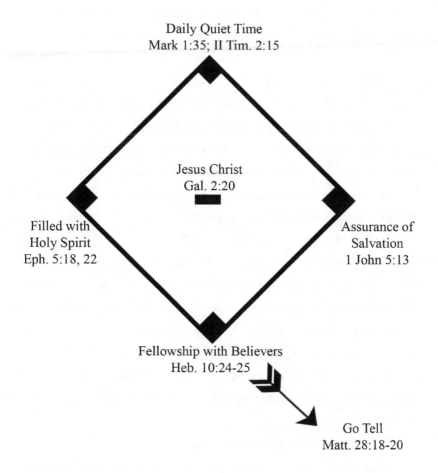

Daily Quiet Time
Mark 1:35; II Tim. 2:15

Jesus Christ
Gal. 2:20

Filled with
Holy Spirit
Eph. 5:18, 22

Assurance of
Salvation
1 John 5:13

Fellowship with Believers
Heb. 10:24-25

Go Tell
Matt. 28:18-20

First Base

When I follow up with a new believer, I always take him to first base in our first session, which is assurance of salvation, because how can anyone prosper in his spiritual life if he has nagging doubts about his salvation? In fact, one of the initial tactics of the enemy of our soul is to sow seeds of doubt. He will whisper in our ear, "You're not a Christian. Who told you that you were a Christian? Look at all the sin in your life. A real Christian doesn't act or think like that. Who are you fooling?" Subsequently, a new believer begins to doubt the legitimacy of his salvation experience. What are the key elements of a genuine salvation experience?

1) An intellectual commitment — We commit to Christ with our mind. We understand the basics of the gospel, and we give intellectual assent to the truth of the message. Different people require different amounts of information in order to give their mental assent. Some are skeptical and require lots of research, lots of information, and have lots of questions. There's nothing wrong with this as long as they are sincere seekers. Some merely need to hear the name of Jesus like a pastor I met in India who was saved after hearing the name of Jesus spoken by a group of Christians.

I was incredulous, so I asked him a few questions through an interpreter. "Had you really never heard the name of Jesus before the day you were saved?"

"No, never," he replied emphatically.

"Had you ever heard a gospel presentation or been to a church?"

He shook his head negatively.

"Had you ever met any Christians before that day?"

Once again, he replied, "No."

"Then how did you get saved?"

Through the interpreter, he explained, "I was walking through the market, and I heard a group of Christians talking. I heard the name of

Jesus spoken. Immediately, I was overcome with guilt for all my sins, and I knew that Jesus, whom I knew nothing about, could take away my sin. I committed my life to Him on the spot. I approached the group of Christians and began to ask questions. They accepted me and answered my questions. Soon I was baptized, and now five years later I am a pastor."

My Christian friends and I on this mission trip were completely amazed at his story and the power of the name of Jesus. Never doubt the truthfulness of the gospel hymn that exclaims, "There's power in the name of Jesus." So, you see, some folks don't require much information, just the bare facts! *Just the facts, ma'am, just the facts.*

2) Volitional commitment — We make a commitment of our will. We choose Jesus. We reject the world, the flesh and Satan, and we choose Jesus as an act of our own wills. Billy Graham's monthly magazine is called *Decision* for a reason. People who become believers have to make a decision to repent from sin and their old way of life and turn toward God and a new way of life. It's a decision. It's a choice. That's why we sing, "I have decided to follow Jesus, no turning back, no turning back."[2] (I know John 15:16 says that He actually chooses us, but that is a discussion for another day.)

3) Emotional — We make an emotional commitment. This looks different for different people. Some folks are very matter-of-fact and unemotional in their salvation experience but just as legitimately born again as the next. Some folks are very demonstrative, tearful, or shouting, "Hallelujah." People are different, and we should allow Holy Spirit to be unique as He works in people's lives. However, we should not doubt our salvation just because we don't have an exuberant emotional experience like someone else we know. Remember: "Different strokes for different folks."

When I was a first grader in Charleston, South Carolina, it was a big deal for every elementary kid to ride on the coal-driven train known as "The Best Friend of Charleston" — "the first commercially operated steamer constructed in America" and first used in December 1930.[3] Each elementary school in town would be bussed out to the old train for a ride. I still remember it clearly fifty-five years later — black smoke bellowing from the engine, kids hanging out the windows of the passenger cars, and the engineer pulling the whistle. What a great day!

After it was over, the engine and coal car disconnected from the passenger cars and pulled away. I thought to myself, "That's not right. They belong together." Now fast forward to today and label the engine "Word of God" and the coal car "Faith." Let's label the passenger car "Emotion." You understand that train will run with just the engine and the coal car just fine. Your salvation experience is legitimate with or without an emotional experience — just like the train can run with or without the passenger cars. Sometimes it may not look right to you, but it's still just fine.

Well, doctor, how can I know for certain I've been born again? I'm glad you asked that question.

1) There is an external witness, which is the Word of God. The Scriptures affirm that "everyone who calls on the name of the Lord shall be saved" (Acts 2:21). If you are confident you have done this in good faith, then you have to trust God that He will keep His promise to give you new life. As long as God is on His throne, you can trust Him to keep His promises.

2) There is also an internal witness, which is Holy Spirit. When we are born again, the Bible tells us the Spirit of God comes to take up residence within us. We become the temple of Holy Spirit (1 Corinthians 6:19), and "the Spirit Himself bears witness with our spirit that we are the children of God" (Romans 8:16). A.W. Tozer made this observation in his book *How to Be Filled with the Holy Spirit*: "Jesus Christ wanted to take religion out of the external and make it internal and put it on the same level as life itself, so that a man knows he knows God the same as

he knows he is himself and not someone else. He knows God the same as he knows he is alive and not dead. Only Holy Spirit can do that. The Holy Spirit came to carry the evidence of Christianity from the books of apologetics into the human heart, and that is exactly what he does."[4] Listen carefully: It is impossible for the Spirit of the most Holy God to invade and possess your physical body and you not know it. Why?

3) It is because of the witness of a changed life. Second Corinthians 5:17 tells us, "Therefore, if any man is in Christ, he is a new creature; the old things passed away; behold, all things become new." Hallelujah! That is so true. When Holy Spirit comes to live in you, and you allow Him to rule over your life, everything changes — the way you think, the way you talk, the way you look at life, your priorities, the way you spend your money — everything. If there is no change, then you've never been born again, or you're not allowing Holy Spirit to rule over your life. You be the judge. In fact, Paul challenges us to "test yourselves to see if you are in the faith; examine yourselves" (2 Corinthians 13:5a)!

But, Doc, why do so many Christians doubt their salvation? I wish I could tell you how many Christian folks have confided in me over the years in my medical office that they doubted their salvation. Why do they tell me? I don't know. I guess they think I'm their pastor. Half the time they call me Pastor or Reverend Jackson instead of Doctor. I just let it go with a smile. I'm honored to be lumped in with my pastor friends. So why do people doubt their salvation?

1) Deception — A person has been deceived by the enemy into believing he made a genuine commitment to Christ when he really did not. Therefore, Holy Spirit is nagging him with conviction of sin and urging him to repent and commit to Christ. He may have joined the church as a child when his friend did, but was never truly born again. Who knows? That person has to look into his heart and decide between himself and God.

2) Unconfessed sin — The Bible calls this a besetting sin. Whenever any Christian has a sin issue he refuses to deal with by repentance and confession, his heart begins to harden and he begins to drift away from God. The inevitable result is doubting one's salvation. Why? Holy Spirit is not working in his life like He once did, and this person knows it. The Bible calls this grieving Holy Spirit and warns us not to "grieve the Holy Spirit of God" (Ephesians 4:30).

3) Inadequate instruction — Sometimes people doubt their salvation due to a lack of good instruction, a lack of good Bible teaching. Unfortunately, some new believers are abandoned at birth. Some new believers are snatched away by the enemy because no one takes them under their wing and instructs them in the basics of the Christian life. This grieves my heart more than anything as a teacher of God's Word. It is so preventable. I have been teaching the basics for forty-one years, attempting to put new believers on a firm foundation. That's part of what prompted me to write this book, the desire to expand my reach to more new believers. You and I both have a responsibility to give a healthy start to all new believers, so that the enemy does not snatch them away.

There is a huge emphasis in medical circles (family practice and pediatrics) to give a healthy start to newborns with proper nutrition, immunizations and intellectual stimulation. All manner of community, medical and government programs encourage all three of these aspects of newborn and adolescent development. But where in the church is the overwhelming concern for the healthy start for newborn believers? Of course, we have Sunday school and small groups, but our attitude is "If you come, we will teach you." When one of my newborns does not achieve his developmental milestones, it is considered a crisis, and I refer him to a pediatric developmentalist immediately. If an elementary school child misses school, a truant officer goes looking for him, but if a new believer misses his developmental milestones (i.e., no fruit of the Spirit, absent from church, doesn't learn how to share his faith, etc.), is that considered a crisis? Is he referred to the pastor or a biblical counselor? What if a new believer drops out of Sunday school or church? Does the Sunday school director or teacher go looking for him or her? Maybe, or maybe not. The point is, we should take seriously the responsibility of nurturing new believers just like we do our newborn infants to insure they prosper in their newfound faith. Never let it be said that we are guilty of abandoning a newborn believer at birth.

> *The point is, we should take seriously the responsibility of nurturing new believers just like we do our newborn infants to insure they prosper in their newfound faith. Never let it be said that we are guilty of abandoning a newborn believer at birth.*

(By the way, a word on the BI-LO baby: He survived and went home with foster parents.[5] Thanks be to God!)

Now our new believer has turned the corner at first base and has been waved on toward second base by the first base coach — his discipler. Will he be thrown out by the opposition? Will his heart be stony ground, thorny thickets, or good soil? What can we do to help him prosper? Read on.

STUDY QUESTIONS | Chapter 16

1. Who or what helped you to grow spiritually when you first became a believer? Was it a person or a group or a curriculum?

2. Did you ever feel abandoned after you first became a believer? How did that feel?

3. What can we do in our churches to prevent new believers from being abandoned or falling through the cracks?

4. Have you ever doubted your salvation? How did you overcome your doubts?

5. Why do people doubt their salvation?

6. What gives assurance of salvation?

17

Second Base: Daily Quiet Time

When I was a freshman in college, I fell in with a group of college kids who were very serious about their Christian lives, growing in the Lord and studying the Word. Even as college kids, they were prayer warriors. Some of them would stay up all night to pray for spiritual awakening at our college. They invited me to come along one time, and I was dumb enough to agree to it. I was dead asleep by 11:00 p.m. I woke up with a carpet impression on the side of my face as they were going to breakfast. The older students who had prayed all night just smiled and invited me to breakfast. I overheard one guy say, "Well, he's mastered the art of sleep praying." Boy, was I humiliated! Nevertheless, they still let me hang around them and learn from them.

When I first met them, they constantly asked one another, "How is your quiet time?" I had no idea what they were talking about but was too embarrassed to ask since they all seemed to be "in the know." They were obviously holding one another accountable about something they called a "quiet time," but I had no clue.

One day, a senior student named Mae caught me in a stairwell, looked me dead in the eye, and asked, "Rob Jackson, how's your quiet time?"

I wasn't about to let on that I had no idea what she was talking about, so I just mumbled, "Fine, fine," and walked briskly past. Oh, man, what a loser.

A week later, they had a seminar entitled "How to Have a Daily Quiet Time." I decided immediately to attend because I was tired of being in the dark. The teacher was a student named John "Stump" Propst, whose nickname was appropriate since he was as wide as he was tall and hairy as a bear. That was forty-one years ago, and I remember it like it was yesterday. John revolutionized my spiritual life. He taught me how to have a daily devotional called a daily quiet time. I call this second base because one cannot grow in one's spiritual life if one doesn't touch second base. Trust me, the devil will throw you out of the game!

In baseball, the runner can be thrown out if he doesn't touch each base as he runs the bases. In like manner on our spiritual journey, you and I will be thrown out of the game by the enemy if we don't touch all the bases appropriately. In fact, we need to camp out on each base and learn the spiritual truths represented by each base.

What did I learn from John that pivotal night? John looked at our group of freshmen and sophomore students and asked, "How many of you understand what a daily quiet time is?"

I looked around at the twenty other college kids in the room and thought to myself, "How many other losers and liars are there in this room like me that have no clue what a daily quiet time is?"

Every hand went up except mine. I felt like an idiot. Even worse, I was sitting on the front row right under his lectern, so everybody could see the long-necked kid with red hair who didn't raise his hand. John looked at me, and I sheepishly said, "I don't have a clue. That's why I'm here."

Then a voice from the back exclaimed, "That's great. I don't have a clue either. I just raised my hand because everybody else did."

Two other voices said simultaneously, "Me, too."

I smiled broadly. I wasn't so dumb after all, and I wasn't the only loser/liar on campus pretending to be a Christian. Well, we all had to begin somewhere.

John began, "Your Christian life is a relationship with God the Father through Jesus the Son. It's not about the rules or regulations of the Bible. You cannot please God by obeying the Ten Commandments. Jesus is your righteousness. Jesus is your life. He is all you need. Seek His face. Get to know Him. Learn to love Him. He will satisfy the deepest longings of your soul."

That was heady stuff from a college kid, but we ate it up — and we believed every word of it. John continued, "Jesus said in John 15:5, 'I am the vine, you are the branches; he who abides in Me, and I in him, he bears much fruit; for apart from Me you can do nothing.' We abide in Jesus, the Vine, by reading the Word and praying. That's how we connect to Jesus, the source of our spiritual life. But if we do not abide in Jesus, we lose our spiritual vitality. 'If anyone does not abide in Me, he is thrown away as a branch, and dries up; and they gather them, and cast them into the fire, and they are burned' (v. 6)."

John asked the group, "How do we cultivate a genuine personal relationship with our Lord Jesus?"

The class stared at him like a bunch of owls in a tree at midnight. One highly intelligent college kid ventured, "Through a daily quiet time?"

John exclaimed exuberantly, "Exactly! Now, let's talk about the practical nuts and bolts of a quiet time. First, you pick a time and place. The best time for most people is early morning before the day begins. Mark 1:35 says, 'And in the early morning, while it was still dark, He (Jesus) arose and went out and departed to a lonely place, and was praying there.' In fact, if you carefully read the book of Luke, you'll find

Jesus had a custom of slipping off alone to pray. Now get this: If Jesus, the very Son of God, who had uninterrupted fellowship with the Father, felt a need to get up early to pray, how much more should you and I do the same?"

He let that hang heavy in the air for a long time while we all digested the significance of that statement. In that moment, I made up my mind to get up early the next day and start a habit of seeking God's face in a daily quiet time. That habit has been with me now for forty-one years, thanks to the challenge of John Propst and the accountability of the other college kids who would often ask me, "How's your quiet time?" By then I knew how to answer truthfully.

In that moment, I made up my mind to get up early the next day and start a habit of seeking God's face in a daily quiet time.

My place became the chapel on the eighth floor of Johnstone Hall at Clemson University. I met Jesus there for two years at 6:00 a.m. At first it was hard because, quite frankly, I didn't know Him very well. I set out to pray and read my Bible for thirty minutes. I took my Bible, an old commentary, and a notepad up to the chapel for my first time. I read one chapter in my Bible, worked on a memory verse, and prayed for everything I could think of. I then looked at my watch; I had been there for seven minutes. Aargh! This was harder than I thought, so I did it all again.

The second time it took only five minutes. I guess I got more efficient or forgot to pray for somebody. This really was harder than I thought. I realized that after being in church all of my life from bed baby to college, I didn't know God at all. My acquaintance was so superficial that we couldn't even carry on a conversation. I was discouraged and embarrassed, but I didn't give up. I kept going to the chapel every morning at 6:00 a.m. I slowly learned how to pray. I learned how to worship God.

I learned how to intervene for my lost friends. I slowly learned how to study the Bible, not just read it. I developed a voracious appetite for memorizing Scripture and actually memorized hundreds of verses my first two years of college. My roommate was not a believer. He grew weary of me excitedly telling him all the things God was revealing to me in the Scriptures and also practicing memory verses on him.

Back to John — he wasn't through with us. He then recommended a Bible, a paper and pen. "Read the Word expectantly. Expect God to speak to you through His Word. Write down the observations you make, the sin He reveals in your life, the character traits of God that He makes plain to you, the commands He expects you to obey.

"Keep an ongoing prayer list of people and events you pray for. Mark them off when God answers your prayer.

"Write down verses that speak to you and begin to memorize them. I recommend memorizing at least two verses a week. Put them on an index card and carry them with you as you walk to class. Spend free time meditating on these verses, and let God speak to your heart about those Scriptures."

I made plans on the spot to do just that. I'm still writing verses on cards forty-one years later. Thanks, John, wherever you are!

John finished by cautioning us, "Don't approach your quiet time as a religious duty or an item to check off each day on your religious check off list. Approach your quiet time as a sacred time alone with the Savior of your soul, getting to know Him and love Him. Just rest in Him a little while every day. Remember what Jesus said in John 15:7-8: 'If you abide in me, and my words abide in you, ask whatever you wish and it

> *Approach your quiet time as a sacred time alone with the Savior of your soul, getting to know Him and love Him.*

shall be done for you. By this is my Father glorified, that you bear much fruit, and so prove to be my disciples.'"

All of this was new to me. I was a church attender prior to that time but not a serious Bible student. I lay awake that night pondering the passage John quoted to us — if I would bear fruit, it would glorify the Father and prove that I was Jesus' disciple. More than that, if I would abide in Jesus through a daily quiet time, the fruit would come as surely as a branch connected to the vine bears fruit. I just had to be patient and wait. It wasn't my responsibility to produce the fruit. That was God's responsibility. All I had to do was stay connected. As time passed, God began to produce the fruit, which leads me to third base.

STUDY QUESTIONS | Chapter 17

1. Has anyone ever taught you the basics of a daily quiet time? Who was it? When was it in your spiritual journey?

2. What should we do in a daily quiet time?

3. Does anyone hold you accountable for your daily quiet time? Why is accountability important? Why do we resist accountability?

4. What is the purpose of a daily quiet time? What is *not* the purpose of a daily quiet time?

5. Why do we memorize Scripture? Do you have a plan for Scripture memorization? Do you have a Scripture memorization accountability partner?

6. Have you ever set aside a half day just to pray, meditate, and read God's Word? Would that be hard for you to do?

18

THIRD BASE:
FILLED WITH HOLY SPIRIT

Ken Kelly and Mike Garber sat across from me in my dorm room at Clemson University, B706 Johnstone Hall. They asked me questions that were destined to change my spiritual journey forever.

Ken looked at me seriously and asked, "Rob Jackson, have you made the wonderful discovery of the Spirit-filled life?"

My mind raced. I had grown up in a Baptist church. I had perfect attendance pins for twelve years. I had sung in the choir from age five until this moment, but for the life of me, I had no idea what Ken meant by the Spirit-filled life. I didn't want to appear spiritually clueless after I had just shared my testimony with them and kinda bragged about all of my church activities growing up. Now I was stumped.

I looked at both of them with vacant, uncomprehending eyes like those of my daughter's never-dying beta fish that would stare back at me from its tiny fish bowl in her bedroom, and I sheepishly acknowledged, "I have no idea what you're talking about."

Mike smiled politely and said, "Don't feel bad; most other people don't know either. Let us explain it to you. Do you know who Holy Spirit is?"

"Well, yeah, He's like the third person of the Trinity — Father, Son, and Holy Spirit. Everyone knows that."

Ken smiled, "Exactly, but everybody doesn't really know that. What does Holy Spirit do?"

Once again, my mind went blank. I stared at them, wishing I hadn't bragged on my perfect Sunday school attendance. Probably, I should know this. In a flash it came to me, and I blurted out, "He convicts of sin. I know I've experienced that!"

Mike and Ken both burst out laughing. Mike said, "Haven't we all, haven't we all." Then he continued, "Holy Spirit also is responsible for teaching us God's Word when we read the Bible. He guides us in prayer. He is responsible for regenerating the new believer — i.e., causing us to be born again. Holy Spirit also produces the fruit of the Spirit in our lives when we allow Him to control us. Does this sound familiar?"

"I'm sure I've heard all of this at one time or another, but it must not have stuck with me."

Ken took up the conversation using a teaching tool, which was a little booklet he had with him. "Robert, we all have a choice to make each day of our lives. That choice is whether to allow Holy Spirit who lives in us Christians to rule in our lives and over every area of our lives, or to arrogate that role for ourselves. When we choose continuously to rule our own affairs apart from Holy Spirit's input, we become what the Bible calls carnal or fleshly. Paul, in Galatians 5:19-21a, describes the characteristics of a carnal man by saying, 'Now the deeds of the flesh are evident, which are: immorality, impurity, sensuality, idolatry, sorcery, enmities, strife, jealousy, outbursts of anger, disputes, dissensions, factions, envying, drunkenness, carousing, and things like these.' Does this ever describe your life?"

I was a little queasy as I looked at the list, because much of the fleshly fruit looked like me at that time in my life. I opened my mouth, but I couldn't find my voice. I just opened and shut my mouth a couple of times like my daughter's beta fish used to do.

Mike confirmed what was going on in my mind. "That's what I thought. Before we learned this stuff, we were all like the carnal man. That's why we're so excited to share with people how they can be Spirit-controlled."

Ken jumped in with, "Yes, now catch this. People who are really born again have Holy Spirit in their lives. They are the temple of Holy Spirit (1 Corinthians 6:19). The Bible teaches that if we submit ourselves to the authority of the indwelling Holy Spirit, He will rule over our spiritual life and produce in us the 'fruit of the Spirit.' This is found in Galatians 5:22-23, which says, 'But the fruit of the Spirit is love, joy, peace, patience, kindness, goodness, faithfulness, gentleness, self-control; against such things there is no law.' Now which fruit would you like to characterize your life?"

I pointed to the verses describing the fruit of the Spirit; then I paused and asked, "How do I know when Holy Spirit is in control of my life?"

Mike clapped his hands with excitement and exclaimed, "I'm glad you asked that question!" He referred me to the booklet again and began to teach me the truths that have directed my spiritual trajectory for the last forty years.

"Robert, the first step is to make sure you keep a short account with God. By that, I mean confess your sins as soon as Holy Spirit convicts you of any particular sin. If you allow sin to find a nesting place in your heart, Holy Spirit won't rule in your life. You will then produce rotten fruit. First John 1:9 tells us, 'If we confess our sins, He is faithful and righteous to forgive us our sins and to cleanse us from all unrighteousness.'

"Second, concentrate on surrendering every area of your life to God every day. Ask Holy Spirit to sit on the throne of your life and rule as king over every part of your life — lock, stock, and barrel — without holding back. He is the Lord of creation and should be Lord of your life. In Romans 12:1, Paul urges us "by the mercies of God, to present [our] bodies a living and holy sacrifice, acceptable to God, which is [our] spiritual service of worship."

"Third, the Bible says, 'As you therefore have received Christ Jesus the Lord, so walk in Him' (Colossians 2:6). How did you receive Him? By faith, right?"

I nodded slowly, trying to discern where this was heading.

Mike continued, "Then you also walk by faith. We trust Him every day to make us more like Jesus and to produce His fruit in our lives. I can't live like Jesus. Neither can you. We have to trust Holy Spirit in us to produce the life of Christ in us. That's where the faith comes in."

Mike added seriously, "Don't think this is a magic formula. Being a Spirit-controlled Christian involves abiding in the Word, abiding in prayer, and connecting with fellow believers. What we have described to you is just the beginning."

I moved my head up and down methodically, trying to absorb all they were saying.

Ken took over with, "Would you like to pray right now and begin a life long journey of every day asking Holy Spirit to control your life and make you a Spirit-controlled Christian?"

I knew without hesitation what I should do — and should have been doing all along. No one had ever explained it to me that simply or that plainly. I answered enthusiastically, "Sure! Let's pray right now!"

That day in B706 Johnstone Hall, I began a forty-year journey of every day subordinating my life under the authority of God's Word and the Person of Holy Spirit who lives in me. I strive to live a clean life, a yielded life, and a life of faith, trusting Holy Spirit to make me more like Jesus every day.

The transformation in my life was immediate and dramatic.

Previously, I was the world's biggest worrywart. If I could have gotten paid for worrying, I would've been rich before nineteen years of age. I worried constantly that I wouldn't make the grades for medical school. I had this constant nausea in my stomach about exams and grades. After Ken and Mike taught me about abiding in Jesus and abiding in His Word, I began to conscientiously submit my life to Holy Spirit every day, including my future plans for medical school. Over a several-month period, Holy Spirit began to produce in me "the peace of God, which surpasses all comprehension" (Philippians 4:7a). I began to rest in Jesus and entrust my future plans to Him. I continued to study hard, but I left all the results up to Him. I was gradually liberated from the excessive fear and anxiety that had plagued me for two years of college life.

I also noticed I wasn't in a hurry all the time. Before, I had been terribly impatient and prone to be angry when people or events got in my way or slowed me down. Gradually, I noticed I wasn't constantly in a hurry. I didn't get in a fizz when things didn't go my way. What's the fruit of the Spirit? Among them are peace and patience and self-control. Now, I can tell you that these didn't emanate from within me. These came from Holy Spirit; they were supernaturally produced.

I was surprised to find that Holy Spirit awakened in me an insatiable appetite for reading and studying God's Word. Beforehand, I had a fairly nonchalant attitude about my Bible reading, but now I couldn't get enough. More than that, I began to read books about theology, about evangelism, missions, and missionaries. Every time I went home from college, I made a beeline to my pastor's study

> *Holy Spirit awakened in me an insatiable appetite for reading and studying God's Word.*

(Paul Sullivan at First Baptist Church, Manning, South Carolina) with a list of theological questions. He would frustrate me by not answering my questions directly. He would simply look at his bookshelves, pull down a book, and hand it to me to read.

I would say, "Preacher, I don't want to read a whole book; just give me the short answer." He would just smile, and I would leave with five or six books to read, in addition to all of my calculus and chemistry. Oh, my! But I read all of them because the Lord gave me an appetite to learn God's Word. I'm pretty sure he helped me get a solid doctrinal foundation my first two years of college.

As mentioned in another chapter, my father called me on the phone at some point and asked, "Son, are you sure about going to medical school?"

"Why do you ask?" I questioned, perplexed.

"You're studying the Bible all the time and teaching Bible studies. I thought maybe you might think seminary would be more appropriate."

I laughed and said, "No, sir, I'm confident God has called me into medicine. I just love studying and teaching God's Word."

This conversation took a lot on my dad's part since he was a family doctor, and I know he loved the idea of me being a family doctor.

Not only did I love to study God's Word, but I also loved to tell people about Jesus. Anywhere from two to four times a week, I joined up with another college friend, and we would go and share the gospel in the dorms at Clemson. The Holy Spirit put in me a compulsion to share the gospel and to help fulfill the Great Commission.

Jesus told His disciples in John 15:26-27, "When the Helper comes, whom I will send to you from the Father, that is the Spirit of truth, who proceeds from the Father, He will bear witness of me, and you will bear witness also, because you have been with me from the beginning." Boy, was that ever true in the lives of the first-century disciples. They were powerful witnesses for Jesus Christ wherever they went, despite persecution and opposition.

I was surprised to find that college kids were open to talking about their spiritual lives, and many prayed to receive Christ. The same has been true of my patients for the last thirty-five years. Paul told the Corinthian church, "For the love of Christ controls us" (2 Corinthians 5:14). I understand this fully because I have a Holy Spirit-engendered love for my patients compelling me to tell them about Jesus.

In medicine, we use a Latin term *sine qua non* — literally meaning "without which it could not be," an indispensable action or condition.[1] This term is used to refer to physical findings that give away or indicate a diagnosis or, in other words, physical findings almost always positively correlated with a certain diagnosis. For example, if one of my patients demonstrates petechiae in the posterior pharynx, he most certainly has strep throat. Therefore, petechiae on the posterior pharynx is the *sine qua non* for strep throat. It is the physical finding that gives away the diagnosis.

Now, let me ask you a question. What is the *sine qua non* for the Spirit-filled Christian life? What is the physical finding that is the positive correlate for the Spirit-filled Christian life? You should have a sneaking suspicion by now that it is a compulsion to share the gospel. Once again, what did Jesus tell His disciples just before He ascended into heaven? He told them, "But you shall receive power when Holy Spirit has come upon you; and you shall be My witnesses" (Acts 1:8). The same is true for you and me. Whenever you see a Christian spreading the seed of the gospel as a way of life, you can mark it down that person is a Spirit-led Christian.

> *You should have a sneaking suspicion by now that it is a compulsion to share the gospel.*

Now, I know what some of you are thinking: *I'm not so certain about submitting to God's control over my life. He might tell me to go to Africa and live in a grass hut and eat bugs for the rest of my life!* Admit it. You're afraid of God and afraid of doing God's will. You're not convinced that God has your best interests at heart.

I'm not going to kid you. God often asks His people to do hard things in order to accomplish His eternal plan and glorify His name. After all, He allowed His only Son to die a terrible death for you and me in order to purchase our redemption. But let's set the record straight. He has a prior claim on our lives by virtue of having created us, by sustaining us daily, and by redeeming us. Who are we to deny Him sovereignty over our lives?

He owns us. He purchased us with the blood of His own Son, and we are now the temple of Holy Spirit. That's why He doesn't give us the option of choosing. In Ephesians 5:18, He says, "And do not get drunk with wine, for that is dissipation, but be filled with the Spirit." That's a command from the Lord God Almighty. He expects us to be controlled by Holy Spirit who lives in us. It's a logical and reasonable expectation. When we review the fruit of the flesh, it is foolishness on our part to choose rebellion and self-rule. So why do we do it?

The answer? It is because we love our autonomy and we love our sin. Each of us loves our old sin nature that we have to contend with every day. The Bible calls it the flesh. Paul challenged the Galatian Christians to "walk by the Spirit, and you will not carry out the desire of the flesh. For the flesh sets its desire against the Spirit, and the Spirit against the flesh; for these are in opposition to one another, so that you may not do the things that you please. But if you are led by the Spirit, you are not under the Law" (Galatians 5:16-18). Did you catch that? The desire of the Spirit is contrary to the desire of the flesh. Have you ever met a "contrary person"? You know the exact person I am talking about, don't you? You have them in your mind already. They are argumentative and always picking a fight. The word for them is "pugnacious." Look it up. It means "quarrelsome." Inside the Christian are two contrary forces that are always quarrelling — the Spirit and the flesh. As the above verse says, the Spirit and the flesh oppose each other. Paul understood this conflict we all face daily, which he described in Romans 7:14-25.

Are you getting the big picture? If we walk according to the flesh (i.e., allow self to rule in our lives), then our minds will be set on what the flesh desires rather than on what the Spirit desires. Make your choice. The mind set on the flesh results in death and the fruits of the flesh described above. The mind set on the Spirit results in life and peace. The truth of the matter is if we refuse to allow Holy Spirit to govern, we become enemies of God (hostile to God) and cannot possibly submit ourselves to God's way of life. That is the struggle. That is the spiritual battle that is waged within all of us.

Here is the good news in Romans 8:10: "Because Christ is in you … the Spirit gives life because of righteousness." Whose righteousness? Christ's righteousness, of course. His righteousness was imputed to us as a free gift at salvation. Walking in the Spirit implies that we tap into the power of indwelling Holy Spirit on a moment-by-moment basis in order to exhibit Christ's righteousness, walk in His spiritual victory, and produce the good fruit of the Spirit in our lives.

So how does a Christian walking in the Spirit think? What is his mindset? Let's get some help from Paul in Romans 6:11-14 (KJV):

> *Likewise reckon ye also yourselves to be dead indeed unto sin, but alive unto God through Jesus Christ our Lord. Let not sin therefore reign in your mortal body, that ye should obey it in the lusts thereof.*

> *Neither yield ye your members as instruments of unrighteousness unto sin: but yield yourselves unto God, as those that are alive from the dead, and your members as instruments of righteousness unto God.*

*For sin shall not have dominion over you: for ye are not
under the law, but under grace.*

Reckon (v. 11): "Reckon ... yourselves to be dead indeed unto sin." This means to count it as true that you are dead to the influence of sin in your life. Sin has no power over you. You are now alive to God in Jesus Christ, whereas previously you were spiritually dead and insensitive to God's influence.

Let me share with you a personal and painful illustration. I was turkey hunting many years ago when South Carolina still had a fall turkey season. I was leaning against a giant oak tree, waiting for three tom turkeys to slowly approach my decoy, when suddenly this little fuzz ball came bounding up the hill barely able to keep his head above the foot-deep deposit of dry leaves. He made such a disturbance that he scared off my turkeys, ruined my afternoon hunt, and almost got his cute little self shot. It was some kind of dog, only a foot long — skinny, long-haired, gray in color, and happy as a clam. He never saw me dressed in camouflage, but he was fascinated with my turkey decoy, which he promptly began to stalk with low guttural growls. I hoped he would eventually go away, but no such luck. Long story short, he ended up riding home with me. Now I had a turkey dog.

He wore a long-haired shirt. He was skinny as a rail, so he must have been eating locusts and honey. I found him in the wilderness, and every time he barked he said, "R-r-repent!" So logically, I named him John the Baptist. Within a year, he weighed ninety pounds, had glorious long, gray and black hair the color of a German shepherd, the face of a bear, and a black tongue like a chow. He was a loving and pleasant dog, and, oddly enough, he never barked. He was a silent dog, which I found intriguing. His presentation was quite imposing, and he scared the tar out of deliverymen and the Mormon missionaries. The only problem was, despite his name, John had a demon. It didn't become apparent until one day my neighbor's twelve-year-old son walked through my garage when John was eating a hambone I had thrown out. A neighborhood dog and the boy entered the garage simultaneously. The twelve-year-old must have been the bigger threat. He ended up with teeth marks on his behind and torn pants. We apologized profusely and passed it off as John being territorial.

Six months later, for no apparent reason, John bit my medical partner's son on the wrist prior to a home Bible study. John went into lockup in our backyard, where he stayed for two years, no exceptions.

We moved to a new home in the country, and John was liberated. Unfortunately, after a period of time, a two-year-old fell on top of this giant fur ball, and John bit him in self-defense. Now, to my dismay, John had to go.

Here's the point. I could not personally put John down. I loved that devil dog. We were emotionally attached, so I carried him to the vet, who said, "Dr. Jackson, I can do for you what you cannot do for yourself. Just give me permission and I can handle it."

I mumbled my thanks, hugged John's neck, and quickly walked out the door. I sat in my truck and snubbed for a few minutes before driving off. John had been a good friend.

Now there's a lesson in this painful, personal illustration. That vet had to do for me what I could not do for myself. I could not bring myself to put down a devil dog that I loved. In like manner, we all have a lower nature that loves to sin — and even though the sin we love brings us harm, we can't bring ourselves to put it down or put it to death. The Bible calls this crucifying the flesh. We know we are dead to sin and alive to God in Christ Jesus (Romans 6:11), yet we still love our sin, and we go back to it over and over. Didn't you think I should have gotten rid of that devil dog much sooner than I did? I mean, he bit several people before I saw the light. Don't be so hard on me. You've got sin in your life like a cancer, destroying you and your relationships, and you haven't been to the vet yet! *Well, Dr. Jackson, what do you mean by that?* Here's what I mean: In Romans 8:13, Paul told the Romans, "For if you are living according to the flesh, you must die; but if by the Spirit you are putting to death the deeds of the body, you will live."

Who's the vet? The Holy Spirit! He will do for you and me what we cannot do for ourselves. We just have to give Him permission, and He will put to death sin in us so that we can live victoriously and walk in righteousness. (And we won't bite people anymore.)

There's only one caveat in my illustration. When John was put down, he was gone for good, and I don't believe he went to dog heaven. We have to take up our cross *daily*. We have to go to the spiritual vet *daily*. We have to be willing to go see "Dr. Ghost," who will do for us what we cannot do for ourselves. We have to rely on Holy Spirit to put the flesh to death *daily*. Remember what Paul told the Romans: "If you live according to the flesh, you will die; but if by the Spirit you put to death the misdeeds of the body, you will live." How painful is that! Why do we have to do that daily? It is because our flesh won't stay dead. We have to contend with our deceitful, fleshly desires every day. Life.Is.Not. Fair! Reckon yourself/consider yourself to be dead to sin and alive unto Jesus Christ every day.

We have to go to the spiritual vet daily. We have to be willing to go see 'Dr. Ghost,' who will do for us what we cannot do for ourselves.

Reject (v. 12): Reject sin and its influence in your life. "Do not offer any part of yourself as an instrument of wickedness" (NIV). You now have power and authority to do this. Previously, you were a slave to sin and Satan. Now you are free.

Righteousness (v. 13): "I am the righteousness of Christ." Say that out loud. Lay your hand on your chest and say out loud three times, "I am the righteousness of Christ." Does that sound weird or untrue to you? Do you really believe it? Well, whether you believe it or not, it is biblical truth. Read 2 Corinthians 5:21: "He made Him who knew no sin to be sin on our behalf, so that we might become the righteousness of God in Him." Now do you believe me? You have been made the righteousness of God in Christ. If you are a believer in Jesus Christ, then you possess

'I am the righteousness of Christ.'

the righteousness of Christ as a spiritual birthday gift. You received it on your spiritual birthday. Now, go — walk ye in it! Say it again three times out loud until the truth of it sinks in. That is how spirit-walking Christians think. How you think changes the way you live, walk and talk, but it all starts with what you believe. Colossians 3:2 says, "Set your mind on the things above, not on the things that are on earth." When we choose to set our mind on things above, we also learn to "present [ourselves] to God as those alive from the dead, and [our] members as instruments of righteousness to God" (Romans 6:13b).

Receive (v. 14): Receive grace. Why is sin your master? It's because you can't go half a day without sinning. That's why. (If you did go half a day without sinning, you'd be proud about it, and, therefore, prideful in your heart, you sinner!) But thanks be to God, we as Christians are not under the law anymore. Why? Because of "Grace, grace, God's grace, grace that will pardon and cleanse within."[2] Come on. Sing it with me. "Grace, grace, God's grace, grace that is greater than all my sin." What an awesome hymn! Why couldn't I have thought that one up?

Christians who walk in the Spirit *gladly* (as Paul says in Romans 7:22, "For I *joyfully* concur with the law of God in the inner man") receive God's grace that washes them as white as snow but also enables them to walk in righteousness. Now that is serious stuff — to be set free from sin is to become a slave of the Most High God, but in the trade He leads me to holiness and eternal life.

What's not to like about this? Now let's flash back to where we started this chapter. After all the good teaching by Mike and Ken, I was trying to assimilate all the instruction into my life, but I was having a hard time with all the new concepts. Initially, things weren't going too well for me. In fact, I was pretty discouraged one day as I sat in the cafeteria in Harcombe Commons, playing with some green Jell-O with a fork, when Mike sat down beside me and asked, "So, Rob Jackson, how are things going in your spiritual life?"

He had this big, mule-eating-briars grin on his face. I looked at him for a moment. He looked so happy, like he had it all together. On the inside I was just confused. So I answered honestly, "Not so good."

"What's the matter?"

"I don't know. All that Spirit-filled-life stuff. It just doesn't work for me."

Mike didn't hesitate. I don't know if he was a prophet or if God just gave him a shot of Holy Spirit insight, but he looked right through me and asked, "Do you really believe Holy Spirit will control your life and make you like Jesus?"

I felt like he had stuck me with a hot poker right in my heart. Instantly, I realized he had put his finger on my problem. I was praying all the right prayers, but in my heart of hearts I really did not expect God to change me in any way. I really did not believe.

Sheepishly, I answered him with, "No, I really don't."

He persevered and inquired, "Why not?"

I didn't know why not. I pondered that for a few moments while he stared at me like an evangelist at invitation time. I grew increasingly uncomfortable until it came to me. I responded, "I'm not worthy, Mike. Why would Holy Spirit change my life with all the sin in my life? I'm constantly confessing my sin. I just don't feel like I'm worthy of His attention."

Continuing to stare at me, Mike answered, "When will you be worthy?"

Now that stumped me. I stared back at him like those folks do on Jeopardy when they're asked the $50,000 question, and they don't have a clue. Finally, it came to me and I dropped my fist on the buzzer. "I don't guess I'll ever be worthy, will I?"

He smiled a big smile and said, "No, sir, nor will I or anyone else." I sighed a big sigh of relief. I didn't win any money, but I was elated nonetheless.

Then he continued with a question, "How did you receive the Lord Jesus Christ?"

I knew the answer to that one since Vacation Bible School in the third grade, so I answered, "By grace. My salvation was a free gift."

"Well, the Bible says, 'As you therefore have received Christ Jesus the Lord, so walk in Him' (Colossians 2:6). You received Him by grace; you walk in the Spirit by grace. Robert, being filled with the Spirit and experiencing the changed life is not dependent upon your worth or my worth. If it were, none of us would be changed."

Now it was my turn to smile. Smiling like the Cheshire cat in *Alice in Wonderland*, I got it. I comprehended, and I was set free to receive God's grace, to freely receive God's grace. After that day, I began to grow in grace and in Holy Spirit. I never looked back. "No one, after putting his hand to the plow and looking back, is fit for the kingdom of God" (Luke 9:62). Not me, brother and sister; I've been attempting to plow a straight row ever since and never looked back at my old way of life.

I rounded third base and stretched out for home plate, the subject of our next chapter.

STUDY QUESTIONS | Chapter 18

1. Who is Holy Spirit? Why did He come?

2. Describe the ministries of Holy Spirit.

3. If a friend asks you how he can be filled with Holy Spirit, what would you tell him?

4. What does it mean to walk in the Spirit?

5. What does faith and grace have to do with being filled with the Spirit? Walking in the Spirit?

6. Has anybody ever taught you this concept? Were you able to learn this on your own just by reading the Bible?

7. Why is understanding the Spirit-filled life so important?

19

HOME PLATE:
FELLOWSHIP WITH BELIEVERS

For three summers in high school, I worked on two of my uncles' pig farms in Clarendon County, South Carolina, one of which was the largest pig farm in the Southeast at the time. They had over 4,000 hogs on the lot and sold 200 pigs at market every other Friday. The pigs were raised on concrete floors that were washed down twice a day (which was my job) to keep them free of parasites, and they were fed a high protein diet to maximize growth. The little 40-pound piglets would be ready for market at 250 pounds in approximately six months on the specialized diet. They had their own farrowing house, where pregnant sows delivered anywhere from nine to fifteen little piglets. That's where I learned to be a pig obstetrician, delivering a multitude of little piglets in sweltering heat and overwhelming stench.

Performing CPR on a slimy, one-pound, premature piglet is an experience of a lifetime. Really, everyone should try it. Every little newborn piglet was worth $250-$325 in six months, depending on market prices, so we tried to resuscitate every piglet, even with mouth-to-nose CPR if necessary! (Yuck!) Actually, I got accustomed to the stink, but my family and friends never did. My mother made me shower at the farm before leaving work, then outside at home, and again inside at home before I could come to the dinner table. Then I would have to sit at the far end of the dinner table all alone. No one would sit by me. I'm not kidding. Oh, the price of an honest dollar. (Well, five dollars. I got paid five dollars a day back then.) If I ever went to town to purchase items for the farm, the hardware store would clear out as soon as I walked in. The store owner would say with wrinkled nose, "You're working for your uncle this summer, aren't you? I can smell — I mean, tell." It didn't bother me; I just got faster service.

I learned to preach at the pig farm. The pigs were raised in a quarter-mile-long building with concrete floors that we called a pig parlor. The building had forty stalls with forty pigs of various ages and sizes in each stall. All they did was eat, sleep and poop. My job was to scrape the floors, then wash them with a high-pressure hose twice a day. This required a highly skilled labor force — hah! More flies dwelled there than in Pharaoh's Egyptian plague. I sprayed fly poison every afternoon, then swept up a five-gallon bucket full of dead flies before leaving work. At break time every morning, I preached to the pigs.

Now the pigs were a good bit nervous like most congregations with a new evangelist. They never sat on the front row. They would run to a far corner of the stall and jump one on top of another to get away from me as far as they could. As I preached my message, their curiosity got the better of them, and they would start sniffing and grunting, all the while sauntering cautiously toward me. I would then start singing an invitation hymn as they got nearer. When they got even closer, I would throw down a little ground corn and switch to "Just as I am, without one plea, but that Thy blood was shed for me." I never lacked for lots of converts at my invitations, no matter how bad my preaching and singing might have been — especially if I had enough corn. Many years later, I heard a preacher say that a famous evangelist he knew could "forevermore shell the corn"! I knew immediately what he meant, and I swelled up with pride because I knew he was talking about me, too. Been there, done that!

When I worked on the farm, my uncle had a friend whom I invited to church on a number of occasions. He was a disrespectful, booze-loving, rough old cuss, but he took a liking to me and laughed at my porcine preaching habits. When I invited him to church, he would respond, "Boy, he who tills the sod, he worships God. I ain't got no need for church or preachers or all those hypocrites going to church. Now leave me be." He was very emphatic about it, but he still came and listened to me preach and sing to my porkers. He laughed at my converts; he just didn't want to be one.

At that stage in my young life, I didn't know how to respond to him. It's manifestly true that all farmers depend upon God for sunshine and rain, but this doesn't mean they reverence God. He certainly didn't. He didn't reverence and respect anybody. In fact, he was quite profane. I would wince when he took God's name in vain. I understood his concern regarding hypocrites. Nobody likes hypocrites in church or in any area of society. I know a cardiologist who smokes, but his hypocrisy doesn't invalidate cardiology. I still send my patients to a cardiologist when they have chest pain, an arrhythmia, or heart failure. Just because some so-called Christians behave poorly does not invalidate the church. In fact, the writer of Hebrews stated, "And let us consider how to stimulate one another to love and good deeds, not forsaking our own assembling together, as is the habit of some, but encouraging one another; and all the more, as you see the day drawing near" (Hebrews 10:24-25). If you take a log out of the fire and place it on the hearth by itself, what happens? That log will stop burning and become cold and hardened. What happens to a Christian taken out of the church? His passion for Christ and Christian service goes out, and he becomes cold and hardened. That's why the Hebrew writer admonished us to encourage one another "to love and good works."

Where does all this encouragement "to love and good works"

happen? At church, my friend, that's where. The local church is an organized assembly of believers gathered together for worship, Bible study, Christian fellowship, observation of the ordinances, promotion of the "one anothers" of the New Testament, and fulfillment of the Great Commission.

What happens to a Christian taken out of the church? His passion for Christ and Christian service goes out, and he becomes cold and hardened.

Before I dissect the definition of church with you (doctors are good at dissecting), let me tell you the tale of two patients. I was privileged to lead to faith in Christ two men in my office in the same week several years ago. I shared with both of them the baseball diamond illustration of the last four chapters. One of them received gladly the challenge to become a part of a local church (not my church) and continued to grow in his Christian life. He is still active in his church, still growing in the Lord, happily married, and goes on mission trips with his church overseas.

The other patient would never agree to join with a local church, even though I challenged him multiple times with the necessity to do so. He has never prospered in his spiritual life. His marriage is on the rocks. He has never shared the gospel or the joy of his salvation with any others. Periodically, he will meet with me and talk about his spiritual life and what he needs to do next, but he never does the next thing. He doesn't have a church family to help him grow, to teach him, to encourage him, to hold him accountable, "to stimulate him to love and good works."

So, what is home plate? Home plate is a home church, a local community of believers who know you, love you, and hold you accountable. A pastor friend once told me the local church should be easy to join but hard to stay in. Why? Because of church discipline (i.e., accountability). If we look out for one another, as we should, we would not allow one another to fall into sin, to backslide, or to fall away from the faith. "My brethren, if any among you strays from the truth, and one turns him back, let him know that he who turns a sinner from the error of his way will save his soul from death, and will cover a multitude of sins" (James 5:19-20).

> *Home plate is a home church, a local community of believers who know you, love you, and hold you accountable.*

A local church, functioning as it should, looks out for the little lambs (and the old goats), protecting them, reproving and rebuking them if necessary, encouraging, loving, teaching and comforting them. Every Christian should be in a small church, or in a small group in a big church where, like on the television comedy *Cheers*, everybody knows your name. Make sure you are a part of a group where everybody knows if you are sick, absent, promoted, fired, or had a baby. You know what I mean. Don't get lost in the crowd. Get in a small group where you can serve and minister and be ministered to. God did not make us as Christians to be independent but to be interdependent. That's why Paul describes the church as a body with different parts. Each part has different functions, but every part is important. The body cannot do without any part. In a nutshell, the message of 1 Corinthians 12:12-27 and Romans 12:5 is we are members one of another.

Why is church important? People have asked me over the years why is church so important. Sometimes the question is sincere, and sometimes challenging in an effort to justify non-participation. My response has always been that we as Christians should love the things that Jesus loves, and it is manifestly evident that He

> *My response has always been that we as Christians should love the things that Jesus loves.*

loves His bride, the church. In Ephesians 5:25, Paul told the Ephesians, "Husbands, love your wives, just as Christ also loved the church and gave Himself up for her." Jesus didn't die for a building or a denomination. He died for a living, breathing bride known as the church of the living God, which is the visible representation of Christ on planet earth to whom He has given the message of reconciliation.

The rest of Paul's challenge in verses 26-27 to the Ephesians states that Jesus gave Himself up for His bride, "that He might sanctify her, having cleansed her by the washing of water with the word, that He might present to Himself the church in all her glory, having no spot or wrinkle or any such thing; but that she should be holy and blameless." Not only are we expected to love His bride, the church, we also have a responsibility to actively participate in the sanctification process whereby He will present to Himself a radiant bride without stain or wrinkle or any blemish — in other words, a holy and blameless bride.

Not only are we expected to love His bride, the church, we also have a responsibility to actively participate in the sanctification process.

How does He accomplish this? He does this by the washing of the Word! Isn't that what Jesus said in His high priestly prayer in John 17:17 when He prayed to His Father, "Sanctify them in the truth; Thy word is truth." There is a supernatural quality about God's holy Word. The more we read, study and memorize God's holy Word, the more Jesus sanctifies us and washes us, removing every stain and wrinkle and preparing us to be a radiant bride, holy and blameless. The hymnwriter William D. Longstaff wrote:

> *Take time to be holy, speak oft with thy Lord;*
> *Abide in Him always, and feed on His Word:*

Make friends of God's children, help those who are weak;
Forgetting in nothing His blessing to seek.[1]

However, this requires cooperation on our part. In the same way He doesn't force salvation on us, He doesn't force sanctification on us either. You and I must sincerely seek to be conformed to the image of Jesus Christ. We must practice the disciplines of the Christian life — prayer, Bible study, confession, repentance, Christian fellowship, worship — in order to grow in Christlikeness. God honors a heart that yearns after righteousness coupled with discipline over years of time. "Blessed are those who hunger and thirst for righteousness, for they shall be satisfied" (Matthew 5:6). The end result of this Christian discipline — plus a passion for righteousness, plus time — is sanctification.

Now where do these activities occur? Two places — your prayer closet, and home plate (a New Testament church). We seek God's face privately at home, and we worship God corporately with the local body of believers at church. At church we receive good Bible teaching, we worship God with like-minded Christian folks, we receive communion, and we baptize new believers. Other believers who love you will encourage you, admonish you, rebuke you, teach you, bear your burdens, rejoice when you rejoice, and weep when you weep. In the New Testament church, we practice the "one anothers" of the New Testament. Why? Because the Bible commands us to, but also because we are a big family and we love each other. This is what families do.

So why should you be a part of the local church? Because you love the things that Jesus loves! Jesus loves the bride, His church, and gave Himself up for her in the greatest demonstration of sacrificial love we have ever seen. This kind of sacrifice and this kind of love demands that we value His bride, the church, to a far greater extent than most of us do. This demands a fiery and passionate love for Him and His church. If you love Jesus, you will love the things that Jesus loves — especially His radiant bride, the church.

STUDY QUESTIONS | Chapter 19

1. If your friend at work asks, "Why do you go to church so much?" what would you say?

2. Who is "the church"? What is the difference between the universal church and the local church?

3. What should a church do?

4. What are the necessary ingredients for a group of Christians to call themselves a church? Can a Bible study group consider itself a church? Can a home group? Can these grow into a church?

5. Can you name the "one anothers" of the New Testament church? Why are these important?

6. Why do some folks have a negative view of the church? What can, or should, we do about this?

20

PANAMA SUMMER

It was a dream job for a college microbiology major/premed student. I had acquired a summer job at a hospital lab in Panama City, Florida. I was in Florida for the summer on a beach project with Campus Crusade for Christ to be trained in evangelism and discipleship. Each of the college students acquired a day job, and at night we participated in Bible studies and discipleship training. On the weekends, we participated in evangelistic events on the beach. It was one of the best summers of my life, considerably better than working on the pig farm!

I arrived at the hospital my first day to find the lab a dark place filled with about fifteen people who didn't get along very well; in addition, almost all of them chain smoked. The smell of tobacco smoke filled the lab (remember, this was the '70s) and a blue haze hung constantly in the air. Profanity, vulgar suggestiveness, and sexual innuendo laced most conversations, despite the fact that only one of the employees was a male. He kept to himself in a separate part of the lab where he conducted blood typing. I was not trained as a lab technologist, so they had no idea what to do with me; plus, I had no idea how to do anything in the lab. Nevertheless, I had been hired, and I was eager to learn and eager to serve.

Michael, the single male employee, was the son of a Methodist minister, but you would never know it from his conduct. He confidently told the other employees, "This little college boy won't last one week."

I spent the first week observing how the various lab tests were performed, and I began to assiduously clean the lab's counters and floors. I also began to pray for every employee by name on my way to work each day, a forty-minute drive.

I discovered that no one liked to place urine and stool specimens on the culture media to discover what kind of bacteria would grow. Since I was a microbiology major, this fascinated me, so I volunteered to do the job daily. (Was this a great job or what? This was a serious upgrade from the pig farm!) I immediately became everybody's new best friend. I also slowly began to learn how to do other more complex lab procedures as time went by. My microbiology studies gave me the fund of knowledge to learn quickly.

One day as I was standing under the hood (a ventilation device that captures harmful fumes and bacteria in the air) spreading pee and poop on culture media, a divorced woman named Susan joined me. Susan was the loudest, most brash, most vulgar woman in the lab. I stiffened up, preparing myself for some kind of embarrassing verbal assault, but to my surprise she said quietly, "Robert, what is so different about you?"

I laughed out loud with relief, then said, "Susan, you already know the difference in me is Jesus. I'm a believer."

"Yeah, I know that, but I know lots of Christian people, just none like you. What's the difference?"

"Susan, not everyone who says they are a Christian really is a true believer, and they give Christians a bad name. Some Christians don't live as they should and give Christ a bad name. Does that make sense?"

"Sort of."

"But listen to this." Then I launched into my three-minute testimony of how I became a Christian, including a gospel presentation and ending with, "So that's how I became a believer."

"I don't think I've ever fully understood all that. Would you come to my house and explain things to me further? I have a lot of other questions."

"Sure, but I don't think it would be appropriate for me to come alone. Can I bring a couple of my friends?"

She stared at me for a moment, then a light went on in her head, and she laughed out loud and said, "Sure, bring your friends, choir boy. I make the best lasagna in town."

We met at Susan's house on a Friday night and answered her questions late into the night. We laughed a lot, but we also had some very serious discussion time. It was obvious Susan had a great time. She was a gracious host. We prayed over her before we left. The lasagna was really great, too!

By Monday morning at work, Susan was a brand-new woman. All she could talk about was Jesus and all the new things we had taught her. Her foul language was gone, and she quit smoking. *Bam!* She was totally transformed. The women in the lab stared at her with their mouths wide open.

One woman asked me, "What have you done to her?"

I replied, "It wasn't me; it was Jesus. You better be careful. You'll be next."

She just shook her head in amazement.

Susan had been the ringleader. As I said previously, she was loud, profane and vulgar. If I had to pick in order who God would save first, it would not have been Susan, but He chose her first to demonstrate His power and His glory. The entire atmosphere in the lab changed. The cursing slowly died down. The coarseness disappeared. The darkness lifted. People began to ask me theological questions, sincere questions that deserved serious answers. They started going to church and would come in on Monday morning and report to me where they went to church and show me the church bulletin! They were like school kids reporting to the headmaster!

One young lady in her late twenties was going through a divorce. She invited me to speak to her over our lunch break for weeks regarding her spiritual life and how she might restore her marriage. She listened intently but could never grasp being born again or being able to forgive her estranged husband. I can still see her face in her hands, weeping over her broken relationship.

As my summer job began to wind down, the lab employees came to me and said, "We don't know how the lab will operate without you. How did we even get along before you came?"

Michael came to me the day I left and said to me, "Robert, I am the son of a Methodist minister. I am ashamed to admit it, but I should be ministering to these employees like you do. I am determined to do better. You have challenged me. I told them you wouldn't last a week, but now we don't think we can get along without you. That's the impact of a single Spirit-filled Christian life. I appreciate your influence here. God bless you."

Looking back on that experience and evaluating what happened that summer, I learned several valuable lessons:

1) Demonstrating a servant's heart
2) Emitting the aroma of Christ
3) The power of a testimony
4) Being prepared to give an answer
5) Praying persistently

First, being willing to do the dirty jobs in the lab that no one else wanted to do endeared me to the other long-term employees. I cleaned. I spread human waste. I filtered chemicals — and the list goes on. I also learned as many jobs as I could so that when people took off for summer vacation, I could fill in where appropriate. Jesus said, "I did not come to be served, but to serve and to give [my] life a ransom for many" (Mark 10:45). Demonstrating a servant's heart in the lab gave me much credibility, whereas I had none when I started. I teach my children that when they take on a new job to do the things no one else will do, work harder than everyone else, learn as many positions as possible, and always do everything "as unto the Lord." That way when it comes time for the company to downsize, you will have made yourself indispensable, and you will be the last person let go.

Second, I learned that a Spirit-controlled Christian has the aroma of Christ about them. That's why Susan asked, "What's different about you?" "For we are to God the pleasing aroma of Christ among those who are being saved and those who are perishing" (2 Corinthians 2:15, NIV). Spirit-controlled Christians have a certain atmosphere created by Holy Spirit that other people notice and appreciate. People who are open to the subtle prompting of Holy Spirit will be drawn to you and to Jesus in you. People who are closed to the ministry of Holy Spirit will be offended and will often ridicule and scorn you. To them, you may present the odor of death, not life. Make sure Holy Spirit rules over your life in every way and every day so the aroma of your life is light and life. Trust me, people notice.

A Spirit-controlled Christian has the aroma of Christ about them.

Third, in Revelation 12:11, the Scripture tells us the martyrs "overcame [Satan] because of the blood of the Lamb and because of the word of their testimony." Did you notice how Susan was influenced by a simple three-minute testimony? I practiced my testimony over and over in my head until I memorized it and could speak out in any situation. Boy, was I glad I had practiced when this profane, loud, intimidating woman sidled up beside me and began asking questions. My mind didn't go blank. I had my three-minute testimony ready. I thanked the Lord for Ralph Vick, my discipleship group leader in college, who challenged me to write out and memorize my testimony. You should do the same!

I still lie awake at night modifying my testimony in all manner of different situations. I have the basic framework, so it is easy to modify to different scenarios. I suggest you write out your testimony describing your life before you met Christ, how you became a believer, and your life after you were saved. Avoid using church lingo that non-Christians would not comprehend. Always end with a meaningful Scripture verse. Time yourself to make sure your story is quick and under three minutes, then commit it to memory. Be prepared, because God will give you opportunities to share it. You watch and see!

Fourth, I was grateful I had embarked on a three-year personal journey in college to find answers to hard questions — not for anyone else, but for my own satisfaction. Susan asked many hard questions that Friday night, and I was prepared to answer them. First Peter 3:15 says, "But sanctify Christ as Lord in your hearts, always being ready to make a defense to everyone who asks you to give an account for the hope that is in you, yet with gentleness and reverence."

All of us have an obligation to study a little bit of apologetics, at least to answer our own questions about how Scripture addresses the difficult issues of life. We also have an evangelistic responsibility to be informed well enough to answer the "yes, but" questions of sincere seekers like Susan.

Finally, did you notice I prayed for that crowd every day on the way to work? Prayer undergirds everything we do. As I've often heard, "Where there is little prayer, there is little power." No doubt the impact of this summer was in large part a consequence of everyday prayers on their behalf. I can't change a person's heart one iota, but God can. Isn't it interesting that the loudest, most brash, most profane person in the lab was the one God plucked up first? That's the way He operates. In the book of Acts, early in the life of the church, He chose Saul, the Christian persecutor — the last person anyone in that day expected God to choose as his missionary to the Gentiles. No doubt some Christians prayed for him daily.

> *'Where there is little prayer, there is little power.'*

My brothers and sisters, never underestimate the power of persistent, concerted daily prayer on behalf of your family, neighbors, or coworkers. God hears, and God answers. Be expectant. Be prepared. *And* keep your eyes on the loudest, the most profane, the last one you would expect to be saved. That's the one God will pick. As my Arab friends in Gaza would tell me, "Believe me, before many years I know this to be true!"

STUDY QUESTIONS | Chapter 20

1. Do Christians really have a different "aroma" about them? What creates that aroma?

2. Have you ever written out a three-minute testimony? What are the elements of a good three-minute testimony? Take time to do so today and practice it on someone.

3. Have you ever had the opportunity to positively influence an entire group of people for Christ? Describe that experience.

4. What is the benefit of a servant's heart?

5. Why should we be "ready to make a defense to everyone who asks us to give an account for the hope that is in us"? How do we prepare ourselves to give an account? What is the best book you've read to prepare yourself, other than the Bible?

21

Nice Guys Don't Go to Heaven

Hollis was a good man. He would literally give you the shirt off his back. Everyone in the community knew him and liked him. He lived across the street from what used to be Rock Hill Baptist Church — a large, rural Baptist church. He helped every pastor who moved into the pastorium, located directly across the street from his house and farm.

There was only one problem. Although Hollis was a good man, he was a dead man — spiritually dead, I mean — and he knew it. Every pastor who came to Rock Hill Baptist befriended Hollis and dutifully shared the gospel with him. Every evangelist who preached a revival at RHBC walked across the street and spoke to Hollis about his spiritual condition. No telling how many times he had heard a gospel presentation, but he was still not a believer. He was a good guy, but a spiritually dead guy.

"Doc, how can you say that? I know plenty of guys like Hollis. They are the salt of the earth. They work hard. They take care of their families. They pay their bills. They pay their taxes. They don't drink, they don't smoke, and they don't carouse. Are you trying to tell me they can't get into heaven?" No, not me. The Bible says nice guys don't go to heaven; only born-again people go to heaven.

You see, your friends and Hollis may be "all-around nice guys," but they all have the same problem: They are still spiritually dead.

"Whoa, take 'er easy there, Pilgrim," to quote John Wayne![1] ("What do you mean by that?" you might add.)

Well, the Bible tells us three truths about our spiritual condition before we come to Christ that we all have to understand clearly and with which we must come to grips.

The first truth we need to understand is that we are all born spiritually dead. The Scripture says, "And you were dead in your transgressions and sins" (Ephesians 2:1). Paul made it plain to the Romans that "the penalty for sin is death" (Romans 6:23). King David tells us in Psalm 51:5, "Behold, I was brought forth in iniquity, and in sin my mother conceived me." The consequence of sin, which we inherit from our parents, is both physical and spiritual death.

When I was in college, I used to go to college classrooms just for fun and write on the blackboards, "Born once, die twice. Born twice, die once! Maybe!" If there were students in the class, some would be totally perplexed, and they would stop me, before I left the class, to ask what it meant. Often, a great spiritual conversation ensued. You and I understand that if your nice-guy friend and Hollis are physically born but never spiritually born again by the grace of God, they will necessarily die twice — the spiritual death with which they came into the world, and the physical death at the end of life.

However, if they accept the free gift of God in Jesus Christ, they are born twice, a physical birth and a spiritual birth, and need only die once at the end of life on this earth. Maybe. Why maybe? It is because if the rapture comes, Jesus will deliver us from the physical death, which all men face (except for Enoch and Elijah). Now wouldn't that be an exciting event!

Why do I say in the title to this chapter "Nice guys don't go to heaven"? Because even well-informed Christians still labor under the illusion that well-dressed, well-educated and socially acceptable folks must be approved automatically by God. Somehow if they look good, smell good, and act right, they must be Christians. And guess what? Nobody bothers to share the gospel with them. Thankfully for Hollis, the pastors who lived across the street from him knew better and persisted in sharing the gospel with him.

If you live under a bridge, smell bad, have a drug or alcohol problem, everybody knows you need Jesus. Somebody will pray for you, give you a gospel tract, and try to talk to you about your eternal, never-dying soul. Why? Well, you don't look like a Christian. You obviously need Jesus.

"But Mr. Nice Guy in his fancy house with his fancy car and clean clothes and good job — well, surely he's got his spiritual act together, don't you think?" No, I don't think. He was born dead in his transgressions and sins. The penalty for his sin is death just like the alcoholic living under a bridge. Just like you and me. Just like Hollis. Jesus didn't come to make bad men good, or good men better. He came to make dead men alive! Jesus said, "I am the resurrection and the life; he who believes in Me shall live even if he dies, and everyone who lives and believes in Me shall never die" (John 11:25). Jesus came to impart spiritual life to all dead men who would receive His life. Speaking to His disciples, Jesus said, "I am the way, and the truth, and the life; no one comes to the Father, but through Me" (John 14:6). Jesus then proved the truthfulness of His claim by rising from the dead.

Jesus didn't come to make bad men good, or good men better. He came to make dead men alive!

The second truth with which we must come to grips is that apart from Christ we are all spiritually blind and unable to perceive spiritual truth. "The natural man does not accept the things of the Spirit of God; for they are foolishness to him, and he cannot understand them, because they are spiritually appraised" (1 Corinthians 2:14). I once led a man to faith in Christ who had been a gambler, womanizer, embezzler and outlaw all of his life. He had been married five times, and when I met him, he was living with a woman to whom he was not married. At one time in his life, he had managed five casinos and five motels in Nevada. At the time I knew him, he worked as a bartender and card shark. He had been in prison in twenty-plus states at one time or another for multiple offenses.

After he became a believer, he ate lunch with my family every Sunday and begged me to teach him about the Bible. Here was this former, big-time casino manager from Reno, Nevada, who would dole out $100,000 every weekend in perks to high-rolling gamblers to entice them to stay at one of his casinos/motels now eating Sunday lunch with a southern-fried, Baptist, homeschooling family every Sunday and craving meatloaf, mashed potatoes and Bible lessons! Without any input from me other than the Scriptures, this previously blind man (spiritually blind) decided on his own to give up working in the saloon and dealing cards.

I asked him, "Why?"

He responded, "It doesn't suit my new lifestyle."

Then to our astonishment, he laid down the law to his girlfriend that if she didn't get saved, she would have to go back to her family in Alaska. With urgency, we explained the gospel to her repeatedly, but she never comprehended. After several weeks, he bought her a one-way ticket back to Alaska, saying they couldn't honorably live together anymore since he was now a Christian. We were all in tears because we had become quite attached to her. Shortly thereafter, he purchased a home, and his female realtor showed up one day unannounced and propositioned him at his front door. (I failed to mention he was a very handsome guy, or so said the womenfolk.) He responded, "Ma'am, a few months ago I would have helped you out, but I'm a Christian now. I'm sorry I can't help you. You will have to leave now!"

Where did all of this come from? I never suggested any of this to him. I'm telling you, the Spirit of God opened his eyes that had been blind for years to the sexual immorality and irresponsibility in his life. Now he could see the value of moral purity and biblical marriage without me ever saying a word. The Spirit of God opened his eyes to see the truth.

My friend was not the only one who was blinded for years. All lost people are blinded by the devil, who is called the god of this world in Scripture. "The god of this world has blinded the minds of the unbelieving" (2 Corinthians 4:4). Not only can they not see the truth about Jesus, they cannot perceive all manner of spiritual truth. Satan causes them to believe his lies in every area of life. Only when God imparts His life can we see life from His perspective. Don't be angry at your lost friends or family who don't comprehend spiritual truth or biblical principles. They can no more see the truth than a blind man can see the sun. We don't get angry with handicapped people. We try to help them. Don't get angry with spiritually handicapped friends; help them, pray for them, and share Jesus' life with them. Only when they possess the life of God can they see truth. "For God, who said, 'Let light shine out of darkness,' made His light shine in our hearts to give us the light of the knowledge of God's glory displayed in the face of Christ" (2 Corinthians 4:6, NIV).

Now the third truth we have to deal with is spiritual bondage. Before we come to Christ, we all live in spiritual bondage to Satan and to sin. I have a medical colleague who shared with me that before he became a believer he was addicted to pornography. He spent thousands of dollars and hundreds of hours in pursuit of pornography of all types. He was in bondage to a sinful and disgusting habit, enslaving him. Ashamed and powerless, he felt like a slave to his porn addiction; he was in spiritual bondage. However, when he became a believer, Christ set him free from that addiction overnight! He went from bondage to freedom in Jesus Christ.

In different but perhaps in less dramatic ways, all lost people are in bondage to sin. They are slaves to sinful conduct and attitudes. Let me say it again: The penalty for sin is death — spiritual death for all eternity. Jesus set my medical friend free when he was born again, liberating him from a degrading lifestyle that had ensnared him for years. Jesus said, "If you abide in my word, then you are truly disciples of Mine; and you shall know the truth, and the truth shall make you free" (John 8:31-32). The truth of the gospel set my medical friend free, not just from pornography but from the eternal consequences of sin. It will set you free if you have never been born again and if you still live in bondage to sin. The truth of the gospel will liberate your lost friend as well. We just have to come to grips with the biblical truth that Mr. Nice Guy is spiritually dead, spiritually blind, and spiritually bound. Only Jesus can give them life, sight and freedom. We will never be effective seed-planters until we understand these basic biblical truths.

> *We just have to come to grips with the biblical truth that Mr. Nice Guy is spiritually dead, spiritually blind, and spiritually bound.*

One Saturday morning, Hollis' wife, Ollie, called me on the phone. I could tell she had been crying. "What's the matter, Mrs. Ollie? What can I do for you?" I took care of her sister and her family in my medical practice. I also knew that fifty to seventy prayer warriors at Rock Hill Baptist Church had been praying for her husband's salvation at her insistence for two years every Wednesday night in prayer meeting.

"Can you come talk to Hollis about his spiritual life?"

"Mrs. Ollie, can Billy Graham preach? Sure, I'd like to come talk to him. I'll be there in fifteen minutes."

As I grabbed my car keys and coat and ran out the door, my wife asked, "Where are you going?"

I called back over my shoulder, "To lead Hollis Jackson to the Lord!"

It turns out Hollis' five-year-old niece, Brandy, had discovered that he was not a Christian. Appalled and quite stricken that her uncle was not going to heaven like the rest of the family, she began to weep and to beg him to give his heart to Jesus. Nothing wrong with that. Second Corinthians 5:20 says, "We beg you on behalf of Christ, be reconciled to God." This so disconcerted Hollis that he started to tear up. Then all three of them were weeping uncontrollably and did so all night. When morning came, it started all over again, so Ollie suggested she call me, to which he agreed. I was honored beyond words.

When I arrived that Saturday morning, the three of them were sitting on the couch with Hollis in the middle, holding hands and dabbing at their eyes with tissues. All three were red-eyed from crying all night.

I asked, "Hollis, are you sure this is what you want to do?"

"Yes, sir."

"You're not just making an emotional decision to make her happy?" I asked, pointing to his pretty little red-haired niece.

"No, sir."

He looked at that little red-haired girl I often saw him riding around in a golf cart on his farm across the road from the church, and he smiled broadly at her. Then he started snubbing again. Really, it was a holy moment.

"Hollis, I know every preacher and every evangelist that's ever been to Rock Hill Baptist Church have all shared the gospel with you. You know what you need to do. Is there any question I need to answer for you?"

"No, sir."

"Can we all kneel right here, and I'll lead you in a sinner's prayer?"

"I'd like that."

We all got on our knees in front of the couch in their den, holding hands, and crying together. I led Hollis Jackson in a sinner's prayer. He apologized to God for waiting so long and thanked Him for a precious niece helping him see the light.

Sometimes leading people to the Lord is like picking ripe fruit. You just lay your hand under the apple or peach, and it just falls into your hand. That's the way it was with Hollis. The hard work had been done in previous years on Wednesday nights with us on our knees for many years previously. The hard work had been performed by all the pastors befriending Hollis and sharing the gospel with him over and over. Jesus told His disciples, "Thus the saying 'One sows and another reaps' is true. I sent you to reap what you have not worked for. Others have done the hard work, and you have reaped the benefits of their labor" (John 4:37-38, NIV).

A week later, Hollis walked the aisle at Rock Hill Baptist Church amidst shouts of "hallelujah" to join the church. Two weeks later, he was baptized publicly, acknowledging his profession of faith in Christ. Now Hollis was a nice guy *and* a born-again guy. Now he was a nice guy who possessed the life of Christ. Now he was a nice guy who *could* go to heaven. Hollis served faithfully at his church until his death in 2015.

Now Hollis was a nice guy and a born-again guy.

Do you know any nice guys who probably are not going to heaven? Go sow a little gospel seed in their direction. They need Jesus, too.

STUDY QUESTIONS | Chapter 21

1. Why don't nice guys go to heaven? Why does any lost person miss heaven?

2. What were three spiritual conditions of lost people mentioned in this chapter?

3. How does Jesus address each of these issues?

4. Why was it so easy to lead Hollis to faith in Christ?

5. What does it mean "I (Paul) planted, Apollos watered, but God was causing the growth" (1 Corinthians 3:6)? What does this have to do with seed-planting?

6. Have you ever harvested where another planted?

7. Do you know any nice guys who look good and smell good but have probably never heard a full gospel presentation? Are they someone you can talk to about Christ?

22

A Fire in My Bones

In Jeremiah 20:9, the prophet exclaimed that he could not hold in the Word of God. Even though he tried to stifle it, he could not because it was like a fire in his heart — like a fire shut up in his bones. Jeremiah was persecuted miserably for his prophetic message of doom and destruction because the people of Judah did not receive his message favorably. He was beaten, put in stocks, thrown in a cistern, and generally disbelieved. Understandably, he tried to suppress the message God gave him for personal safety and because it was an unpopular message. However, like a true messenger of God, he could not. It was like a fire in his bones.

Do you remember having money in your pocket when you were a little kid? It burned a hole in your pocket until you spent it, right? Well, God's message burned a hole in Jeremiah's heart until he spoke it. It had to come out regardless of the consequences. That's why our brothers and sisters in Islamic and communist countries end up being persecuted for their faith. They can't keep it in. Like Paul, they are "compelled by the love of Christ" to speak the message, regardless of the consequences. Many end up as martyrs for the cause of Christ. Why? Because the good news burns like a fire in their bones!

When I was last in India, I met a pastor who became a believer as a teenage boy. When his father found out, he choked him until he thought he was dead. An hour later, his mother and sister revived him, but he could not talk. In fact, he could not talk for months. They secretly moved him out of the house, and some Christian friends placed him in hiding. He left for another city for several years, where he attended Bible school. He is now an evangelist and church planter. He got his voice back and never stops talking about Jesus, although it is risky business in his predominantly Hindu culture. Why would he do such a risky thing? Because of the fire in his bones!

In 1965 in the state of Kerala of India, a man named Cherian Mathews heard the call of God to go to northern India where the gospel had rarely been preached, where millions of Hindus lived in spiritual darkness. He and his wife, Grace, lived in southern India where the coconut trees rustled with gentle warm breezes, where food was plentiful, and where the Christian population was around 30 percent. It was a safe and comfortable place to live, work and worship.

Nevertheless, they both had a fire in their bones to carry the gospel message to Indian people in the north who had never heard the good news. Their family and friends questioned them severely, "Are you crazy? The people will hate you. They will hurt you. How will you find work? Who will support you?" Despite these dire warnings ringing in their ears, Cherian and Grace boarded a steam-engine-driven train for a three-day, two-night journey north to Gujarat at twenty-eight years of age to begin an unwelcome ministry of preaching the gospel to an unappreciative, hard-hearted, idol-worshiping people.

They arrived with one son and were five months pregnant. They rented an apartment from a Hindu landowner who proved to be a thorn in their side for many years. As time went by, God gave them five sons and two daughters. One of their precious daughters died at two years of age due to inadequate medical care. Thus, a twenty-two-year ministry of preaching the gospel began with a vision, a bicycle, and a Bible. And, oh, yes, a fire in his bones that would not be extinguished.

How the enemy tried to extinguish his evangelistic fervor! Without any financial support, this missionary family lived in poverty, hunger and hardship. Many nights, the children thanked God for the food that was not there and then went to bed hungry, wondering why their idol-worshiping friends had plenty to eat and they had none. The landowner hated Cherian with a passion. He hated what he stood for, and he hated the gospel message that he preached. He hated the worship services and the singing emanating from the Mathews household on his property. He would grab hold of the iron grill on the doors or windows during worship services and shake them vigorously, making an awful racket just to disrupt the services. He would do the same thing at random times just to frighten Mrs. Grace and the children when Cherian was away. He was a mean and hateful man, but the little church and Mathews family only prayed for him. "Love your enemies and pray for those who persecute you" (Matthew 5:44). Eventually, the landowner filed eviction notices against Cherian when he fell behind on his rent. He taunted the preacher from southern India with, "I thought you served a living God, Mathews, but you are dirt poor and cannot pay your rent. Where is your God now?" Thankfully, the law in India favored tenants, and they were able to stay until they caught up on their rent.

The enemy continued to try to extinguish the fire in Cherian's bones. As he rode his bicycle from village to village, preaching the good news, he was run out of many places and physically abused, pushed around, and slapped on the face. After one year he had one convert, and after three years there were enough converts to have a small group of believers meet at their home for a church service on Sundays.

Then in 1998, the enemy had all he could stand. It was time to throw cold water on the fire, not just on Cherian but on all of his converts as well. A Bible conference was being conducted in Gujarat for pastor training. Several hundred pastors, the fruit of forty-plus years of Cherian's ministry, were in attendance. Dr. Bill Bennett from Southeastern Seminary in Wake Forest, North Carolina, was the primary instructor at the conference. The Bible teaching was excellent, the worship was exuberant, and the Spirit of God was moving. The local people started attending in addition to the pastors. On the fifth night, ninety local people were converted to Christianity and became believers. The word of this spiritual awakening got out, and a group of militant Hindus attacked the premises where the pastors were staying. With heavy sticks and chains, the pastors were brutalized. Some were even thrown from the second-story windows. Many experienced deep lacerations, concussions and broken bones. Thankfully, no one was killed. The local police stood by as spectators, not intervening. Grace Mathews refused to allow Cherian or his sons to intervene, but went herself to plead for the lives of the pastors with, "What have these men done that you allow the men to brutalize them so?" She was promptly arrested and spent the night in jail, a terrible humiliation for her.

While in jail, her captors tormented her, saying, "Why don't you just praise our gods? What is so special about Jesus?"

With defiance and strength that surprised and silenced her jailers, she responded, "You can slit my throat before I will allow another god's name in my mouth."

They could have kept her in prison for many days and even forced her to go to trial, but the pastors prayed for her all night. Miraculously, she was released the next day on medical grounds.

Cherian encouraged the pastors to go home for their safety and their protection, but they refused, saying they rejoiced that God considered them worthy to suffer for Christ's sake. The following Sunday morning, they showed up for the evangelistic service in bandages or on crutches, ready to worship the God whom they joyfully served. There was a huge celebration of worship that day. The enemy could not extinguish the fire in their bones, even though some of their bones were broken.

Dr. Bennett said, "I have read the book of Acts. I have preached the book of Acts. But that night, I saw the book of Acts come alive before my very eyes!"

In the last ten years, Cherian Mathews has baptized more than 7,000 converts in northern India and Nepal. He and his son, Finny, supervise a network of hundreds of pastors and children. God has certainly honored his faithfulness and the gospel message burning in his bones.

This begs the question: Why don't we in America speak up more? Why don't we have a fire in our bones like Jeremiah and Cherian Mathews? I have been teaching evangelism classes for years in American churches, and I have pondered this question frequently. Here are some of my thoughts:

I. Carnal — In Acts 1:8, Dr. Luke tells us that when we are filled (controlled) by Holy Spirit, we will be witnesses — not *might* be, but *will* be. When I see a congregation full of people who rarely talk about Jesus outside of the church building, I am looking at a bunch of people who don't know what it means to be controlled by Holy Spirit. They may understand the concept, but they don't experience walking in the Spirit in their daily lives. When I was in college, I read a column in a local newspaper where an evangelist stated that in his opinion the American church was filled up with about 95 percent carnal Christians. Then he justified it by saying 95 percent of the Christians he knew never shared the gospel. You have to remember that the litmus test (the *sine qua non*) of a Spirit-filled believer is witnessing to the good news. Self-controlled (carnal) Christians and lost people do not talk about Jesus. This brings up the next question: What must a believer do to be a Spirit-filled Christian? There is no magical formula, but here are a few necessary ingredients in a nutshell. (This is discussed at greater length in Chapter 18).

    A) 'Fessed up — Confess all sin (1 John 1:9)

    B) Yielded up — Surrender to Holy Spirit's lordship (Romans 12:1)

    C) Faithed up — Trust God to make you like Jesus (Ephesians 5:18)

II. Fearful — Some folks are just plain fearful. I had a friend that lived down the street from me who was a big fisherman. He had an awesome bass boat that would go eighty miles an hour on the lake. The boat itself was a thing of beauty and had all the electronics one could possibly desire with a fish finder, depth gauge and GPS. He attended seminars on bass fishing regularly and attended every wildlife expo in South and North Carolina annually. He purchased every new fishing lure on the market, and I knew he had at least thirty fishing rods of all sorts. There was only one problem: He.Never.Went.Fishing! He had the boat, the gear and the training — but he never went to the lake. He always had an excuse for not going. It was too hot, too cold, too windy, or he was too tired. You get the picture! Sound like anybody you know?

Does it sound like any Christians you know? They go to all the evangelistic training seminars every year. They buy all the evangelistic tools (tracts, videos, CDs, and NOW links). They buy books on sharing the gospel and make a renewed commitment to share the gospel with ten lost friends this year, but there's one problem: They.Never.Go.Fishing. Just like my fishing buddy, they never talk to anybody about Jesus. They have lockjaw! They remind me of a high school kid I took to the beach one time for an evangelistic outing. We stood on the beach and looked both ways. There were hundreds of people on the beach in both directions. Then he said, "I guess there's no one here to talk to today." I just busted out laughing. The beach was white unto harvest, but his fear made him blind to it; he was ready to leave before we had even started.

I had personally trained him in evangelism, so I knew he was equipped, but fear gripped him even though he was with me, someone he knew to be experienced in beach evangelism. Does any of this sound familiar? Does it sound like you? Be of good cheer! There are very few assertive evangelists in America. I'm not excusing you; I'm just saying you're in good company.

Now, this is a good time to make a distinction. I have a patient named Dave who is an evangelist, both professionally and in his gifting. What do I mean by that? Well, he travels all over the southeastern United States, speaking/preaching in evangelistic crusades. That is his profession. Wherever he speaks, many people give their lives to Christ. He is very effective at what he does. He is what we call a gifted evangelist. Why do we say gifted? Because God has given him the supernatural gifting of evangelism. Whenever Dave preaches, people respond to his message and invitation. It is remarkable and supernatural. More than that, wherever he goes he leads people to the Lord in restaurants, retail stores, parking lots — everywhere. It's his gifting. When he comes to my medical office, he can't walk from the waiting room to the exam room without talking to people about Jesus, and he often leads people to faith in Christ in my office. He is an amazing evangelist.

It sometimes makes me feel like I don't even know how to share the gospel or that I don't even try, but I have to remind myself that Dave has a supernatural gifting from God and he is a gift to the church. Ephesians 4:11-13 tells us that Jesus gave to the church as a gift "apostles, the prophets, the evangelists, the pastors, and teachers, to equip his people for works of service, so that the body of Christ may be built up until we all reach unity in the faith and in the knowledge of the Son of God and become mature, attaining to the whole measure of the fullness of Christ" (NIV). Dave is one of those evangelists given to the church as a gift to equip God's people. He is both gifted as an evangelist, and he is a gift to the church. Most of us are not gifted in the same way as Brother Dave. We shouldn't beat ourselves up if we can't win lost people like Dave does. In like manner, not all pastors are gifted to be evangelists like Dave, so don't expect your pastor to perform like Dave in the pulpit. Your pastor may be gifted as a pastor/shepherd/teacher. Let him be unique in his gifting from God. Nevertheless, neither you nor your pastor nor I are excused from sharing the gospel at every opportunity. Indeed, it should be like a fire in our bones.

So how do we overcome fear? We overcome fear by practice. I remember the first time I sang in church. I was nearly paralyzed with fear, but later I overcame the fear by virtue of practice and got to where I loved to sing at every opportunity. My first public speaking opportunity was at a Civitan Club meeting in my hometown. I was frightened to death. I was told later that I reversed my age and grade stating, "I am six years old, and I am in the twelfth grade." I wondered why all those men laughed at me. I thought I was on my way to being a comedian. I just didn't know why. Now I jump at every opportunity to speak, preach, or share my testimony. Why? Practice!

A violinist with his violin in hand on the street of New York stopped a bystander and asked, "How do I get to Carnegie Hall?"

The bystander replied, "Practice. Practice. Practice."

How do you and I get over our fear of sharing the gospel? Practice. Practice. Practice.

During my first four years of sharing the gospel when I was in college, all I ever did was read the same gospel tract over and over to hundreds of college kids until I had it memorized. This gave me comfort and confidence. Over years of time, I have memorized several different ways to share the gospel that I can utilize in different situations. You can, too, but you have to start somewhere. Find a tract you like, memorize it, and read it verbatim to every person you can. Millennials prefer to use evangelistic apps on their smart phones. Whatever suits your fancy. Just use something that will provide comfort and encouragement and the opportunity for practice.

III. Unclean or Ashamed — I knew a guy one time who had the fire in his bones. He was the chairman of the deacons in a rural Baptist church. Every Monday night, he attended church visitation and brought a little black book with a list of names of people he knew in the community who did not attend church or had visited his church. He kept that black book wrapped alongside a little New Testament with a rubber band in his front shirt pocket. He rarely missed a Monday night visitation. He was skilled at sharing the gospel, exceedingly pleasant, and friendly. His wife went with him most Monday nights.

There was only one problem. He kept a pack of Marlboros right behind his New Testament in his shirt pocket. He smoked two packs per day, and he reeked of tobacco smoke. His thumb and index finger were stained green from tobacco smoke. He had been confronted by several Christian friends about this inconsistency, but he couldn't break the habit. More than one person had commented, "Don't you think it a little odd for a Baptist deacon to be a chain-smoker?"

Sometime later, there was a Sunday school revival at his church designed to teach the finer points of growing a church through Sunday school evangelism. The evangelist, in the course of his teaching, commented one night, "I've never seen a cigarette smoker who was a consistent soul winner." He wasn't being vindictive or harsh; he was just making an observation. As soon as he made that comment, a pack of Marlboros came flying from the back of the church all the way to the altar, surprising everyone. Nobody said a word. The evangelist kept preaching, but that was the last day this deacon ever smoked a cigarette. You see, his desire to be an effective seed planter exceeded his desire for nicotine. He repented that day and turned away. He didn't want anything unclean in his life to prevent him from being effective as an ambassador for the Lord Jesus Christ. I have talked to many Christians over the years who are not only ineffective, but who are also unwilling to speak up. They are not vocal because they do not want to be perceived as a hypocrite. They either have glaring public sin, or secret sin in their lives that shuts them up. In good conscience, they know better than to be vocal because of their personal sin. They are too ashamed to speak up for Jesus. They do not want to be called out by those who know their sins, or they don't feel qualified by their sinful past. They haven't removed the beam from their own eye.

> *He didn't want anything unclean in his life to prevent him from being effective as an ambassador for the Lord Jesus Christ.*

What is the remedy? If the sin is current, the only solution is to do like this deacon. Confess and repent. Walk away from that sinful behavior — no, run! Run away as fast as you can, and give glory to God for delivering you. That is your story. That is your testimony. Nobody is perfect. Somebody will identify with your story and crave the same deliverance God gave you. Own it and tell it. Don't be proud of your sin, but don't drown it in shame. Jesus took our sin and shame at the cross. That is the beauty and the glory of the cross. Now go proclaim it! If we hadn't done so poorly, the cross wouldn't be so wonderful!

If your sin is a distant past sin that still haunts you, the same process applies. Make sure it is under the blood of Jesus, fully confessed, fully repented, and no going back. Fully receive His forgiveness and the righteousness of Christ. Walk in that righteousness every day (2 Corinthians 5:21). Again, none of us are perfect. If we have to wait until sinless perfection, none of us would qualify to share the gospel. As soon as you realize that your sins are under the blood, then tell somebody and don't stop telling. When Jesus transformed the lives of people in the New Testament, they immediately went away to tell everybody what Jesus had done for them. They had a fire in their bones, and they couldn't keep it in.

If you are a true believer, there is a fire smoldering in your bones. Don't allow carnality, besetting sin, fear or shame to smother the flame that Holy Spirit produces in you. If you would be an effective seed planter, live a life of confession of sin and submission to Holy Spirit. Deal with besetting sin and walk in righteousness. Put off the old man and put on the new man so you need not bury your head in shame or defeat. Allow Holy Spirit to fan the smoldering flame into a fiery passion for speaking the truth of the gospel. How hot is the fire burning in your bones?

STUDY QUESTIONS | Chapter 22

1. What inhibits Christians from sharing the gospel freely?

2. How do we overcome these inhibitions?

3. Would you say you have a fire in your bones to share the gospel? What does it take to stoke the fire?

4. Do you think you would ever be a martyr for Christ? Can you withstand the everyday pressure and temptations to violate your convictions?

5. Do you speak out against moral evil around you, or do you let it slide to avoid conflict? Jeremiah tried to keep silent but couldn't. Do you think we should be more prophetic as Christians?

23

PERMANENCE

My physician assistant student and I sat politely and listened enthralled as an attractive and animated middle-aged oriental woman told her story. Along with her mother and nine other siblings, she had escaped from Laos to Thailand in the 1970s. After some years in a refugee camp, a church in Spartanburg County agreed to sponsor her family through a refugee resettlement program. They were shipped first to the Philippines and then to South Carolina in the early 1980s, where they settled in Camp Croft with numerous other Laotian families. Interestingly, while in the Philippines, they saw the *Jesus* film, which she said "terrified the entire family" but produced no spiritual conversions.

In 1985, our church — Rock Hill Baptist in Inman, South Carolina — began an outreach program to the Laotian community in conjunction with our county Baptist association. Two days a week, volunteers from our church would assist with after-school homework and English language skills at a Baptist mission center located in Camp Croft near the Laotian community. On Sunday afternoons, we sent a bus thirty-plus minutes from our church to Camp Croft to pick up about forty to fifty Laotian children and their mothers at the center. We brought them to our church, fed them supper, and included them in our discipleship training classes and evening worship service. The bus driver then returned them to Camp Croft. This took place over a one and a half- to two-year period. My current patient was an adolescent girl included in this group of Laotians who came to our church in the mid-1980s.

Sometime later after I entered my private medical practice in 1985, she ended up at my office and remembered me immediately. As I walked into the exam room, this teenage girl said, *"Sabaidi,"* with her hands placed together in front of her face and bowing respectfully.

I responded in like manner, *"Sabaidi,"* placing my hands in front of my face and bowing respectfully as East Asians do.

She looked at me inquisitively and asked, "Do you speak Laotian?"

I responded, *"Nony nung,"* meaning "only a little bit."

She clapped her hands and laughed, saying, "You do speak Laotian. How?"

I reassured her, "I don't speak Laotian, only a few phrases I heard from my father when he returned from Vietnam. He was a doctor like me and ran a medical clinic in Laos during the war, caring for Laotians and downed American airmen. He learned Laotian and often spoke it for years after he came home."

She was duly impressed and told all her Laotian friends that I spoke Laotian despite my protests otherwise. That's how I ended up with a large contingent of Laotian patients. I didn't get to go to the mission field as a missionary as I once desired (due to uncontrolled glaucoma and numerous surgeries on both eyes), but God brought the mission field to me.

Years later after completing her physical exam on one particular visit, I asked her about her spiritual life. She responded that she was Buddhist. I then asked if any of the Bible lessons at our church had any impact on her, to which she responded, "Oh, yes, I received Catholic instructions in the Philippines and Baptist teaching here. I understand that I must be good."

"Do you understand what it means to be born again?"

She stared at me blankly and admitted she did not.

I described the encounter between Jesus and Nicodemus, and explained, "You must acquire the life of God in order to know God personally. More than that, God is a holy God. He doesn't allow anything sinful into His holy dwelling place in heaven. What can you do to erase any of your sin?"

She just shrugged.

"When Jesus died on the cross, He shed His perfect blood to pay the price for all of our sin. More than that, when we trust in Him, He not only takes away our sin, but He also gives us His righteousness so that we may qualify to live in God's holy heaven."

Her response was, "But I believe in Jesus and Buddha. My parents are Buddhist."

"Yes, ma'am, but Jesus said, 'I am the way, and the truth, and the life; no one comes to the Father, but through Me' (John 14:6); then He proved the truthfulness of that claim by rising from the dead. Neither Buddha nor any other world religious leader has done that — only Jesus! When you say you believe in Jesus and Buddha, you are putting one foot in quicksand and one foot on the Solid Rock. You will still sink. You are like a 'double-minded man, unstable in all his ways' (James 1:8)."

I handed her a gospel of John that I keep in every exam room and suggested she read it and ask God to reveal the truth to her. She agreed to do that.

As she left, I put my hands together and said, *"Khob chai,"* meaning "thank you."

She smiled broadly but had a troubled look on her face. I could tell she was already pondering the things I had shared with her. Afterwards, my PA student and I prayed that God would take away the spiritual blindness from her eyes, so she would see and comprehend spiritual truth and Holy Spirit would impart the life of Christ to her.

Now why do I share this story with you? This evangelistic encounter occurred in the life of this oriental woman and this family doctor because of stability. By this, I mean my stability in my community. I have been in the same community — in fact, in the same office building with many of the same employees and longtime partners — practicing medicine for thirty-three years and in residency for four years before that, all in the same city. Many of my patients have been with me for thirty-plus years. I am now taking care of their children and grand-children. I have attended three churches within ten miles of each other and lived in three homes within fifteen miles of each other.

I had one of my longtime patients tell me just a month ago that his grandson was a marine recruit at boot camp at Parris Island. He reminded me that I prayed for him in the delivery room minutes after he was born, dedicating him to the Lord. He said, "Doc, I've reminded him many times over the years that he belonged to God because Dr. Jackson dedicated him to God right after he was born. He's a fine Christian young man now, fully committed to the Lord Jesus Christ." Then he broke down in my office and began to sob uncontrollably. I put my arms around this grandfather's shoulders and rejoiced with him. This is what long-term stability in a community allows us to accomplish in terms of Christian ministry.

In medieval times, an order of monks took a vow of permanence. This meant they would not be roving teachers like most monks, but would commit to staying in a certain city over a lifetime to build relationships and demonstrate integrity.[1] Why? They did this because so many people did not know the itinerant (traveling) monks and did not trust them. They would show up for a little while, teach about God's Word, expect food and money in exchange, then leave. They didn't stick around long enough to build any lasting connections. Sadly, unscrupulous monks sometimes stole from the people, giving the rest a bad name and making the whole situation worse. No wonder folks were skeptical.

To solve the problem, a certain order of monks took a vow of permanence, deciding they would stay in their individual communities for a lifetime to demonstrate service, faithfulness and integrity. They believed this would enhance the gospel message.

Let's make a few observations. I have lived in the same community for thirty-seven years. I travel the same roads, I shop at the same stores, and I know the same people. I try to purchase fuel at the same location every time because the owner of the gas station is from India. And guess what? He is from the same town in India where our church supports a Bible college. We know some of the same people in a city halfway around the world. He was astounded that I knew of his city, much less people in his city. What a great evangelistic opening! I don't pay at the pump. I go inside so I can speak to him and his brother personally. I blew him out of the water when I showed him a picture of my nine kids. Eventually, I will get to share the gospel with both of them.

I know the pastors of most of the large churches in my town, and when I ask my patients where they go to church, I can converse with them about their church and their pastor. (It's sad when a patient tells me they go to a particular church regularly. Then I say, "Remind me of your pastor's name," and when they look at me blankly I know they probably don't go to that church as much as they let on.)

You understand permanence has benefits. It allows us to build connections and relationships. If we possess integrity, then it shines through brightly when we live, work and worship in one place over a lifetime.

When I first moved to Spartanburg, I bought my new bride a little Toyota. The very nice lady who handled the paperwork for us ended up being the mother of one of my favorite patients. Why do I say favorite? Because she had glorious, long red hair, and I've always been partial to red hair. (I had carrot-red hair when I was a little boy, although it has turned darker over the years.)

I took care of her, her children, and her husband for years. She had frequent, severe migraine headaches, which were disabling at times. At one point, she had an unrelenting headache that lasted for weeks, along with intractable vomiting. She had blurred vision and poor concentration, just like with all her other headaches. However, this one just would not go away, so we ordered a brain scan. She turned out to have an inoperable brain tumor that ultimately took her life within two years. It was a devastating blow to her family; I grieved over the loss of that precious red-haired patient of mine, but no one grieved as hard as her husband, Daryl.

Daryl was a giant of a man, standing six feet two inches and weighing 310 pounds. He had chronic back pain from arthritis, coming to see me every three months for treatment. He was like a Neanderthal man. Because he spoke mostly in grunts and hand motions, I often had a hard time comprehending him. However, we shared our grief over the loss of his wife and my patient; we cried together, bonding as we did so. Daryl slowly became addicted to alcohol over three years after his wife died. He admitted it to me but was unwilling to do anything about it. I placed him on antidepressant medication, but it didn't seem to help.

Every time Daryl came to see me, I would say a prayer over him, which initially seemed to disconcert him terribly, but later he came to expect it. Then I began to share the gospel with him and told him bluntly he would never give up his booze or depression unless Jesus gave him a new heart. That did not register with him at all.

After three years of every-three-month visits, he came into my office one day and asked, "Where do you go to church?" I knew immediately that God had prepared his heart. That was the first spiritual question he had ever asked me other than why God had allowed his wife to die. Rather than telling him where we went to church, I invited him to eat breakfast with me. For the next six months, we ate breakfast together every Saturday morning. The medical man and the Neanderthal man — we became best friends. I began to teach him all about Jesus and Bible doctrine while he spat his chewing tobacco in a plastic drink bottle. Daryl was like a sponge. He quit drinking booze. He gave up his live-in girlfriend. He began reading his Bible every day. The depression disappeared.

Nowadays, I take care of Daryl's sister and brother-in-law, and I have crepe myrtle trees in my yard donated by his father. Do you get the picture? What if I had moved to the beach or the mountains for a better opportunity or different scenery? I would have lost all of the opportunities that have come my way by staying in one place for a lifetime and by being a constant ministering presence in the life of a single family over multiple generations and many issues.

I understand that sometimes jobs and the failing health of elderly parents cause us to move when we don't plan to. Nevertheless, I would encourage you to have a ministry mindset and realize that when moving about from one part of the state to another or one part of the country to another just for adventure or job advancement, you willingly choose to be counter-productive for your personal impact for the kingdom of God. Why? Because it takes a decade for the average person to build up integrity and reputation in a new community. It takes a long time to rebuild connections in a new location.

Please understand that I am not in any way abrogating the call of God on some of our lives to go to faraway places to fulfill the Great Commission as missionaries. When God calls us, we must say as did Isaiah, "Here am I, Lord. Send me." However, a missionary on the mission field will have to build connections the same as we do here — over years of time by practicing stability and seeking permanence in a community. That way, the people they seek to minister to will learn to trust them.

I have a large extended family in my hometown of Manning in the lower part of the state of South Carolina (thirty-one first cousins and a gazillion second cousins). They always ask me if I'm going to come back to Manning when I retire. Now, that's appealing to me because I love the Lowcountry; the hunting is great, and I would reconnect with my extended family. The only problem is, I have thirty-seven years of ministry connections and relationships that I value here in the Upstate. I have a ministry mindset. I can't just sacrifice all of these relationships to satisfy my personal desire to relocate to the Lowcountry. I would have to start all over building relationships with people who haven't seen me much in thirty-seven years (really longer, counting college and medical school). I would be no different than the traveling monks.

That's why I'm surprised at Christian friends who retire and move to the beach or the mountains or wherever. They lose all their connections. They have to start all over — that is, if they haven't retired from ministry, too. We don't retire from ministry when we retire from our jobs. The work of sharing the gospel with our circle of influence never stops as long as we live. Jesus said, "We must work the works of Him who sent Me, as long as it is day; night is coming, when no man can work" (John 9:4). Perhaps we should take a cue from the monks and consider taking a vow of stability. It might enhance all of our respective ministries.

STUDY QUESTIONS | Chapter 23

1. How long have you lived at your current residence? Why did you move from your previous home?

2. How hard was it to make connections after you moved? How long did it take to make close, intimate friends?

3. Do you think your personal ministry for the kingdom of God suffered when you last moved? Did it take long to gear back up?

4. How hard was it to find a church home after your last move? Was it emotionally hard? Do you feel a part of the "in crowd" at your new church?

5. Do you intentionally try to connect with business owners or clerks in businesses in your town for the purpose of building relationships in order to eventually share the gospel? Name a few places where you could do that easily.

24

THE FLIGHT OF CHURCH KIDS

"Dr. Jackson, would you please say something to my son? He is coming to your office in the morning. He's a good boy. We raised him right, but I'm ashamed to admit he has a drinking problem. His mother and I are afraid his alcohol use will get him into trouble with the law, or worse. We don't like the crowd he runs with because they are a bad influence on him. He won't listen to us anymore, especially since he moved out. Do you mind trying to talk some sense into his head?"

These words were spoken to me by a pastor friend of mine. He was an evangelist and had been a missionary overseas for many years. His son had been raised in a strong Christian environment all of his life. He had heard the gospel message preached since he was a child, yet somehow he had rejected the sincere faith of his parents and, like Rehoboam, Solomon's son, had listened to the advice of his friends and chosen an unwise and destructive path.

The next morning, the pastor's son came into my office with a minor medical problem, which we quickly addressed. I did not approach his alcohol problem because, as I have stated in a previous chapter, the alcohol and drug abuse in my patients' lives is just a superficial manifestation of a deeper root issue, which is sin. Only Jesus can solve the sin issue in any of our lives. The heart of the human problem is the problem of the human heart. As Jeremiah said, "The heart is more deceitful than all else and is desperately sick; who can understand it?" (Jeremiah 17:9).

"Luke, tell me about your spiritual life."

He immediately began to look around the room like a trapped animal. I just waited patiently. He finally calmed down a bit and made eye contact with me when he realized I was not going to attack or bite him.

He sighed heavily and said, "I really don't have a spiritual life."

"Well, then, tell me: Have you ever been born again?"

He squinted his eyes and looked at me through narrowed slits. Slowly shaking his head back and forth, he answered, "I don't know what that means."

It was my turn to stare. "Luke, you have lived in the home of an evangelist for twenty years. How can you not know what being born again means?"

I could tell he was thinking hard, but finally a blank stare surfaced, and he replied, "Really, I don't know."

I was incredulous, but I pressed on with a gospel presentation, explaining carefully about Jesus' encounter with Nicodemus and the challenge to be born again. I carefully explained the new birth to this spiritually blind preacher's kid. I finished by saying, "Luke, salvation is a free gift from God that we receive by faith. We trust that what Jesus did on the cross for us is sufficient to satisfy the just demands of a holy God. You must confess your sin, repent, and receive the Lord Jesus Christ as your personal Savior. Holy Spirit will then impart to you the life of Christ. Does this make sense to you?"

He was looking at me, but the light was not on. We were not connecting. Then a silly grin came on his face, and he looked around the room before saying, "Doc, all of that is well and good. I'm sure I have heard it before, but it's really not for me. I'm just not into that religious stuff." Then he covered his face with his arm, and I realized he was actually laughing at me. In all of my years of sharing the gospel in my medical office, I do not remember anyone laughing at me or mocking me. I was actually stunned. I was thirty years older than him and having a very serious conversation regarding the condition of his eternal, never-dying soul, and he was laughing at me. I simply handed him his papers and dismissed him with a grieving heart.

Two weeks later as I walked into my office, my receptionist asked me, "Dr. Jackson, have you read the papers today?"

"No, ma'am. I don't usually read the paper until after work."

"You need to see this." She showed me an article describing a motor vehicle accident in which a twenty-two-year-old male had been killed instantly in an alcohol-related incident. It was Luke. Of course, there was no consoling his parents.

"Do not be deceived. God cannot be mocked. A man reaps what he sows. Whoever sows to please their flesh, from the flesh will reap destruction" (Galatians 6:7-8a, NIV).

♦ ♦ ♦ ♦ ♦

"But, Dr. Jackson, I don't understand. I thought the Bible promises that if we 'raise them up in the way they should go, when they are old, they will not depart from it.' Did not these missionary parents raise Luke in a Christian home and tell him about Jesus and take him to church? Where did they go wrong? What more could they have done? Why didn't God keep His promises?"

First, let's talk about what this verse actually means; then, let's talk about child evangelism. Next, we'll talk about what it takes to keep our children from departing from the faith, because, as we can all observe, there is a huge problem with church kids leaving church after high school and never coming back. I call it "the flight of the church kids."

1) Proverbs 22:6 — My *Unger's Bible Dictionary* says the phrase "train up" actually means "to imbue one with anything, to initiate." I like what "imbue" means: "to inspire, to influence, or to permeate." Other Bible dictionaries say "train up" means "to dedicate." The Hebrew word translated "train up" challenges us parents to actively engage in the ongoing process of shepherding our children's hearts into adulthood. (For that matter, my wife and I consider ourselves to be a source of counsel for our adult children if they want and need it.) We must imbue — inspire and influence them — but how? According to *Unger's*, the next phrase, "in the way he should go," reads literally, "according to his way, according to his disposition and habits."[1] Put these phrases together, and the verse reads, "Imbue (inspire/influence) a child according to his way."

That begs another question: What is a child's way? Considering *Unger's* definition and my own experience of parenting nine very different children, it could mean that I, as a parent, must guide my child according to his own "disposition and habits." I have certainly found this to be necessary as each child has his or her own set of strengths and weaknesses, personality traits, preferences, aptitudes and attitudes. As tempting as it is to box them into my paradigm (I mean, why can't they all be doctors, right?), my wife and I have always encouraged our children to pursue their own dreams, their own interests, their own giftedness — with our input, of course. (The result? Not one doctor among them. One daughter is about to enter nursing school.)

No matter what "their way" is, however, Deuteronomy 6 admonishes us to instruct our children in the Word, and Ephesians 6:4 says to "bring them up in the discipline and instruction of the Lord." My wife and I have intentionally attempted "to imbue" our children toward walking with our God. We do not apologize for this.

Our children's hearts are filled with foolishness. "Foolishness is bound up in the heart of a child; the rod of discipline will remove it far from him" (Proverbs 22:15). This is why we parents must discipline (train up, shepherd, dedicate) our children and instruct them in wisdom. "The rod and reproof give wisdom, but a child who gets his own way brings shame to his mother" (Proverbs 29:15). Without proper training the way leads to folly and shame, and possibly even death — eternally.

What about the promise that they will not depart from it (their training)? We would all like to think that our early, intentional spiritual training will leave a lasting impact on their lives for their good. This verse certainly seems to imply that; however, this verse is not a guarantee, because the Book of Proverbs makes it absolutely clear that our youth have choices to make. They can choose roads leading to life or roads leading to destruction. We wish we could make those choices for them, but we cannot. You and I have both seen children raised well by the same parents where one chose to follow the wicked unto death (Proverbs 22:12-19), and another chose the wisdom of his parents and the good path of the righteous unto life (Proverbs 22:1-11, 20). Conversely, I have seen the children of poor parenting choose wisely the path of righteousness that leads to life. It has been a marvel to me of God's mercy and grace. Our children grow up to make their own choices.

Proverbs challenges parents to be faithful in establishing a positive, moral and spiritual course for the lives of their children while also challenging our children to heed their parents' faithful and wise instruction, to be more like the Master.[2]

> *Our children grow up to make their own choices.*

2) Let's talk a little bit about child evangelism. I learned the importance of reaching children while attending a men's breakfast sponsored by Child Evangelism Fellowship. More than a thousand men attended.

At one point in his presentation, the speaker asked all of the men who had become believers as adults to stand up, whereupon about fifty men stood. Then he asked everyone who had become believers before the age of eleven to stand up. I was astonished, as fully 95 percent of the crowd stood up. It made a huge visual impact on every man, including me, in attendance. He made a strong point that most people become believers as children, and do so before the age of eleven. That's why child evangelism is so critical. I'm not saying that God can't or won't save people as adults. He can do anything! However, most people who choose Christ do so as children.

Then the speaker asked everyone to stand who had been saved at an evangelistic crusade or at church. Once again, about fifty people stood. Then he asked those who had been led to Christ by a friend or a relative at home or at work to stand. Once again, I was stunned to see about 95 percent of those 1,000-plus men stand up. A great standing ovation erupted from the crowd, with many of the men hugging the man standing next to them. It was obvious to all of us that many of the men were attending with someone who had led them to Christ. It was an emotional, inspiring educational moment for all of us. It drove home the point that all of us should focus our efforts on winning our children to faith in Christ before the age of eleven. This event occurred in the late 1980s.

Consider the trend in late 2017. According to research conducted and reported by veteran researcher, George Barna, for the American Culture and Faith Institute (ACFI) in November 2017, 68 percent of believers are born again by the age of eighteen, two-thirds of these under age thirteen, while another 24 percent become believers between the ages of eighteen to thirty-nine.[3] Only 9 percent of believers accept Christ after the age of thirty-nine.[4] In the same ACFI survey, "parents emerged as the most likely dominant influence, named by three out of every ten born-again Christians (29 percent), as responsible for their conversion to Christ."[5] Barna notes:

> Fewer churches emphasize and equip people for evangelism these days, and the results are obvious and undeniable. The implications of ignoring gospel outreach — especially among children, who are the most receptive audience to the gospel — are enormous. All the "church growth" strategies in the world cannot compensate for the absence of an authentic transmission of the good news of what Jesus Christ has done for humanity.

> Parents, who have more influence on the spiritual choices and development of their children than anyone else, are ill-prepared these days to lead their children to a genuine, life-changing relationship with Jesus. ... Worse yet, surveys conducted by ACFI earlier this year revealed that most American parents are not interested or engaged in helping their kids to know Jesus personally.[6]

Therefore, it is a serious responsibility for parents to "dedicate their children in the way that they ought to go" while they are young, and to pray desperately that they will make a sincere commitment to Christ during those early years.

By the same token, we should involve ourselves in churches and other organizations that are aggressive and focused on child evangelism. Such churches have evangelistic Sunday schools purposefully sharing the gospel as a part of their curriculum. They believe in the power of

Vacation Bible School, Awana, and other child-friendly events to reach children inside and outside the church. Our family participated in Child Evangelism Fellowship, an organization attempting to reach children through backyard Bible clubs. It taught my children to be comfortable with sharing the gospel when they were summer missionaries with CEF. You will never know how my heart thrilled sometime later to observe my teenagers sharing the gospel comfortably and authoritatively in a cross-cultural event in Haiti (with an interpreter, no less) because of their CEF training.

There are plenty of good evangelistic organizations that focus on reaching and discipling children. Involve yourself and your children, first in your local church, and then in an organization that focuses on reaching children. Once they are past the age of eleven, the evangelistic going gets tougher — not impossible, just harder.

3) "But, Dr. Jackson, be real. Our church reaches many people when they are young. We have a huge youth group because of this, but after they graduate from high school, they disappear. We never see most of them ever again. What are we doing wrong?" According to George Barna, 61 percent of teens leave the church by the second year of college.[7]

Let me give you my perspective on this issue. When I speak to youth groups, I sometimes start by asking them the top ten country and western songs to break the ice. That gets all the youth involved. They have no problems naming the current top ten. Then I ask them to name the top ten beer producers. Now mind you, these are church-going kids. They laugh themselves silly as they name dozens of beer producers. After I have set them up, I lob softballs and ask them easy questions about Moses, David, and Jesus. Usually, all I get is crickets. For you see, our church-going kids are culturally savvy but biblically illiterate. Barna "discovered that 85 percent of 'born-again' teens do not believe in the existence of absolute truth, while over 60 percent agreed with the statement, 'Nothing can be known for sure except for things you experience in your own life'"; plus, "more than half of those surveyed believe Jesus sinned in His early life"![8]

Christian Smith and his research team at the University of North Carolina in Chapel Hill studied teen religion and published their research in a book entitled *Soul Searching*.[9] They discovered that the religion of U.S. teenagers is largely "ambiguous" due to the disparity between the time and attention devoted to their spiritual life compared to their social life, academics and athletics.[10] Supporting the everyday observations of many pastors and youth pastors, Smith states:

> Our research suggests that religious congregations are losing out to school and the media for the time and attention of youth. When it comes to the formation of the lives of youth, viewed sociologically, faith communities get a very small seat at the end of the table for a very limited period of time. Hence ... most teens know details about television characters and pop stars, but many are quite vague about Moses and Jesus. Most youth are well versed about the dangers of drunk driving, AIDS, and drugs, but many haven't a clue about their own traditions or ideas. Many parents clearly prioritize homework and sports over church or youth group attendance. ... The majority of American teenagers appear to espouse rather inclusive, pluralistic, and individualistic views about religious truth, identity boundaries, and the need for religious congregations.[11]

In the words of Rev. Voddie Baucham: "The culture of secular humanism appears to have co-opted America's Christian teens."[12] Why should we be surprised when our teens leave the church after high school graduation? All through high school, their parents have emphasized academics, athletics and their social life more than their spiritual life. Their parents have effectively secularized their own teenagers by teaching them that church and spiritual development is not that important. I submit to you very respectfully that these teens are *not* leaving Christianity; they probably *never* became Christians! I don't believe I am alone in this assertion! Reverend Baucham agrees.[13] Dr. Norman Geisler and Jason Jimenez agree in their book *The Bible's Answer to 100 of Life's Biggest Questions*. One of their answers to Question 95 — "Why are so many young people abandoning the faith?" — is "Many millennials (eighteen- to twenty-nine-year-olds) who claim to be Christians never had a true conversion to begin with. The pat Sunday school prayers that churches and revivals have people recite don't guarantee salvation."[14] John explained this phenomenon in 1 John 2:19: "They went out from us, but they were not really of us; for if they had been of us, they would have remained with us; but they went out, in order that it might be shown that they all are not of us." Ooh, this is painful. Teens who are not born again are nominally participating in church as long as they are under their parents' roof, but as soon as they have some independence, they discard a belief system with which they disagreed, and which was relegated to the margin of their lives as they grew up.

> '*The culture of secular humanism appears to have co-opted America's Christian teens.*'

> *The responsibility for raising your child in the nurture and admonition of the Lord was not delegated to the youth pastor or the Christian school. God gave that responsibility to you.*

So, Mom and Dad, what is the solution? Should you squeeze them into the mold of the youth group? No, absolutely not! The responsibility for raising your child in the nurture and admonition of the Lord was not delegated to the youth pastor or the Christian school. God gave that responsibility to you. In Deuteronomy 6: 4-9, the Lord told Moses:

> *Hear, O Israel! The Lord is our God, the Lord is one! And you shall love the Lord your God with all your heart and with all your soul and with all your might. And these words, which I am commanding you today, shall be on your heart; and you shall teach them diligently to your sons and shall talk of them when you sit in your house and when you walk by the way and when you lie down and when you rise up. And you shall bind them as a sign on your hand and they shall be as [a]frontals [b]on your forehead. And you shall write them on the doorposts of your house and on your gates.*

Whether they admit it or not, your children look up to you and respect you more than anybody else, and whether you like it or not, they will grow up to be like you more than anybody else. What an amazing opportunity for you to influence your children for the kingdom of God! So what do you do?

1) Be like Jesus. You must have the real disease if you want your kids to catch what you have. By that, I mean you must have a passionate love for Jesus, His Word, and the church if you expect your children to catch from you a love for Jesus and a desire to follow Him. Our kids hate hypocrisy as much as we do. In their book *Abandoned Faith*, Alex McFarland and Jason Jimenez

quote Andy Lawrenson, student pastor of Nags Head Church of North Carolina. He says, "When young people see hypocrisy and misplaced priorities in the lives of their parents, they often will look elsewhere for role models and guidance."[15] We have to be consistent and honestly confess when we fail. Jesus is altogether beautiful and infinitely attractive. The more you and I are like Jesus, the more our kids will desire the Jesus life. We have to walk the walk before we can talk the talk, because our walk walks farther than our talk talks.

2) Disciple your own children. It is my responsibility to train my own children in biblical truth. It is your responsibility to train your children in biblical truth. It goes way beyond reading them Bible stories when they are young. Yes, we should take our children to Sunday school, VBS, and church summer camp. We as a family take advantage of all of these things, but we cannot overcome the steady drumbeat of the world's secular input if that is all the spiritual input our children receive. We taught our children Bible stories at the dinner table every night from the time they were young even until now, graduating from simple truth to more complex doctrinal concepts. We taught our children to pray from an early age. We all memorized Scripture together. We worked through the catechism together. Both my wife and I were deeply committed to discipling our own children. We wanted to see them born again, growing in grace and the knowledge of our Lord Jesus Christ, understanding the Spirit-filled life, able to share their faith, loving the local church, and committed to world missions. Mom and Dad, if these things are not deeply rooted in your own heart, you will never pass them on to your children. The apple doesn't fall far from the tree. I'm just saying.

3) Establish a family altar/worship time. Fathers, you are the priest in your family. This is your responsibility. You are the one primarily responsible to "teach them diligently," as God commanded through Moses in Deuteronomy 6:4-9. You and your wife decide on the best time of day. Be consistent and start simply. Let it grow over time. Read from the Bible. Sing with a Christian CD or a hymnbook and pray together. You must prepare in advance. Your family will know if you are ill-prepared, just as a congregation knows if the pastor is unprepared. You are the pastor/priest, and they are your congregation/flock. Shepherd them well. Your ministry to them should consist of the overflow of your personal relationship with the Lord in your own daily quiet time. Your family will understand and appreciate that. Here are several additional suggestions:

a. Pick a consistent time. We have a family time after the evening meal. Nobody leaves the table until Daddy reads the Bible and has question time/prayer time. I usually ask thought-provoking questions to make everybody think and stimulate conversation. My children are adults now, and this can be a lot of fun and sometimes controversial.

b. No electronic devices. Cell phones, laptops, TV, house phones, etc., can be the death of a serious family worship time. My landline house phone rarely rings anymore since everyone has a cell phone unless it's a telemarketer. Nevertheless, it always rings during family devotional time. My wife is always immediately concerned that it is a family emergency, although we've not had a family emergency call on that phone in twenty years. In the earlier years, my children would break furniture racing each other to answer that phone during devotional time. I learned an important lesson forty years ago sitting outside of a general store in Jordan, South Carolina, one day with my good friend Jim Poe eating Moon Pies and drinking RC Colas. There were two older gentlemen sitting on the front porch of the general store leaning against the wall on wooden Coca Cola crates and chewing on straws. The phone (a rotary dial) started ringing inside the store. It rang about ten times, when finally one of the men took his straw out of his mouth slowly and says, "Earl, are you gonna answer that blankety-blank phone?" Earl slowly responded, "I reckon not. I put that there phone in there for my convenience, not his'n!" Well, I realized right then that I should not be terrorized or ruled by modern conveniences. Don't allow electronic devices to rule your household or to interrupt your family altar time. That's why God made answering machines.

c. Vary your approach to prevent boredom and becoming stale. Over the years we've read passages of Scripture and discussed them. Sometimes, we address current events and how they line up with a biblical worldview. Sometimes we talk about issues in the family or of people in the news but bring it to a discussion of biblical principles. Sometimes we pray or just sing. Occasionally, I delegate to other family members for variety.

4) Your ultimate goal is to teach your children the main characters, events, doctrines and principles of life contained in the Scriptures. Over the eighteen years of time God will allow you stewardship of your children's lives, you will be amazed at the knowledge you and your children will gain together. The resources out there are unlimited, but we personally focused on helping our children establish a personal quiet time, memorize Scripture, and acquiring a biblical worldview. We even decorate

our home with Scripture in creative ways, so that everywhere they turn, our children see the Word of God being impressed on their fertile young minds. One day at the dinner table, my oldest son spontaneously quoted a verse from the Psalms. We had no idea where he had learned that verse since we did not recall memorizing that as a family. We inquired, "Where and when did you learn that verse?" He responded quickly, "It's on the wall in your bedroom. Every time you sent me to your room to discipline me when I was young, I had to sit on your bed and wait on Dad. I sat and stared at the cross-stitched picture of that verse on the wall. I guess I just memorized it over the years." We all got a good laugh over that one. It pays to put God's Word on the wall of your home.

5) Be sure to include visitors and extended family in your family devotions. If they are not accustomed to a family worship time, it will have a profound effect on them. Adult visitors will often realize they should, and could, be doing the very same thing. Friends of your children may come face-to-face with Jesus for the first time. Your family altar can be encouraging and evangelistic. Remember: God inhabits the praises of His people. Some folks have never been in the atmosphere of holiness. It should be a sacred event in your home.

What is the outcome of Dad, the family shepherd, leading his flock in family devotions over years of time? The little olive plants growing around your table will grow strong and straight and true, turning into legitimate disciples of the Lord Jesus Christ. They will, in all likelihood, adopt the sincerely held values of their Christian parents. Is that a guarantee? No, because children make their own choices — but at least you have been a good and faithful steward of the life God has entrusted to you. Your conscience will be clear. In my opinion, parents who personally disciple their own children rather than delegating that to the youth pastor have a far less likelihood of experiencing the flight of the church kid. The greater likelihood is that you will pull back your bow and shoot that carefully crafted arrow out into the world, confident that it will fly strong and straight and true.

STUDY QUESTIONS | Chapter 24

1. What does it mean to "train up a child in the way he should go, even when he is old he will not depart from it" (Proverbs 22:6)?

2. Does this training guarantee a child will become a believer and remain faithful to the Lord? Why or why not? Is this hard to accept?

3. What can we do as Christian parents to avoid the flight of church children in our family?

4. What does it mean to disciple our own children? What does that look like?

5. What does your family altar look like? How can you improve it? Do you use a curriculum? Do you sing?

6. Do you know anyone whose children departed from the faith after high school? Are you concerned about your children or grandchildren?

AFTERWORD

I was standing in line at our local polling location to vote on a cold November morning with my wife and my daughter, Rebecca. My sweet, blue-eyed baby doll Rebecca had just returned from a three-year missionary journey to the Middle East with the Southern Baptist International Mission Board, where she learned to speak Arabic fluently as an Arabic language student and where she ministered to young Arabic women. She absolutely loved her ministry there, as well as the many young women whom she met and with whom she was able to share the gospel message.

As we stood in line talking with folks and trying to stay warm, someone inquired about Rebecca's position in life, so she excitedly began to share about her three-year adventure in the Middle East. While listening in, a rather portly gentleman in line became quite agitated the longer she talked. He had already told us he was a truck driver who drove a route to Alabama and back every day. Suddenly, he couldn't stand the conversation any longer, so he interjected, "Well, I can share the gospel with more people between here and Alabama. I don't need to go over yonder to talk to those 'ferners.'"

The whole crowd of listeners suddenly quieted down. They all looked at me and Rebecca. My wife grabbed my arm. I admit my blood pressure was rising, but Holy Spirit was still in control. I quietly asked him, "Sir, how many people have you talked to about Jesus between here and Alabama in all your years of driving back and forth?"

His wife responded, "Yeah, Earl, tell him if you are such a great evangelist!"

He just kicked the dirt and stared at his shoes. Somebody in the crowd started snickering. I was still a little hot under the collar in my daughter's defense. "Well, I like her way of sharing the gospel both here and there better than your way of not sharing the gospel."

Some lady in the crowd said, "Preach it, Brother!"

A recent research conducted by George Barna for American Culture and Faith Institute revealed that only two out of five Christians (39 percent) believe they should share their faith with others.[1] I don't know what was in the heart of this truck driver. Maybe he was a churchgoer who had never been born again. Maybe he was a true believer but just didn't have an evangelistic bone in his body, or maybe he didn't have a burden for lost souls between here and Alabama or in the Middle East. I've met plenty of Christians just like him.

I remember clearly when God began to put a genuine burden in my heart for sharing the gospel, a burden that has only intensified since that day. I was sitting in a motel ballroom in Atlanta with about 1,000 other college kids the week after Christmas in 1974 listening to Charles Stanley talk about the need to take the gospel to all the world. I wrote down what he said — about two billion people (at that time) had never even heard the gospel. He talked about 146,000 people dying worldwide every day, and 117,000 of them never even hearing a gospel presentation in their entire life. I was stunned to hear that and attempted to grasp the magnitude of the thought. (Don't quote me on those numbers. I'm remembering from forty years ago, but you get my point.)

He challenged us to be the generation that made a difference, taking the gospel to all the world. Then he reminded us that we would be fooling ourselves if we thought we would be cross-cultural missionaries if we didn't share the gospel with our lost roommate or next-door neighbor. That made perfect sense to me, so Holy Spirit began to light a fire in my heart to not only share the gospel but to make a difference around the world (i.e., fulfill the Great Commission).

I trust that you have enjoyed traveling with me as I shared with you many of the adventures in seed-planting that God has allowed me to experience over the years. Every adventure I shared was designed to teach a different principle of evangelism. Please take advantage of the study questions with answers at the end of the book, so you may think more deeply and use it for group discussions or Sunday school classes.

Do you remember the parable of the sower and the seed? We tend to focus on the different soils and who they represent, but don't forget the one who sows. There is no seed to sprout and no harvest to gather in if there is no farmer who is willing to sow. Did you notice that this farmer was quite liberal in his sowing? He was not stingy; he didn't hold back. He lavished the seed on his field. He didn't even mind throwing his precious seed in the thicket or on the stony ground where the yield would be minimal or none, but he knew if he didn't throw seed there, the possibility would be nil. He risked some of his seed on the outside chance that some would survive.

We do the same thing. We share "the word implanted which is able to save our souls," knowing that not all the seed we sow will take root or flourish. Nevertheless, out of love, compelled by the love of Christ, we sow liberally and sometimes in stony hearts, hoping for the seed to find a nesting place; just like any good farmer, we pray over it, we fertilize it, we protect it, and we drive away the wild animals — deer, rabbits, demons. Like our Heavenly Father, who is the original sower of the seed, we are "not willing that any should perish, but that all should come to repentance" (2 Peter 3:9).

"He who goes to and fro weeping, carrying his bag of seed, shall indeed come again with a shout of joy, bringing his sheaves with him" (Psalm 126:6).

Brothers and sisters, sow the seed. Sow it liberally. Sow it freely.

Trust God that He will bless the seed that you sow, that He will not allow it to return void or empty but will cause it to accomplish His eternal purpose in the life of those who hear. Remember: The power is not in you or me the messenger, but the power is in the gospel message. "For I am not ashamed of the gospel, for it is the power of God for salvation to everyone who believes" (Romans 1:16). Also remember: The gospel message is like a lion. It doesn't need to be defended. It merely needs to be released!

ANSWERS TO STUDY QUESTIONS

Chapter 1

1. In the context of this chapter, it would mean that we are not ashamed or embarrassed to share Jesus with alcoholics or drug addicts. In our heart of hearts, we are convinced that Jesus can meet every need of the human heart, even the hard cases like Lenny who saw no need to change.

2. AA and NA provide accountability for those trying to leave a life of drugs or alcohol abuse, often by people who have been victorious already so they understand the battle. All of us need accountability in our Christian journey in order to overcome temptation and improve Christian discipline in Bible study, Scripture memorization, prayer, etc. Without accountability, we get slack and slide backwards.

The danger of AA and NA meetings is being in a room with a group of people who were ordered there by a judge or counselor, but don't want to be there and are not intrinsically motivated to change. They can poison an entire group and undermine the good intentions of a sincere attendee. Sometimes they meet former friends who steer them back into abuse.

(I don't mean to imply that all AA and NA meetings are potentially negative experiences. It all depends upon the leadership and the participants in each individual group meeting. I have many patients who have been helped tremendously by the accountability provided by these meetings.)

3. The transforming power of the gospel. Jesus changed his heart and his desires — simple as that, supernatural as that.

4. It means the old man is dead, and you have been raised to a new way of life in Jesus Christ. It means to be born again, to be washed in the blood, to have a new heart, to be transferred from the domain of darkness into the kingdom of God's beloved Son, to be set free, to have your eyes opened to spiritual truth, to be made spiritually alive, to have your name written in the Lamb's book of life, to have eternal life. That's a good start!

5. It is persistence in prayer and multiple exposures to the gospel over time.

Chapter 2

1. Your answer

2. Because God meets us there. Because kneeling at the altar demonstrates humility on our part and complete dependence on God. We are admitting that we are depending on Him to intervene in the life of our loved ones and do for them what we cannot do.

3. I think there are two reasons:

1) Pride — we are too prideful to kneel in front of God and everybody. Remember: "God is opposed to the proud, but gives grace to the humble" (James 4:6). Put on your humble shirt and go to the altar. If this bothers you, go in private when no one is there.

2) We are not convinced that God will answer our prayers, nor are we convinced that the altar is a sacred place. The remedy is more Bible reading, because "faith comes from hearing, and hearing by the word of

Christ" (Romans 10:17). The more we read the Word, the more our faith in God and His willingness to answer our prayers grows.

4. Impatience and lack of faith. We don't understand the value of persistence in spiritual warfare.

5. If God could rescue Saul, who was persecuting and murdering Christians, and turn him into a missionary, He can rescue and save anyone.

6. Name them and write them down.

Chapter 3

1. It's the appropriate response in a Christian home that is raising well-mannered children according to biblical principles.

2. Why should our children obey in that way if we don't obey our Heavenly Father sweetly, completely and immediately? That's a double standard, and our children will see through it. All of us, including our children, hate hypocrisy.

3. The Bible is full of illustrations of spiritual activity going on that we cannot see. Read 2 Kings 6:15-17. Can you think of others?

4. We never know what circumstances Holy Spirit has orchestrated in advance to protect us or prepare someone's heart. Disobedience could cause us harm or a lost opportunity to lead someone to Christ.

5. We become attuned to the voice of Holy Spirit by prayer, reading the Word, and memorizing Scripture.

6. Ninety percent of God's will for your life and mine is contained in God's Word. If we get busy obeying God's Word, the rest comes easy. For the other 10 percent, seek wise counsel from mature and godly Christian people, learn biblical principles of life, and determine to follow where God leads you. He is a capable shepherd.

Chapter 4

1. Learning the importance of a daily quiet time and Spirit-controlled life.

2. Your answer

3. Your answer

4. Your answer

5. Your answer

6. Your answer

Write down these names, pray for them, and schedule a time to go see them. If you don't set a time, you probably will let other things interfere, and you will never go see them.

Chapter 5

1. Many people, including Christians, believe there is another option for getting to heaven other than believing on the name of Jesus Christ. We call this universalism, which believes all people will be saved because God is merciful and good. This concept doesn't take into account God's wrath or justice.

2. Because God is just and the righteous Judge. As Abraham asked God before He destroyed Sodom and Gomorrah, "Shall not the Judge of all the earth deal justly?" (Genesis 18:25). God is just and "does not leave the guilty unpunished" (Exodus 34:7). More than this, Peter tells us emphatically, "And there is salvation in no one else; for there is no other name under heaven that has been given among men, by which we must be saved" (Acts 4:12). Jesus himself asserted, "I am the way, and the truth, and the life; no one comes to the Father, but through Me" (John 14:6).

3. Because they are spiritually dead.
The better question is this: Is it fair for you and me to be saved by grace and not have to pay the penalty of our sin? Is it fair for us to live in a land with a church on every corner, multiple Bibles in every house, TV and radio evangelists on every other station, Bible colleges and seminaries in every state, while other people groups live and die for generations in spiritual darkness, never hearing Jesus' name?

4. He rose from the dead. "[He] was declared the Son of God with power by the resurrection from the dead" (Romans 1:4).

5. To fulfill the Great Commission and take the good news to every part of the globe.

6. To take ownership of the Great Commission.

We assume it applies to missionaries and church staff, but the Great Commission was given to every one of us. We have to personally ask ourselves, "What am I doing to take the gospel to all the world?"

7. No evangelical church or organization is actively working to spread the gospel within that people group.

6,945 unreached/unengaged people groups!

Chapter 6

1. Your answer

2. Your answer
Apply for your passport by faith!

3. Make plans to put missions giving in your monthly budget. Why is being out of debt so important to being a missions giver?

4. Who is the missionary with whom you could correspond?

5. Cocooning is a modern trend of returning from work, closing the garage door, locking the front door, turning on the television, and never leaving the house until the next morning to return to work. People live in a cocoon, never socially interacting with neighbors and friends. Often people don't know their neighbors and have limited numbers of

close friends. If we don't make a plan to reach our neighbors and friends by first socializing with them, we never have the audience with which to share the gospel.

6. Share your mission trip story.

7. If you cannot visualize yourself in full military regalia with a sword upraised in one hand and a warhorse beneath you ready to lead the cavalry across the battlefield, you probably won't lead the charge! In like manner, if you can't see yourself landing in a third world country airport with chicken wire around the terminal, goats and chickens wandering across a dirt floor, armed guards with machine guns, passport in hand, ready to make disciples of all the nations, then I don't think you will go on any mission trips. Not all mission trips are like that, but some are. It depends on the country. If you can't see yourself conducting Bible schools through an interpreter with children of another ethnic group, you'll never go on a mission trip. Simple as that! Get a vision! Pray first!

Chapter 7

1. Both God and Pharaoh.

2. Both God and Mr. B.
This doesn't happen in one instant but over years of time.

3. Your answer
People can be deceived by Satan.
Children make decisions with their friends but are not truly born again.
Adults make emotional decisions but are not truly born again.

4. People are often offended by a balanced, biblical perspective of the true God. He is as Mr. Beaver told Susan in *The Lion, the Witch, and the Wardrobe*. "Safe?" said Mr. Beaver. "Who said anything about safe? 'Course he isn't safe. But he's good. He's the King, I tell you."[1] As Susan was afraid of the Lion, most people who are not biblically grounded are offended by many aspects of a holy and just God.

5. We all have people in our lives like Mr. B. who put off making a decision for Christ and who are daily hardening their hearts toward God. This should create an urgency in our hearts to pray for them and share the gospel with them.

Chapter 8

1. Reaching friends, relatives, business associates and neighbors.
The point of this acrostic is that these people represent our circle of influence (COI). Most folks have between ten to twenty people in their COI when you add up FRANs.

2. Name them and write them down and begin to pray for them. Make plans to share the gospel with them.

3. Dr. Jackson took the time to be his friend.

4. Your answer
Many evangelistic organizations have follow-up materials that are five-week studies on the life of Christ and how to get started in the Christian life.

5. Your answer

Divide your FRANs into two lists — those you could talk to right now, and those you would need to pray for first.

The first group: Go talk to them about Jesus.

The second group: Pray first, then go.

Chapter 9

1. God is holy. He is the absolute standard of righteousness by which all men will be judged. There is none good but God. Those who think they are good are deceiving themselves, comparing themselves to other people worse than themselves rather than to God, the true standard.

2. The Pharisees who kept the Law stringently were the cultural standard for human righteousness acquired by adhering to the Law. Jesus made it plain that with God we had to exceed even that standard, which was incredibly difficult. That's why the disciples asked, "Then who can be saved?" They thought to themselves, "No one." Jesus replied, "The things that are impossible with people are possible with God" (Luke 18:27). Hallelujah! God has set us free from the requirements of the Law and has saved us by grace through faith in Jesus Christ.

3. *Solus Christus* — Christ alone

Sola gratia — grace alone

They were called Protestants because they protested the Roman Catholic insistence on adding to the doctrine of salvation by grace through faith in Christ alone. Their rallying cry was *solus Christus* and *sola gratia*, as well as *sola scriptura*.

4. Doug's heart was not changed. Drug rehab provided account-ability, which is necessary, but heart transformation must come first. Only Jesus can change a man's heart from the inside out.

5. Of course not. Jesus can save anybody. He can make the foulest clean. Sometimes He even delivers them from the consequences of their choices in life, but not always. I know Christians who, after being saved, still go to prison, die from alcoholic cirrhosis, or end up divorced due to an alienated spouse because of their serial adultery. Nevertheless, they have a new heart, a transformed outlook, and a new home in heaven.

6. Write down your list of names.

Go ask them, "If you die tonight and stand before God and He asked you, 'Why should I let you into my heaven?' what would you say?" I de-double-dog dare you! Ten times!

Chapter 10

1. To win lost people to Christ

Our organized, collective efforts are often better than our individual efforts. People will often respond to a special event if it catches their fancy or arouses their curiosity. Our responsibility is to help promote, organize, invite and pray.

2. Holy Spirit anoints the efforts of His people. Lost folk respond to different things, like fish respond to different lures. Some will never come to a regular church but gladly attend a wildlife banquet.

3. He came because Mark prayed for him, and Holy Spirit softened

his hard heart just like He will your hard-hearted friend.

4. Your answer
Write down their names and start praying.

5. Is the gospel powerful enough to save the people you listed in #4 above?

6. God "desires all men to be saved and to come to the knowledge of the truth" (1 Timothy 2:4). Some people resist Holy Spirit. Perhaps no one is praying for them or sharing the gospel with them. All some people need is a simple invitation.

Chapter 11

1. Lemon juice! (No, silly goose, you get Jesus!)

2. Your answer
You don't have to answer publicly.

3. Your answer

4. I don't think most of us, including me, are sufficiently like Jesus that we attract much opposition. He was a prophet who called out hypocrisy and sin constantly. Most of us don't do that. We just tolerate sin around us and rarely rebuke or call out sin. Try that a few times and see what happens. You'll learn the meaning of that verse.

5. I find that praying for people on the spot when they share

a problem with me is a huge ministry, especially with my patients. I frequently hear patients say, "Wow, I've never had anyone do that for me," especially lost patients. I had an eighty-two-year-old tough guy break down and weep when I prayed over him prior to a knee replacement surgery. He then told me I was his best friend and that no one had ever prayed with him in his whole life. Prayer is a ministry. Be the priest in your lost friend's life.

6. As above

7. Abide in the Lord and in prayer; submit to His lordship. It's automatic. It just happens. "This little light of mine, I'm gonna let it shine."

Chapter 12

1. Your answer
Not just lost people, but socially unacceptable people.

2. Using your home as a place of ministry to people less fortunate than yourself. What? You think God gave you that big, fat house just for you and your kids? Oh, come on!

Yes, it's a lost art. Very few people invite lost people to their home for the purpose of making friends and sharing the gospel. Make a list of who you would/should invite — poor, homeless, hungry, just out of jail, jobless, homosexual, transgender, depressed, alcoholic, drug-addicted, divorced, foster kids. Dr. Jackson, we could never do that! Chicken heart! Invite a sheriff's deputy, too, then. Who cares? Just do it!

3. Your answer

I'm not asking you to do anything I haven't done. I still see a patient named Rodney, who I visited in prison twenty-five-plus years ago (sometimes with my family). I helped him get his life back together when he got out, but, more importantly, I was his friend when he was in the slammer and loved him to faith in Christ after he got out.

4. Your answer

We have to be convinced in our deepest core that Jesus can help and transform anyone.

5. Every Christian is a member of the body of Christ. Every member has his or her unique giftedness provided by Holy Spirit. The body suffers when any of us fails to contribute our gift of service to the local church.

6. Your answer

"Root, hog, or die" means we get in the trenches with whomever we minister to, and we stay with him until he overcomes his difficult circumstances.

Chapter 13

1. Your answer

I had a college professor who intimidated me terribly at Clemson. He was six foot six, loud, brash, and profane; however, I respected him for his academia and enjoyed his classes. For some reason, God put it on my heart to share the gospel with him. We became friends because I asked a lot of questions in class. I prayed for months but was deathly afraid because of his persona. I finally got up the courage to go to his office and share my testimony with him and a gospel presentation. Turns out he was bitter at God because he had an infant son who had died young. Nevertheless, he listened politely, and we had a great conversation.

2. We can be full of fear and still be obedient like when I talked to my professor.

3. No, and no.

I've led lots of people to Christ after saying, "That's a good question. I'll get back to you on that one."

4. You will never share the gospel because we never learn all the right answers to all the possible questions.

5. Not at all.

I place a premium on apologetics. I think we should all learn as much as we can for our own sakes to answer hard questions to shore up our own faith.

6. No, of course not.

But some who say "no" will say "yes" to Jesus later. One of my best friends in Christian ministry today said "no" to a gospel presentation in college, but a few months later Holy Spirit got a hold of him at a revival service at his church. He told me about it later when we met in medical school in anatomy lab.

Chapter 14

1. Friendliness and a big smile/winsomeness.
Ask questions to draw your customers into the conversation.
Make a strong transition statement into your sales presentation.
Make the presentation clear and quick, using visual aids if possible.
Make a strong closing statement/answer questions.
Invite your customer to make a purchase.

2. Distractions — television, other people, pets, small children.
Unkempt personal appearance, bad breath, body odor.
Bad timing, being in a hurry, interruptions.

3. Same as #1, except we don't have a customer; we have a friend, relative, business associate or neighbor, and our visual aid is a gospel tract. We don't ask them to make a purchase. We ask them to make a decision.

4. We contend with spiritual opposition. Pay attention to your gospel presentation, and you will notice that when you get to talking about the blood of Jesus or repentance, there will often be interruptions. This is not accidental; it is demonic!

5. "Drawing the net" is offering people an opportunity to receive Christ. No sales presentation is complete without an invitation to purchase a product. No gospel presentation is complete with an invitation to receive Jesus Christ. We never know how Holy Spirit is working in a person's heart. Always conclude with: "Would you be willing to confess your sins right now and receive Jesus as your Lord and Savior?" You may be surprised at how often people will answer affirmatively.

6. Your answer. You'll never be successful as a salesman unless you make a lot of sales presentations. You and I will never lead a lot of people to Christ unless we sow a lot of seeds.

Chapter 15

1. Worship sets the stage for evangelism by welcoming divine intervention, expelling demonic opposition, and preparing human hearts.

2. Your answer
Describe your experience.
It is effective in some parts of the country and with some personality types. Some people are gifted at that type of evangelism. Warm contact evangelism (i.e., those in your COI) is much more effective.

3. The presence of God and the praise of His people are mutually inclusive. Where praise exists, the presence and power of God is manifested. No, it wasn't logical to put the choir up front, but spiritual warfare is not rational; it is spiritual (2 Corinthians 10:4).

4. Take the dare! Praise God seven times a day. Memorize a few verses. Your brain won't explode!

5. Gospel conversations plant seeds of thought about Jesus, biblical principles, moral or ethical truth, etc.
Gospel presentations are formal, structured presentations of the gospel with an invitation to respond.

Chapter 16

1. Your answer

For me, it was 1) a small discipleship group in college, 2) the books provided by my pastor, and 3) solid Bible teaching by a series of pastors in my life. I am an avid reader, and in my thirst for answers to life questions I have read hundreds of Christian theology, Christian living and apologetics books over the years. I laughingly tell my friends that I attend KTBS when they ask how I know so much Bible information. "Aren't you a medical doctor?" KTBS stands for Kitchen Table Bible School!

2. Your answer

Who delivered you into the kingdom of God?

Who was your spiritual pediatrician?

3. Follow-up, hospitality, adoption.

To ensure that no one falls through the cracks, every church must have a system for follow-up. There must be one church member/staff member devoted to working the follow-up system of calling, visiting and writing notes. Every Sunday school or connection class should be committed to shepherding their members and visitors so that no one gets lost. Hospitality ministry cements relationships. When you and I invite new believers into our home for a fellowship meal, they become a part of our family and the church family. Then we adopt them into our family and the larger church family by loving them and seeking to meet their spiritual needs. As we mentor/disciple them, they become our children in the faith, and we become their adopted parents. We can't lose people like that.

4. Your answer

5. Deception

Unconfessed sin

Inadequate instruction

6. The Word of God

The indwelling Holy Spirit

Faith in God's promises

Chapter 17

1. Your answer

2. **A**-doration, **C**-onfession, **T**-hanksgiving, **S**-upplication

Read the Word with pen, paper, purpose, prayer.

Remember that the most important part of Bible study is Scripture memorization.

3. Your answer

Who asks you "How's your quiet time?"

I've been doing this for forty-four years, and I still have an accountability partner who asks me a list of questions, including about my daily quiet time. Accountability is important because "iron sharpens iron, so one man sharpens another" (Proverbs 27:17). We applaud accountability in government, the military, the education system, but we reject it in our personal lives. Why? We don't really want anyone else holding our feet to the fire regarding spiritual and moral disciplines in our lives, even though we all know we desperately need it.

4. To meet the Master face to face and love Him more. Sleeping or preparing Sunday school lessons are not the purposes of a daily quiet time. If we go to our daily quiet time looking for a message, we will miss the Master. If we go looking for the Master, we often come away with a message or two.

5. Hebrews 4:12

It is the offensive part of our spiritual armor and protects our mind from the attacks of the enemy. If you don't plan to memorize Scripture, trust me, you never will. You must plan your work, then work your plan.

6. Your answer

Why is that hard? We are so attached to electronic devices that most of us don't know how to be quiet — much less quiet in the presence of God (unless you are a deer hunter). I challenge you to set aside two hours initially to just sit quietly in God's presence, reading His Word, listening to Him and praying a little here and there. Memorize a verse or two and meditate on them. Put it on your calendar to do this once a month, then once a week (with no phone). You won't die! Your spiritual vitality will grow exponentially.

Chapter 18

1. Holy Spirit is God; third person of the Holy Trinity; coequal with God the Father and God the Son; possessing all the attributes of deity.

2. He came to glorify the Son. Holy Spirit came to guide us into all truth (John 16:13), to glorify Christ (John 16:14), to tell us what is yet to come (John 16:13), to convict of sin and righteousness and judgment (John 16:8), and many other ministries.

3. Your answer

Confess all known sin; submit every area of life to Christ; faith —
trust Holy Spirit to rule in your life and reproduce the life of Christ in
you.

4. Daily dying to sin and choosing to submit to lordship of Christ
in our lives (i.e., taking up our cross daily and following Christ in
obedience) (Luke 9:23).

5. Faith is the catalyst (like in a chemical reaction, requiring a
catalyst to energize the reactants). Faith is required in our lives to
energize our daily walk with Christ. "Without faith it is impossible to
please Him" (Hebrews 11:6). God's grace is a divine, enabling influence
in our lives that empowers us to walk in righteousness, reject sin and
choose obedience. It is God's grace that brought us here (salvation) and
God's grace that will lead us home (sanctification).

6. Your answer

7. The abundant Christian life promised in John 10:10 depends on
an understanding of the Spirit-filled life. Producing fruit of the Spirit
also requires an understanding of the Spirit-filled life. Being an effective
seed planter requires an understanding of the Spirit-filled life.

Chapter 19

1. I love what Jesus loves. Ephesians 5:25 says, "Christ also loved
the church and gave Himself up for her." The church is also called "the
pillar and support of the truth" (1 Timothy 3:15).

We as the church are responsible for teaching the truth — about God, Jesus, salvation, Christian living — to a lost and dying world that lives in spiritual darkness confused by Satan's lies. The church is a bastion of light and truth.

I need the fellowship and the accountability. I am weak, and my heart is "prone to wander, Lord, I know it, prone to leave the God I love" as the hymn writer put it in "Come Thou Fount of Every Blessing." That's why I need the body of Christ to "stimulate [me] to love and good deeds" (Hebrews 10:24).

My heart longs to worship God. I do that best in concert with other Christians.

2. The church is composed of believers of all ages justified by faith. The universal church is all believers of all time. The local church is a group of believers in a localized community gathered for worship, Bible study, prayer and outreach.

3. A church should be organized according to New Testament guidelines with a pastor, deacons, and elders. Churches teach the Word, worship, pray, evangelize, observe the ordinances (Lord's Supper and baptism), ordain pastors and send out missionaries. We practice the "one anothers" of the New Testament within the body of Christ.

4. Paul sent Timothy back to various locations where they had established groups of believers with instructions to organize these groups — probably home groups — into churches with pastors, deacons and elders, outlining the qualifications for each. So, yes, a Bible study or home group can grow into a church but cannot consider themselves a church without proper New Testament organization and leadership.

5. Your answer

How well do you and your church practice these?

6. Bad experiences personally or bad reputation of some churches in a community. We are the church, and we represent Jesus Christ. We have to walk in integrity and police ourselves and one another. Reprove, rebuke and exhort if we have to, in order to maintain a good testimony.

Chapter 20

1. Sure they do! I walked up to the ticket counter in a Cincinnati airport dressed in blue jeans and a T-shirt, and the lady at the counter said, "Let me guess: You're a preacher!" I was astonished. I hadn't said a word yet. I looked at her, held out my arms to my side in bewilderment and asked, "Why do you think I'm a preacher?" "You just look like one." I looked around at my friends going to India with me, only one of which was a pastor, and inquired, "What does a preacher look like?" "I don't know, but I'll bet you're a preacher!" I said, "Well, ma'am, I'm a medical doctor, but you're half right because I do a lot of preaching, and I'm on my way to India to preach the gospel. How did you know?" She responded, "I can just tell."

Have you ever had a lull in the conversation and someone said, "An angel just flew over"? The original Dutch saying was "A pastor just walked by," because it usually represented a lull in the coarse jesting. Yes, indeed, you have an aroma about you. That's why people at work apologize to you when they curse; at least they should. That's why they ask you to explain hard Bible questions. You're the priest in their midst, and you have the aroma of Christ about you.

2. Elements of a three-minute testimony:

Before you become a believer

How you became a believer

After you became a believer

Concluding verse — *Bam!*

Practice, practice, practice!

3. Your story

4. A servant's heart opens doors and creates credibility.

5. We never know when someone with a sincere, seeking heart will come to us with questions. We prepare by diligent study.

Recommended reading:

Evidence That Demands a Verdict by Josh McDowell

Who Moved the Stone by Albert Henry Ross

Case for Christ by Lee Stroebel

More Than a Carpenter by Josh McDowell

So What's the Difference by Fritz Ridenour

Chapter 21

1. Everyone assumes they have their spiritual house in order because they look good, smell good, and live in a nice house. If they are morally good, they must be saved, right? Wrong. They could be as lost as a long-necked goose in a bucket of juice! Lost people miss heaven because they are not born again. They don't have the life of God in them.

2. Spiritually dead — Ephesians 2:2

Spiritually blind — 2 Corinthians 4:4

Spiritually bound — 2 Peter 2:19

3. Jesus gives life — John 10:10

Jesus opens blinded eyes — 2 Corinthians 4:6

Jesus sets us free — John 8:31-32

4. Holy Spirit had prepared his heart by virtue of multiple gospel presentations and many people praying for him over years of time.

5. Effective seed planting is a team sport that involves multiple players working in concert with Holy Spirit over years of time. Sometimes we know each other, sometimes we don't. The hard work in Hollis' salvation was done by the pastors, evangelists and prayer warriors. I just happened to be there at harvest time, which was easy in his case. Seed planting and watering with prayer is a labor of love, but make no mistake — it is a labor of hard spiritual work.

6. Your answer

Chapter 22

1. Your answer

The fire is stoked by reading the Word and being filled with Holy Spirit. There is a supernatural quality about God's Word that affects our spiritual life toward evangelism/seed planting. However, we have to choose to be obedient to God's Word, which means we have to move out of our comfort zone and talk to people about Jesus intentionally, even though it makes us uncomfortable and wrecks our schedules. Every time I show the gospel in my office, it wrecks my schedule. My patients and employees get upset, but God didn't put me there just to take care of sore throats and hemorrhoids. He put me there to minister in Jesus' name.

2. Being unprepared
Unconfessed sin
Not being filled with Holy Spirit
Fearfulness

3. Learn a gospel presentation and practice it; memorize your three-minute testimony.

Confess all known sin.

Submit daily to Holy Spirit.

Choose obedience. Fear may never leave, but remember courage is doing the right thing in spite of our fears.

4. I doubt that we would lose our life for Jesus in America, but I foresee a time when we could lose jobs and businesses if we stay true to our moral convictions, like the cake shop and flower shop owners over the homosexuality issue. We are all tempted to say, do, or look at things daily that violate our convictions. If we cannot withstand these minor temptations, how can we think that we would be willing to suffer martyrdom? "He who is faithful in a very little thing is faithful also in much; and he who is unrighteous in a very little thing is unrighteous also in much" (Luke 16:10).

5. There is a personal cost to speaking out against moral evil around us. People around you will label you. They will ridicule and scorn you,

they avoid you, and they flaunt their sin in your face. For example, I routinely challenge cohabitating couples in my medical practice to consider marriage as the best option for their relationship. Sometimes I lose patients. Sometimes they listen and thank me, but I have a hard time letting it slide. Like Jeremiah, there is a fire in my bones to speak the truth.

Chapter 23

1. Your answer

2. Your answer

3. Your answer

4. Your answer

Making connections at a new church can be difficult. It depends on how hard you work at it. It depends on how intentional the church family is at welcoming new families. It also depends on your personality type. Some folks are just more extroverted than others and can make friends more easily than others. Whatever the case, you have to intentionally strive to make yourself a part of the family of God. Otherwise, you will feel "on the outside" emotionally and unable to find a place of ministry.

5. Your answer

If we don't have a ministry mindset, we won't even think about building relationships with clerks, store managers, or business owners for the purpose of sharing the gospel. It's out of a keen desire to plant the seed of the gospel that we seek to make connections with our neighbors and coworkers.

Chapter 24

1. Literally, it means "to dedicate a child according to what his way demands." We all understand that the way of our children without proper parental oversight and discipline is more negative than positive. Without proper training, their "way" leads to folly and shame.

2. No, there is no guarantee. Why not? It is because our children grow up to make their own choices in life. This is hard to accept because we falsely understand Proverbs 22:6 as a promise that our children will not depart from the faith if we "raise them right."

3. We have to engage in a discipleship process with our own children, not merely delegating this to youth workers at church. This is not to minimize the importance of youth, Sunday school teachers, and youth staff who augment and supplement what we teach at home. However, they cannot be the only source of biblical instruction for our children. Our children have to see our love for Christ passionately lived out in our lives first before they will adopt biblical values in their own lives.

4. First of all, recognize that the apple doesn't fall far from the tree. When you have a passionate love for Jesus, Bible reading, prayer, church, sharing the gospel with your neighbors and going on short-term mission trips, guess what? Your kids will, too. They will do what you do and talk about what you talk about.

Discipling our children is intentional, not accidental. I recommend finding a curriculum that teaches Bible doctrine at a level appropriate for their age and advance as they grow older. Make sure your children know Bible events, characters, doctrine, and principles of life.

5. In the Jackson family, we have evolved over time from just reading Bible stories when our children were young to reading passages with an intent to teach an application to life nowadays. I try to tell them stories from my life or my patients (anonymously, of course) or current events, and bring a biblical application. We sometimes sing, especially at holidays.

6. Sadly, we know several friends whose children departed from their faith and their family. We pray for them and ask God to restore them to their family, to God, and to their spiritual upbringing.

Endnotes

Chapter 3

[1] John H. Sammis, "Trust and Obey," *The Baptist Hymnal*, (Nashville: Convention Press, 1991), hymn #447.

Chapter 4

[1] "Oh Happy Day" by the Edwin Hawkins Singers, released in 1968 on the album called *Let Us Go Into the House of the Lord*, http://www.songfacts. com/detail.php?lyrics=2032, an adaptation of original song "O Happy Day, That Fixed My Choice" by Philip Doddridge, 1755, https://hymnary.org/ text/o_happy_day_that_fixed_my_choice, [accessed July 31, 2018].

Chapter 5

[1] "2016 State of American Theology Study," sponsored by Ligonier Ministries and conducted by Lifeway Research, https://thestateoftheology. com/assets/downloads/2016-state-of-america-white-paper.pdf, [accessed November 27, 2017].

[2] "Should Christians Stop Trying to Convert Jews," *Larry King Live,* aired January 12, 2000, http://transcripts.cnn.com/TRANSCRIPTS/0001/12/ lkl.00.html, [accessed November 7, 2017].

[3] Ibid.

[4] John Wayne quote as Wil Anderson in *The Cowboys*, released in 1972; *Newsmax*, "25 Greatest John Wayne Quotes Ever." http://www.newsmax. com/TheWire/john-wayne-greatest-quotes/2015/10/01/id/694217/, [accessed November 8, 2017].

[5] Joshua Project, "Global Statistics," http://unreachedresources.info/global_ statistics, [accessed November 7, 2017].

Chapter 6

[1] Bob Finley, *Reformation in Foreign Missions*, (Charlottesville, VA: Christian Aid Mission, 2010), pp. 156-160.

Chapter 7

[1] Joseph A. Alexander, "The Doomed Man," first published in the *Sunday School Journal*, Philadelphia, April 5, 1837, https://hymnary.org/text, [accessed November 27, 2017].

[2] "Quotes on Repentance," *Ministry 127*, http://ministry127.com/resources/ illustration/quotes-on-repentance, [accessed May 15, 2018].

Chapter 8

[1] Dallas Frazier and Sanger Shafer, "The Baptism of Jesse Taylor," released by the Oakridge Boys in 1978, https://www.youtube.com/watch?v=ps-27RD8rrWQ, [accessed November 27, 2017].

[2] Ibid.

Chapter 9

[1] Fritz Ridenour, *So What's the Difference*, (Ventura, California: Regal Books, 2001), p. 39.

Chapter 12

[1] David Kinnaman and Gabe Lyons, *unChristian*, (Grand Rapids, Michigan: Baker Books, 2007), p. 28.

[2] Michael Lipka, "Millennials are Increasingly Driving Growth of 'Nones,'" *FactTank: News in the Numbers*, *Pew Research Center*, http://www.pewresearch.org/fact-tank/2015/05/12/millennials-increasingly-are-driving-growth-of-nones/, [accessed January 4, 2018].

3 Sam Eaton, "12 Reasons Millennials are Over Church," *Recklessly Alive*, http://www.recklesslyalive.com/12-reasons-millennials-are-over-church, [accessed December 27, 2017].

Chapter 13

1 John McCain and Marshall Salter, *Why Courage Matters: The Way to a Braver Life*, (New York City: Ballentine Books, 2008), p. 9.

Chapter 15

1 Keith Shorter, "The 365 Challenge," *The Courier*, Rudy Gray, ed., (Greenville, S.C.: The Baptist Courier), August 2017, p. 17.

2 Ibid.

3 "Statistical Summary and Tables," *South Carolina Baptist Convention 2016 Annual*, Jan Berrian and Gary Anderson, eds., p. 176, http://www.scbaptist. org/wp-content/uploads/2017/05/sc-baptist-convention-2016-annual-with-links-and-formatted.pdf, [accessed November 28, 2017].

4 Ibid.

5 Alex McFarland and Jason Jimenez, *Abandoned Faith*, (Carol Stream, Illinois: Tyndale House Publishers, Inc., 2017), pp. 56-58.

Chapter 16

1 "Baby Clings to Life After Being Abandoned in S.C. Arena Toilet," CNN Wire Staff, posted February 9, 2011, www.cnn.com/2011/US/02/07/south. carolina.baby/index.html#, [accessed July 14, 2017].

2 Garo Christians and John Clark, "I Have Decided to Follow Jesus," *The Baptist Hymnal*, (Nashville: Convention Press, 1991), hymn #305.

[3] "The Best Friend of Charleston," American-Rails.com, https://www.american-rails.com/friend.html, [accessed November 28, 2017].

[4] A.W. Tozer, *How to Be Filled with the Holy Spirit*, (Chicago: Moody Publishes, 2016), pp. 16-17.

[5] "Baby Found in Toilet Out of Hospital; Custody Plans Underway," WBTV and Associated Press, posted February 7, 2011, updated April 3, 2011, http://www.wbtv.com/story/13981962/sc-police-looking-for-woman-who-left-baby-at-arena, [accessed July 17, 2017].

Chapter 18

[1] Definition as found at https://legal-dictionary.thefreedictionary.com, [accessed November 29, 2017].

[2] Julia H. Johnson, "Grace Greater Than Our Sin," *The Baptist Hymnal*, (Nashville: Convention Press, 1991), hymn #329.

Chapter 19

[1] William D. Longstaff, "Take Time to be Holy," *The Baptist Hymnal*, (Nashville: Convention Press, 1991), hymn #446.

Chapter 21

[1] John Wayne quote as Tom Doniphon in *The Man Who Shot Liberty Valance*, released in 1962, *Newsmax*, "25 Greatest John Wayne Quotes Ever." http://www.newsmax.com/TheWire/john-wayne-greatest-quotes/2015/10/01/id/694217/, [accessed November 29, 2017].

Chapter 23

[1] Gretchen Rubin, "Monks Take a 'Vow of Stability.' Maybe You Should, Too," *The Happiness Project*, http://www.slate.com/blogs/happiness-project/2009/01/26/, [accessed June 6, 2018].

Chapter 24

[1] Merrill F. Unger, *Unger's Bible Dictionary*, (Chicago: Moody Press, 1966), p. 1111.

[2] Jason DeRouchie, "Train Up a Child in the Way He Should Go," *Desiring God*, https://www.desiringgod.org/articles/train-up-a-child-in-the-way-he-should-go, September 20, 2016, [accessed December 12, 2017].

[3] George Barna, "Survey: Christians are Not Spreading the Gospel," http://www.georgebarna.com/research-flow/2017/11/30/survey-christians-are-not-spreading-the-gospel, November 30, 2017, [accessed May 14, 2018].

[4] Ibid.

[5] Ibid.

[6] Ibid.

[7] Ken Ham, Britt Beemer, and Todd Hillard, *Already Gone*, (Green Forest, Arkansas: Master Books, 2009), p. 24.

[8] Voddie Baucham Jr., *Family Driven Faith*, (Wheaton, Illinois: Crossway Books, 2007), p. 11.

[9] Ibid.

[10] Ibid.

[11] Ibid.

[12] Ibid., p. 12.

[13] Ibid.

[14] Alex McFarland and Jason Jimenez, *Abandoned Faith*, p. 27.

[15] Ibid., p. 61.

Afterword

[1] George Barna, "Survey: Christians are Not Spreading the Gospel," http://www.georgebarna.com/research-flow/2017/11/30/survey-christians-are-not-spreading-the-gospel, November 30, 2017, [accessed May 14, 2018].

Answers to Study Questions

[1] C.S. Lewis, *The Lion, the Witch and the Wardrobe*, (New York, New York: Collier Books, 1950), pp. 75-76.

Jackson Family minus three — a son-in-law, a grandson, and a baby not yet born.

The Family Doctor Speaks:
The Truth About Life
Robert E. Jackson, Jr., MD

*Also by Robert Jackson: "The Family Doctor Speaks:
The Truth About Life." Available at Amazon, Barnes
& Noble and other major online booksellers.*